D0204808

Pedal to the Metal

In the series

Labor and Social Change,

edited by Paula Rayman and Carmen Sirianni

Pedal to the Metal

The Work Lives of Truckers

Lawrence J. Ouellet

Temple University Press

Philadelphia

Temple University Press, Philadelphia 19122
Copyright © 1994 by Temple University. All rights reserved
Published 1994
Printed in the United States of America

The paper used in this publication meets the minimum requirements
of American National Standard for Information Sciences—Permanence
of Paper for Printed Library Materials,
ANSI Z39.48-1984 ⊗

Library of Congress Cataloging-in-Publication Data

Ouellet, Lawrence J., 1947–
    Pedal to the metal / Lawrence J. Ouellet.
      p. cm. — (Labor and social change)
    Includes bibliographical references and index.
    ISBN 1-56639-175-X (alk. paper). — ISBN 1-56639-176-8 (pbk.)
    1. Truck drivers—United States. 2. Trucking—United States.
  I. Title. II. Series.
  HD8039.M795U56 1994
  388.3′24′0973—dc20
                                        93-38954

Lyrics from "Asphalt Cowboy" on p. 105, written by Clark Bentley and Lawton
Williams, © Shelby Singleton Music, Inc., and Western Hills Music Corp. Used
by permission, International Copyright secured.

For my parents:

Joseph "Willie" Ouellet and Zelda Shelton

CONTENTS

ACKNOWLEDGMENTS

THIS BOOK does not rely on interviews with fellow drivers, but I am indebted to all who enriched my understanding of trucking by sharing their lives with me. In particular, I would like to thank George Seibert, who took me under his wing when I entered trucking and, to this day, remains a close friend. Evelynn Seibert also has been a good friend and teacher. I thank my brother, Bill, an ex-trucker with whom I was able to discuss some of the pleasures of driving that truckers tend not to talk about. And I appreciate the time AgriHaul's owner spent describing for me the dimensions of competition between AgriHaul and its rivals. George Lines, a friend from my first days in trucking, not only helped me better understand trucking but also generously let me photograph him at work. I thank Bobby Johnson Trucking for the opportunity to photograph one of their beautiful Peterbilt trucks for the photo gallery and Kenworth Sales of Nashville for permission to photograph one of their beautiful Kenworth trucks for the cover. Several truckers who were strangers to me put aside their suspicions and permitted me to photograph them at work, and I thank them. None of the photographs included here are of trucks or drivers attached to the companies in this book.

Although I had Howard Becker as a teacher and carefully read his book *Art Worlds*, the large number of people involved in developing and completing this book comes as quite a surprise. My greatest debt is to Arlene Kaplan Daniels. From the day I spoke to Arlene about my plans, she provided unflagging support. Arlene encouraged my fieldwork, read untidy field notes and working papers, criticized my thinking and suggested alternatives, and was a tireless editor. Howard Becker and Bernard Beck read early drafts of the manuscript and helped guide its development. I also wish to acknowledge the indirect, but substantial, contributions of three of my earlier teachers, Charles Moskos, Sigrid O'Neill, and Ivan Vallier. Others who assisted me include Rod Nelson, Suzanne Staggenborg, Gary Hender, Beth Campbell, Gary Grizzle, Margaret Grizzle, Judy Stephenson, and Gus Alevizos. I thank Joseph Blake for finding the song lyrics quoted in Chapter 5. The book in its final form benefited from the contributions of Michael Ames of Temple University Press, whom I also thank for his faith and patience; Paula Rayman, coeditor of the Labor and Social Change series; an anonymous, very thoughtful reviewer who clearly was generous with his or her time; Bobbe Hughey, whose acumen and thoroughness as a copy editor I greatly appreciate; and Debby Stuart for her assistance during the final period of editing.

I deeply thank my wife, Ardy, for her patience and support as I finished this project. And I apologize to Carrie and Stephanie for my attempts during periods of writing to achieve librarylike quiet in our house.

Finally, I wish to dedicate this book to my parents, Joseph "Willie" Ouellet and Zelda Shelton, for—among a universe of debts—a home that valued both reading and working with one's hands, and career direction that stressed personal satisfaction.

Pedal to the Metal

CHAPTER 1

Driving Trucks,
Driving Ourselves

BEFORE AND WHILE becoming a sociologist, I drove trucks for a living. Choice, not chance, led me to truck driving. When I was a youngster, trucking captured my imagination. I still vividly remember summer nights when my family set out on vacation, journeying into an unfamiliar but alluring world with trucks at its center. We departed near midnight, when temperatures were relatively cool, in hopes of keeping our car from overheating in the mountains north of Los Angeles. As we headed out of the city, I was fascinated by the number of trucks on the road at that time of night. Often they traveled in packs, on some stretches roaring along at frightening speeds and in other places barely moving. Crawling up mountain grades among the most extreme in the United States, truckers sought relief from the heat of their cabs by hanging out their windows, sitting with a door open, or, like circus performers, standing on the cab's steps with one foot on the throttle. After passing one another, often an inch at a time, drivers flashed a code with their lights— an indication, said my father, that one truck had safely cleared the other. To leave these mountains, northbound trucks had to negotiate a steep, winding, dangerous stretch that my parents called "the grapevine." Escape ramps and the pungent odor of hot, sometimes flaming, brakes testified to the risk truckers ran descending to the valley. Just the sight of an escape ramp scared me.

Farther up the road, along Highway 99, were towns like Bakersfield that seemed to exist only for the endless stream of trucks passing through. Their streets were filled with Ken-

worths, Internationals, Macks, Autocars, Freightliners, Peterbilts, and "Jimmies." Trucks were parked at cafés, at neon-
lighted motels, under palm trees at the side of the road. Truck
stops teemed with rigs, drivers, and action. Spicing the night air
were the scents from loads of onions, cattle, hay, and citrus
fruits. Nearly everything about this world seemed different from
the one I knew. The noise, the smells, the night filled with activity, the humidity of the heavily irrigated San Joaquin Valley, the
hugeness of the vehicles, the lights that covered some of them
like Christmas trees, the danger, the cafés and motels and truck
stops, the driver-to-driver signaling, the secret society drivers
seemed to belong to—this was the stuff of high adventure.

Over time these images diminished in scale, but the attraction remained. Shortly before my discharge from the army, I applied for training to drive diesel tractor-trailers, but the army did
not include this trade in their vocational skills program for departing G.I.'s. Back home, I had no job waiting and searched
unsuccessfully for work as a truck driver. Finally, I turned to a
day-labor job on a loading dock. Work was strenuous, and our
pay in cash at the end of each day was only $14.80. Then a
friend told me that the small trucking company where his father
worked was willing to train a driver.

Beginning with that first job, I drove heavy-duty diesel trucks
approximately 800,000 miles, working full-time and part-time
for eight transport companies over a period of thirteen years. All
these firms were based in California, with the exception of a Chicago outfit. Only one company had a union, but I was hired by
its nonunion division. I hauled locally, coast-to-coast, throughout many of the western states, and into Canada.

In these jobs I drove alone and with partners. I operated tractors pulling a single trailer, tractors pulling two trailers, and
truck-and-trailer combinations. I transported fresh produce,
rock and sand, freight, gasoline and oil, jet fuel, asphalt, lum-
ber, pipe, and dry bulk commodities including grains, chemical
fertilizers, and feeds. I hauled these loads in dry vans, refrigerated trailers, tankers, flatbeds, hoppers, pneumatics, end-
dumps, transfer-dumps, and bottom-dumps. To pull these
loads, I drove tractors ranging from first-class Peterbilts and
Kenworths to utilitarian Macks and beat-up Jimmies (GMC
tractors). Pick-up and delivery sites included factories, con-

struction sites, garbage dumps, refineries, warehouses, carnivals, slaughterhouses and rendering plants, vegetable sheds, produce markets, farms, ranches, quarries, harbors, silos, rail sidings, peat bogs, and service stations.

As a truck driver I experienced a wide range of emotions and feelings, maybe more than people in most other jobs. I had episodes of utter boredom and times of depression at the thought that this life might be my fate. There were periods of great stress, jobs so physically demanding that I wondered if I could make it through the next shift, and work so devoid of joy that getting out of bed in the morning was a supreme act of will. The bleakness of concrete and smog at high noon, traffic jams on urban freeways, and mindless and seemingly endless thirty-minute circles from quarries to construction sites and back numbed my mind. Driving long hours was tiring; at times I felt at the brink of exhaustion. There was the pain of friends injured or killed. Once two of us saw a school bus full of children shortly after it plunged off a ramp and landed upside down thirty feet below. Injury and death are familiar sights for commercial drivers.

Yet trucking has another side. Driving can be a source of great joy, satisfaction, and even enchantment. As a trucker, I probably saw more sunrises and sunsets than most people see in their lifetimes. I drove across mountains and prairies, deserts and farmlands, and throughout the paradise that is the Pacific Northwest. There were nights of magic: crossing the snow-covered Cascades under a full moon so bright that I could drive with my headlights off; a summer moonrise over Alberta wheat fields; two A.M. on Highway 99, windows down and the air full of the smells of the Valley's farms and ranches. I felt a sense of accomplishment in handling an eighty-thousand-pound rig, particularly over challenging roads and in poor weather conditions. I found gratification in seeing the end stage of a haul: food in a supermarket, concrete made into a road, a diving board above the swimming pool in someone's backyard. And driving could be great fun, especially trips with friends. At most companies I found a nourishing camaraderie with co-workers, and I maintained friendships with drivers I knew at other companies. Finally, I found the act of driving at times utterly and addictively pleasurable.

The Meaning of Work

Slowly—even gracefully, if you have an eye for it—the Peterbilt tanker cut an arc across the company yard as it rolled toward the service island. With its fancy paint, shiny aluminum, splashes of chrome, and immaculate condition, this was a fine-looking truck. In the short trip to the island no gears were shifted—J.W., the driver, was not a cowboy. He homed in on the pumps and eased the tanker to an almost imperceptible stop. I watched as I waited in the shade of the nearby shop for my truck to arrive; this was a victory dance of sorts.

J.W. let the engine idle, to cool its turbocharger, and then shut off its fuel. As soon as the engine shook itself into silence, he opened a gadget mounted on the dashboard, removed a round chart, and placed it with his other paperwork. From the moment J.W. first climbed into the truck until now, at shift's end, that gadget tracked his time, the truck's speed, and the operation of its engine. Later, he would add handwritten explanations to certain variations on the chart, but first he needed to service the vehicle. Ralph, the tanker's other driver, was anxious to get under way.

J.W. climbed down from the cab, began refueling, and pushed up the truck's hood/fender assembly to expose the engine. But before he made his final inspection, he returned to the cab, retrieved his time chart, and jumped back out. As if flaunting a trophy, he waved the chart at his partner. "Check it out, Ralph. I set me a new Calexico record today: fourteen hours and twenty-three minutes."

Across town, on another day, a similar scenario unfolds. This time the driver is behind the wheel of a brightly painted Kenworth cabover pulling two high-cube, bottom-dump trailers. An hour earlier, the trailers held over fifty-two thousand pounds of wheat, but now they have been unloaded and the driver needs only to service the truck and turn in his paperwork before heading home. While refueling, he brags to a fellow driver, "I turned two out of Imperial today in fifteen hours; I'd say that's kicking ass." In this case, the driver offered no time chart to back up his claim, because charts are not used by this company.

Veteran drivers at these firms would not think twice about the events just described, but for students of work they raise at least two sets of questions. First, why did the drivers complete their work as fast as possible? More broadly, why did drivers at the three trucking companies I examined *routinely* exert high levels of effort? The answer is not entrepreneurship; these people are company employees, and they operate company equipment. Nor, as I show, do explanations that focus on coercion, paternalism, monetary rewards, or the labor process—all of which are, in effect, "done to" the driver—sufficiently explain this behavior.

A second problem appears: how do drivers explain and justify this high level of effort to themselves, to co-workers, and, in a sense, to the world in general? In their studies of class dynamics, both Willis (1977), who focused on English working-class "lads," and Sennett and Cobb (1972), who interviewed working-class people in Boston, suggest that the problem of justifying effort occurs first in school, where working-class children are likely to be labeled low achievers. To protect their self-worth, "to create among themselves badges of dignity that those in authority can't destroy" (Sennett and Cobb 1972, 84), these children—or at least the boys—form a "counter-school culture" (Willis 1977, 11) in which the central ethos is rebellion against authority. For these boys, trying to achieve the school's manifest goals is a betrayal of self and peers and therefore dishonorable. Upon entering the workplace as young men, they strive for acceptance by their peers, with whom they continue to experience class-based injuries to their self-worth that further bind them to workmates. Workers thus face a paradox: the "contradictory morality of craftsmanship" (Sennett and Cobb 1972, 101). To advance at work and thereby assert one's worth requires effort superior to that of workmates, but because making that effort may, in effect, denigrate workmates and mark one as having surrendered to those in authority, it may cost individuals their workmates' support.[1] This tension around acceptable work effort is perhaps most visible in the transition from school to full-time work.

During my own high school years, I was employed at various times cleaning offices, doing odd jobs at a movie theater, taking customers' orders at a fast-food restaurant, and loading and unloading trucks. My male friends, most of whom also were from working-class or lower-middle-class families, had similar jobs:

pumping gas, rebuilding brake shoes, washing dishes. Generally, we behaved at work much as we behaved at school: we wanted to do well enough not to embarrass ourselves, but rebellion against authority figures was expected and even a source of pride. We wanted to become competent at what we undertook, but we went to work determined not to be embarrassingly subservient. As at school, too much effort at work was potentially dishonorable, a sign that we had given in to our employers or managers and sometimes a betrayal of workmates. We felt we were men, and we tried to act as we thought men should. We sought the respect owed men as men, and excessive subservience was not manly. Intertwined with these concerns was a certain ill-defined class hostility. I believe that, for most of my friends, life in high school began to make it clear, if it was not already apparent, that others had advantages associated with wealth that could be used to humble us.

Coming from a home in which my father, most of his friends, and nearly all my adult male relatives were in labor unions, and graduating from high school with at least one foot rooted in a counter-school culture, I found a surprise waiting for me in the world of full-time, blue-collar work: no viable counter-culture opposed high levels of effort. At first I was happy to find that almost every one of my new workmates, male telephone installers, had also been "one of the boys" in school. I expected to join them in a reconstituted version of counter-school culture, this time teamed against our employer. Instead, I found that these one-time rebels worked with considerable diligence and offered little resistance. Their behavior was especially mystifying given that we were paid by the hour and not by the amount of work we produced, that no one stood over us as we worked, and that we could easily have explained low production by citing any one of the many contingencies that regularly slowed us.

If work at the telephone company was surprising, work at my first trucking company left me stunned. In both the army and the warehouse where I worked on the loading dock, my peers and I tried to do as little work as possible, and we often clashed with those who would have us do otherwise. We hated the warehouse foreman so much that by the time I left, my co-workers were plotting an accident to disable him. The trucking company was different. My new co-workers worked with almost no supervision, yet they put forth great effort. Moreover, drivers seemed to judge themselves and one another by how hard they worked; high levels of work were prized. I was also shocked that frequently drivers did work they were not paid for. That most of these men described themselves as rebels in their school days and still displayed attitudes consistent with that claim—if only superficially—made their workplace behavior all the more puzzling. I laughed at them because they seemed not to understand the absurdity of their conduct, and I felt superior knowing that I would never be so deluded. But within a short time, I became much like them.

In this book I explore drivers' high effort levels at work and how they justify these efforts without branding themselves fools or class traitors. The issue here is a worker's sense of honor—how it is created and maintained. It is an issue often overlooked in studies of work.

When I began my research, it seemed to me that examinations of work too often depicted blue-collar workers only as people to whom things are done. This simplified image is summarized by Hodson (1991): "Most theories of the workplace anesthetize workers, considering them merely as objects of manipulation. This is equally true of management theories from scientific management to human relations (Argyle 1972; Mayo 1945) as it is of radical theories which focus on the structural determination (or overdetermination) of workers' actions and consciousness (Braverman 1974; Edwards 1979; Poulantzas 1975)" (48).

Studies that cast workers in a more active light frequently define workers' creativity as acts of resistance directed against management. For example, conflict theorists (e.g., Roy 1952), especially Marxists (e.g., Shapiro-Perl 1979), in their emphasis on workers' attempts to oppose capitalist exploitation, view slowdowns, restrictions of output, absenteeism, sabotage, and quitting as weapons workers use in their war with owners and managers. This approach generally turns a blind eye toward both conflict between workers and worker agendas that include nonsubversive goals. When these issues are recognized, they too often are dismissed as "false consciousness," an analytical decision that undermines a deeper understanding of work.

In his rich ethnography of machinists and shopfloor dynamics in a multinational corporation, Burawoy (1979) noted that both consensus and conflict theorists tend to frame their interests in workers' on-the-job performance with the same question: why don't workers work harder? Consensus theorists (e.g., Mayo 1933) believe workers fail to understand that their interests coincide with those of their employers; they blame this failure on poor communication, employers' lack of concern for workers' human needs, and even workers' laziness (Burawoy 1979, xi). A theme that underlies the consensus approach is that workplace conflict is not a necessary feature of capitalism and can be eradicated by addressing whatever irrationalities are causing it (Burawoy 1979, 10). Conflict theorists, to the contrary, see worker slowdowns as a rational response to attempts by management to unfavorably alter the relationship between effort and wages.

Burawoy had a different vision. He argues that, given the intensity of work on the shopfloor, the appropriate question is, why do workers work as hard as they do? (xi). Burawoy and, by implication, certain other theorists who looked to the labor process to explain shopfloor activity (e.g., Edwards 1979) suggest that the answer to this question depends most significantly on the size and stage of development of the organization within which work takes place. In small entrepreneurial firms where the owner is involved in day-to-day operations—exactly the sort of firms I looked at—these theorists assume that coercion adequately explains why workers work hard. Edwards (1979, 26) maintains that effort in such firms also could be inspired by the owner's charisma.

These explanations of work effort at small firms fail when applied to the truckers I studied. In none of the three companies was coercion a major feature of the organization of work. Charismatic leadership that inspired workers to expend more effort was not as rare as coercion, but in only one of the three companies did it appear to motivate more than a couple—but far from all—of the drivers. At all three companies drivers thus worked hard, but neither coercion nor charismatic leadership adequately explain why.

In the large multinational corporation Burawoy (1979) studied, he found coercion an inadequate explanation of shopfloor behavior. Coercion was almost absent, but Burawoy's fellow machinists labored intensely and displayed almost no resistance. Burawoy explained that work there had been constituted as a game in which workers tried to earn a bonus ("making out") by exceeding a quota. Rather than turning excess production against the worker by lowering piece rates—a practice Donald Roy (1952) observed three decades earlier—management usually left the rates intact as long as production remained within 140 percent of the quota. Contrary to the interpretations of quota restriction by many Marxist researchers (e.g., Lamphere 1979; Shapiro-Perl 1979), what quota restriction existed in this machine shop—that is, the observing of the 140 percent limit—was aimed at preserving the game, not destroying it.

Though the game was based on economic incentives and provided higher earnings to workers able to master it, Burawoy (1979) argues that its primary rewards were social and psychological: "Making out cannot be understood simply in terms of the externally derived goal of achieving greater earnings. . . . The rewards of making out are defined in terms of factors immediately related to the labor process—reduction of fatigue, passing time, relieving boredom, and so on—the social and psychological rewards of making out on a tough job as well as the social stigma and psychological frustration attached to failing on a gravy job" (85).

Could it be that the drivers I studied were responding to some version of "making out," even though they worked in small firms and not in the advanced capitalist organizations Burawoy believed gave rise to this game? I do not think so. Burawoy's machinists earned bonuses by playing the game, even though these were not held to be the game's primary benefits, but harder work by the truckers I studied did not necessarily translate into more money. For example, one of the drivers, J.W., was paid an hourly rate, so his notable effort cost him in lost wages. By no stretch of the imagination did he make out in an economic sense. While I will argue that the driver did, in fact, reap social and psychological benefits through his work effort, I do not believe this event can be viewed as the product of a game in Burawoy's terms—where money provides both a tangible reward and a justification for playing. And if employers allow or encourage high effort even when it does not increase profits—in fact when it reduces them, in the case of truckers, through excessive fuel consumption or wear on expensive equipment—then surely something other than Burawoy's game is taking place.[2]

Burawoy's conception of a game embedded in the labor process depicts workers as caught in a device of management's creation: workers react to a situation they find themselves in and try to make the most of it. It is to Burawoy's credit that he identifies positive social and psychological rewards in the machinists' response to their working conditions, rather than simply characterizing their actions as resisting exploitation, but he came up short in two ways. First, if these rewards are important to workers and they see the chance to obtain them through work, workers probably play a more active role in insuring that they get them than Burawoy's analysis allows for. Second, Burawoy does not explain the nature of these rewards or workers' need for them. In his review of the shortcomings of labor process theory, Knights (1990) states: "But Burawoy fails to theorise subjectivity or identity sufficiently to account for the workers' preoccupations with production output at Allied Corporation. His analysis of the game of making-out is not so much wrong as incomplete" (310).

Whereas Burawoy sees workers as little more than straw blowing in the wind of advanced monopoly capitalism, William Finlay (1988) rejects this image in his study of longshoremen. Finlay reinterprets games to assign a more central role to workers. Using Manwaring's and Wood's (1984) notion of "tacit skills," Finlay accepts that "cooperation is internal to production" and then argues, "The game is a compromise between managers and workers. Neither is supremely powerful on the shopfloor, and the game and its rules are symptoms of their jockeying for position" (29).

Finlay calls bargaining from this perspective a "deal" and defines it as "an unofficial agreement between a worker (or gang of workers) and an employer (as represented by a supervisor, usually a foreman) which gives both parties economic benefits in addition to those mandated by the contract" (29).

In conceptualizing informal workplace relations as a deal, Finlay goes further than Burawoy by recognizing the ability of workers to affect workplace activity. Unfortunately, Finlay paints the deal as almost wholly economic. "Economic interests lie at the heart of the deal: workers are interested in increasing their earnings relative to their hours worked; employers are interested in good production rates" (29). Thus, where Burawoy recognizes noneconomic motivations but sees them only as making workers vulnerable to the manipulations of management, Finlay sees workers as having more power to affect their workplace but attributes their motives almost entirely to economic self-interest.

Lost in these formulations is a full understanding of workers' needs and motives and how these shape workplace activity. In the case of trucking, work is more than a battle for more money or better pay rates and against monotony and fatigue. It is a place where the self is forged. Truckers attempt to manipulate the workplace to construct a positive self, a self they can live with, that places them in a satisfactory relation to their social world. Among the truckers I studied, the meaning of work and understandings of the self were fluid and constantly attended to (cf. Harper 1987). Conflict was plentiful, but most of it did not represent resistance against management. The most serious resistance concerned the meaning and nonmonetary value of work, not its conduct. Gender, which is often ignored in studies of mostly male workplaces, was central to drivers' agendas, strategies, and interpretations of the work experience. So was the pursuit of some sense of freedom, often with antibureaucratic overtones. Finally, it is impossible to do justice to the work of truck driving without recognizing the role of feelings and emotions ranging from frustration and boredom to contentment and exhilaration, from fear of death and injury to excitement at challenging these possibilities, and from despair to something quite the opposite.

Driving and Researching

Between August 1981 and October 1982, I drove trucks at two California-based companies: five months at PetroHaul, a tanker outfit that hauled oil, gasoline, and other petroleum products, and nine months at SandHaul, which hauled raw materials into factories.[3]

I chose these companies for several reasons. On the pragmatic side, I was a graduate student at a time when dissertation funding had disappeared, so I needed a job that provided decent income. I also wanted employment at a company that operated well-maintained (safe) equipment and whose drivers returned home daily. Within these parameters, my selection of PetroHaul and SandHaul was by chance; friends or relatives directed me to both companies because each met my conditions and happened to be hiring.

PetroHaul and SandHaul also provided the settings necessary for my theoretical interests. To explore the meanings work holds for blue-collar workers and how these meanings affect their on-the-job goals and behaviors, it seemed best to study cases where workers have a variety of possibilities for self-expression. If I wanted to look at the importance to blue-collar workers of extrinsic rewards such as pay, benefits, and security compared to the importance of intrinsic rewards such as autonomy, variety, and good equipment, I needed to study an occupation that offered intrinsic rewards. Research on blue-collar workers often focuses on occupations in which the on-the-job choices of workers are highly circumscribed (e.g., Chinoy 1955; Haraszti 1978; Howe 1977; Willis 1977; Lamphere 1979; Shapiro-Perl 1979; Linhart 1981). While such studies may reveal much about how workers respond to a barren work terrain, researchers frequently draw from them overly broad conclusions regarding the motivations of blue-collar workers (e.g., money is their primary interest in work), working-class consciousness, and the blue-collar work experience.

At the other extreme are studies of blue-collar elites such as journeymen in the building trades (e.g., LeMasters 1975; Riemer 1979). Elites, in comparison to other blue-collar workers, tend to have it all: high skill levels, good pay when they work, control over their tools, prestige, considerable autonomy, and other significant intrinsic rewards, and the benefits and protection of a union. Studies of elites act as a corrective to images of blue-collar work and blue-collar workers based on occupations with few rewards other than a paycheck. Here, for example, we see workers who value their skills, autonomy, intellectual challenges, and opportunities for creative expression, not just monetary rewards. However, if workers do not have to choose between types of rewards—and therefore between meanings of work as they define the self (e.g., high wage earner vs. king of the road)—then we will learn less of the relative importance to workers of these issues. In blue-collar occupations that limit on-the-job choices, the struggle for meaning is stunted because work provides so little material for developing the self, while blue-collar elites have comparatively little need to choose between possibilities.

I selected for study an occupation that provides a middle ground. These drivers are nonunion, but they make decent wages and enjoy some job benefits such as medical insurance and paid holidays. More important, the industry provides drivers with considerable latitude in deciding which occupational rewards they most wish to enjoy, extrinsic or intrinsic, though often at a cost of having to choose between them. By studying an occupation that offers these choices, researchers have a better chance to examine the full meaning of work for those doing it, the processes by which meaning is created and maintained, and how workers' needs shape the workplace.

By selecting nonunion companies, which typically are the gateways into trucking, I was sure to find drivers who were at various stages in the process of deciding what sort of driver/worker/person they wanted to be. At most large union companies, drivers have made the decision to pursue extrinsic over intrinsic rewards (see Chapter 9).

The final consideration in selecting SandHaul and PetroHaul was that they satisfied important methodological needs. To avoid writing an autobiography, I needed frequent contact with my workmates. This condition ruled out most long-distance haulers, because drivers in these operations have only sporadic contact with the company's other drivers and may go weeks without seeing the same driver twice. By hauling locally, as was the case at both SandHaul and PetroHaul, I knew that I would see a good deal of my fellow drivers. At both SandHaul and PetroHaul drivers interacted daily at a variety of locations: the company yard, loading and unloading sites, cafés, on the road by CB radio, and after-work drinking areas.

In addition to PetroHaul and SandHaul, I examined a third company, AgriHaul, where I accrued about half of my driving experience and maintained some contacts. While I did not work at AgriHaul after formulating this study, I talked to its drivers whenever possible at loading and unloading sites frequented by both AgriHaul and SandHaul, on the road or at roadside stops, in after-work drinking spots, and occasionally in AgriHaul's company yard. While at PetroHaul, I sometimes delivered diesel fuel to AgriHaul and used those occasions to socialize with employees. Thus, though I did not systematically collect data on AgriHaul, I feel comfortable including it in my analysis.

When I supply numbers for the three companies, such as the number of employees, I use AgriHaul's numbers from 1976, when I last worked there as a full-time driver.

During the time I worked at PetroHaul and SandHaul, neither owners nor employees, with one exception, knew I also was conducting a study, a choice I made for a mix of practical and methodological reasons.[4] As noted, I needed a driving job to get the type of data I wanted and to meet personal financial responsibilities. Landing a driving job seemed impossible if I announced my intention to do research. I knew from experience that most trucking companies in the sector I planned to examine regularly engage in illegal activities, including some that violate criminal statutes. The consequences of being caught for these violations range from minor to quite serious penalties. Unless an owner already knew and trusted me, I doubted that he or she would offer a job knowing that I planned to gather and record information about company operations.

Market conditions made rejection even more likely. When I began my job search in July 1981 and again in December 1981, work was hard to find. Business generally was slow, the United States was heading into a recession, and few companies were hiring. I wanted a job with good pay, safe equipment, and the opportunity to return home daily—in short, a desirable job—and these were even more scarce.

Covert research also seemed to solve a vexing methodological problem. Whenever I had previously interviewed blue-collar workers after identifying myself as a researcher, I had been disturbed by problems that seemed to be the result of perceived status differences. In particular, blue-collar workers, except perhaps those whose skills generally are thought to be considerable like electricians or carpenters, appear reluctant to give full due to those aspects of their work that please and satisfy them. The reason for this reluctance, it seems to me, is that workers find some of these satisfactions embarrassing to talk about to a highly educated person engaged, or about to be engaged, in an occupation with high social prestige, like a college professor, researcher, or author.

If a job is seen by society as lacking inherent worth (e.g., noble service, intellectual challenge, valued skills) and serving mainly to provide a living, then these utilitarian aspects are likely to be emphasized when workers holding such jobs discuss their work with outsiders, especially higher status outsiders. For example, such workers seem to find it embarrassing, perhaps even dishonorable, to explain career decisions oriented toward an intrinsic reward, such as operating first-rate equipment, especially if those decisions mean forgoing more pay, benefits, or other extrinsic rewards. These workers seem likely also to hide constructions of self rooted in their work's intrinsic rewards.

Even blue-collar workers in occupations seen as noble, challenging, and somewhat skilled may hide from outsiders the work's intrinsic satisfactions when these are intertwined with traditional conceptions of masculinity. In her study of firefighters, people who clearly are engaged in noble work, Kaprow (1991) observed that male firefighters "downplay the excitement and say it simply is a well-paying job allowing them to help people" (98). "[They] eschew the word 'hero' and sedulously cultivate a modest, disclaiming attitude, even asserting that their work is mundane" (99). While trucking rarely presents dramatic opportunities for heroism, it offers considerable satisfactions associated with machismo. And, like firefighters, drivers do not readily reveal these satisfactions to outsiders. Such talk typically happens in code terms and among peers.

The honorable response for most blue-collar workers when asked, "Why do you do what you do?" is "Money"—whether in terms of rates, totals, or a secure flow. Money as a motive is not silly, irrational, or provocative. The worker who talks of money or related satisfactions is less likely to be thought a fool by the researcher. Douglas (1976) discusses these sorts of deceptions.

> Most people are concerned with appearing to be rational, systematic, ordered, and so on, almost entirely in those public settings in which they may be attacked by enemies for not being those things. And one of the public settings in which they most commonly fear such attacks is precisely that situation in which they are being studied by religiously rationalistic, systematic and ordered academic scientists. One of the first things they reach for when the so-

cial scientist approaches them is the front of rationality and order.
. . . [The researcher] can rarely rely on the members to tell him
about [problematic feelings and meanings] because they are not
generally conscious of them, but also because they are commonly
anxious to appear to researchers to be rational and ordered (non-
problematic) in their lives because the researchers are "scientists."
(89–91)

Douglas (Douglas and Johnson 1977) suggests that, in this situation, most people are likely to "put on the best rational rhetoric
for the social scientists studying them, and strive valiantly to
keep them all out of the of the back regions where they do their
living and life building" (28).

Even when I interviewed drivers whom I first knew as co-
workers, I felt pronounced changes in our relations once my social scientist identity was announced. It seemed to me that these
drivers became somewhat stereotypical in their responses. That
is, the driver as informant or interviewee seemed to become the
worker he supposed he ought to be, given my status. I often felt
that the driver was apologizing for being "only a driver." Perhaps
this reaction was exacerbated by drivers sometimes believing I
had "made it." In that case, given our similar class origins, they
may have perceived me as living proof of their individual—as
opposed to class—failure to be more successful. The extent to
which class and social status differences can amplify such deceptions (and self-deceptions) is noted by Douglas (Douglas and
Johnson 1977).

Another realm in which self-deceptions, combined with other deceptions, are crucial in understanding what is going on is that of
economic success, status, class and social prestige in general. In a
society as intensely competitive as ours and in which so much in
our lives is determined by our success in economic and general
status striving, yet in which many must be losers by the very nature of the struggle, it is certainly to be expected that this will be
an area of intense emotional conflicts . . . we get all kinds of secret,
often self-deceptive hatreds and resentments that pervade our economic, political and private lives in complex ways. (98)

Thus, those who would conduct cultural studies among their
own people (Hayano 1979), and whose people command less
prestige than their own current reference groups, may face three
less-than-ideal choices: covert research with its ethical prob-

lems and diminished ability to interview; overt research with the possibility that researchers' upward mobility will expand the social distance between themselves and the people they study and lead to greater defensiveness; or rejection of this approach, auto-ethnography.[5]

The objections to covert research generally are premised on a picture of the researcher assuming a fake role and then spying on indigenous folk (e.g., Gold 1958). This depiction has little to do with the auto-ethnographer. I never felt I was faking it. My "true self" includes a quite visceral sense of being a truck driver as well as a sociologist. And, though I certainly was doing research, I also was doing survival. I needed the job. Truck driving is the work I did when I needed money, and it was work with which I had a considerable history. Furthermore, trucking also is a world that I had long thought about in a sociological way. The difference this time was that I intended to record my observations and feelings, and to think about them in a more disciplined manner. This seemed no more like spying than did my reports to trucker friends about university life.

This is not to say I had no qualms about doing covert research. In fact, I imposed a quite serious limitation on myself: to function in this world as much as possible as I would have before doing research. In other words, I felt spying was an issue, and I did not want spy. To satisfy this condition, I never consciously and covertly probed fellow drivers to unearth data useful for my research interests. Nor did I create situations for the purposes of research. For example, at times I fought with owners and management, but never more than was normal for me and never over issues chosen for their research value. I tried to stay within the bounds of my typical conversations and behavior. In other words, I tried to be just another driver, though one who noted what was said and done. This stance, in fact, came almost automatically. As in prior years, I quickly became caught up in my job, yet I also thought about it by using the sociological tools I had so far acquired.

In order to get a job, I did not lie about my background. I told interviewers about my education but emphasized my driving record. Potential employers often remarked about my having an M.A. degree, but only one made an issue of it—he suggested that my future would be better served in freight sales. Since I was experienced and had a virtually spotless record, employers found me attractive. In addition, I had references who knew the general manager at PetroHaul and the owner at SandHaul. The PetroHaul reference was especially helpful, because the general manager had to be convinced I was worth training in the operation of tankers. I also possessed the driving skills needed to pass the formal road test required by PetroHaul and the informal road test at SandHaul.[6]

My role as a covert researcher appeared to leave no residue after I left PetroHaul and SandHaul. At PetroHaul, I was one of several low-seniority drivers put on "temporary lay-off" because of the sudden evaporation of work. Since I lacked the financial means to survive more than a brief period without work, I sought another job. When I left SandHaul, I told everyone that I was returning to school. In this sector of trucking, it is common for drivers to come and go, and, in fact, one other SandHaul driver left about the same time I did to attend college. Thus my leaving SandHaul was not out of the ordinary. I kept in contact with several SandHaul drivers after leaving and, to the best of my knowledge, no one saw or came to see my time there as faking it or spying, a perspective I share (cf. Erikson 1967).

The actual recording of data was simple and unobtrusive. I carried a tape recorder in my tool bag and used it to record my observations and ruminations. I never recorded a conversation, secretly or otherwise, but I sometimes made verbatim notes of conversations as best I could. Later, I transcribed my tapes, coded the transcripts, and used them as a data base.

To overcome the limitations on interviewing that are inherent in covert research and that stemmed from my self-imposed restrictions, I returned to SandHaul a year after quitting, told its owner and drivers that I was "thinking about writing a book," and overtly interviewed some of them. The interviews were open-ended discussions related to my concerns. I supplemented this data with articles collected from newspapers, industry trade magazines, and independent magazines aimed at drivers and owner-operators.

Like many contemporary ethnographers I am struggling to find the voice that best represents to the audience the truths of those I study, while also making clear my place in this enterprise. I have consciously tried to move away from the sort of third-person, omniscient presentation Van Maanen (1988) associates with "realist tales" and toward forms that make the author's presence clear and admit more of the sense of an experience, so that readers can both "feel" it and render their own interpretations.

Overview

Two questions organize this book: Why did drivers work so hard? How did drivers make sense of their high effort? I begin in Chapter 2 with a brief overview of the trucking industry and the niche occupied by the three companies in this study so that the reader will have some understanding of the forces that shape them. I then examine the problems inherent in each company's type of hauling and how work was organized to overcome these problems. In Chapter 3, I detail the responses of drivers to the organization of work they encounter. I found that drivers labored diligently, but this diligence is not explained by coercion. Piecework, which was used at two companies, is shown to be a powerful incentive for drivers, yet drivers who were paid hourly wages behaved much like those who worked for piece rates. I argue that money alone is not enough to explain this high level of effort by hourly wage drivers in the absence of notable coercion.

In Chapter 4, I discuss workplace conflict. Here, I have two goals: to better understand the motivations of drivers, and to challenge misconceptions about conflict that permeate the literature on work. At two companies I found much less driver-owner conflict than most studies suggest. Typically, conflict was greater among drivers than between drivers and owners. In addition, I question depictions of small entrepreneurial firms that emphasize coercion as a means of control and show the issue to be more complex than usually supposed. Finally, significant conflict between drivers and an owner is shown to be a struggle not so much over control of the labor process as over the amount of respect truck driving and individual work performances deserved.

In Chapters 5–9, I examine the meanings of work for drivers, the construction and maintenance of these meanings, and the impact they have on career decisions. In Chapter 5, I discuss self-identity and work, and I detail the problems drivers have in knowing and evaluating their work skills. As a consequence of these problems, drivers and owners search for alternative ways to measure performance, the subject of Chapter 6. I argue that drivers turn to measures that are associated with sheer effort. Because male role definitions put a high value on physical strength and exertion, these become strong indicators of task performance.

Since effort at work, however, is not necessarily honorable in jobs without high social standing, there is a tension between showing how much one can do and not doing so much that one seems to be groveling before the employer. This potential for dishonor is underscored by traditional definitions of masculinity that greatly devalue subservience and submission. Thus effort may be both an attractive measure of task performance and a mark of dishonor. If dishonor is successfully countered, drivers work with great diligence. I argue that the companies in this study countered dishonor by, in effect, constituting drivers as owner-operators. Drivers had considerable freedom to plan their work, seemed to own the means of production, and were able to act out occupational myths that attested to their masculinity and set them apart as special. Sometimes dishonor was further countered by blaming the market rather than company owners.

Beside turning to effort as a measure of skill, drivers also looked to nondriver audiences for validation of their work. In Chapters 7 and 8, I discuss drivers' relationships with government officials, company support personnel, shippers and customers, motorists, and drivers who are not co-workers. Some of these relationships have a particularly theatrical quality, and for them I adopt a dramaturgical perspective.

In Chapter 9, I summarize the experience of driving, present career choices that revolve around this experience, and discuss the significance of this study for understanding workplace behavior. I argue that to understand workers' behavior, workplace conflict, the durability of certain work systems, and the willingness or unwillingness of workers to challenge production relations seriously, it is necessary to look beyond the idea of workers as fixated on money or as puppets of the labor process. As an alternative, I focus on the need of workers to make sense out of their work and their lives.

A final note: because all but one of these drivers were men, and because I believe gender roles are an important element in my analysis, I use the male pronoun when discussing drivers.[7]

CHAPTER 2

The Organization of Work

*H*ow a company is categorized within the trucking industry greatly influences how it conducts its business. The industry is legally divided into interstate and intrastate hauling.[1] Interstate carriers haul between states and are governed primarily by the Interstate Commerce Commission (ICC). State agencies oversee intrastate carriers; in California the Public Utilities Commission (PUC) has this responsibility. The three companies in this book are intrastate carriers, although AgriHaul occasionally secured temporary permits enabling it to transport interstate loads. Three of my other five employers performed interstate hauling.

The trucking industry also is divided into two major groups: private and for-hire carriers. Private carriers primarily haul their own products, while for-hire carriers haul commodities belonging to others. The three companies in this study and all but one of my employers were for-hire carriers.

When I was conducting this investigation, the ICC and California PUC divided for-hire carriers into common, contract, and exempt carriers.[2] Differences exist between ICC and PUC rules for each type of carrier, but they are fundamentally similar. Common carriers serve any shipper within their territory as long as the commodity is appropriate, while contract carriers serve a limited number of shippers, with whom they enter into contracts for high-volume hauling. Interstate common and contract carriers until 1980 were governed by ICC rules that set prices or minimum prices for hauling and imposed considerable restrictions on the ability of new companies to compete, the territories companies could serve, and the routes open to travel.

Common and contract hauling in California continues to be regulated by the PUC, including rules for price minimums (though some say enforcement is much less strict than in the past). Compared to nonexempt interstate haulers before they were deregulated, California's nonexempt intrastate haulers were less restricted in entering the business and gaining access to territories and shippers. Thus, though California's nonexempt intrastate carriers benefit from regulations establishing price minimums, there are many haulers competing for business.

Exempt carriers generally do not have to abide by rules regarding hauling prices, access to shippers, or restrictions on routes. The commodities the ICC and PUC deem exempt differ; the most common exempt carriers at the interstate level are haulers of livestock, fish, and unprocessed agricultural commodities. One characteristic of exempt hauling is a highly volatile market given to considerable fluctuations in supply, demand, and prices. For example, in 1981 the average monthly payment for a load of produce hauled from Southern California to New York ranged from $2,225 to $4,275 (*Overdrive*, March 1982, 88).

Two of the companies in this book, AgriHaul and SandHaul, did common, contract, and exempt hauling. More than a few of their contracts were with customers for whom rail transportation was a viable option. The PUC recognized this competition and allowed lower rates. The sum effect of these arrangements was that in most cases there were price cushions; that is, minimum rates were established by the state, but rates often were low (rail rates), and competition for customers was intense. The third company, PetroHaul, mostly hauled commodities that were deregulated a short time before I was hired.

It is fair to characterize the large, interstate, unionized carriers before deregulation as members of trucking's monopoly sector. Entering the business was difficult, because most operating rights were limited to those owned by companies in existence when federal regulation was established in 1933 (MacAvoy and Snow 1977, 4). Companies in the business were restricted in the territories they could serve and routes they could use. Prices were regulated, and, since most drivers worked under a master contract, increases in pay were easily passed on in prices. On the other hand, the three companies in this book could be characterized as operating in the industry's competitive sector. Some prices were regulated, some regulated prices were quite low, and some prices were left to the market. Entry and access to customers, territories, and routes were far easier for these companies and their competitors than for those in the monopoly sector. Drivers at these companies were nonunion, and pay increases were not easily rolled over into higher hauling charges.

Among drivers of large (Class 8) trucks there were, at the time I drove trucks, no formal occupational gradations based on skill that acted to differentiate them. Until the Motor Carrier Safety Act of 1986 changed licensing by penalizing states that failed to adopt and administer by 1993 a single and uniform commercial driver's license (CDL) for truck and bus drivers, only thirty-one states including California even required truck drivers to hold a special license (*Heavy Duty Trucking*, October 1985, 68). The basic CDL allows drivers to operate a tractor-trailer or truck-and-trailer and to haul loads not classified as hazardous. To operate a tractor pulling multiple trailers or to haul hazardous materials, drivers need to pass additional tests. However, I am not aware of drivers seeing these added qualifications as indices of meaningful skill differences.[3]

Beside not rising through a formal hierarchy based on skill, drivers in these three companies usually do not progress to other jobs within the industry. The only position filled regularly from the ranks of drivers is that of dispatcher, but there are few dispatcher slots relative to the number of available drivers. If drivers stay in the industry, they usually stay as drivers.

Organizing Work at a Trucking Company

Trucking companies of all sorts need to accomplish similar tasks. Their trucks must be driven, loaded and unloaded, serviced, and repaired. Each day's hauls need to be organized and assigned. Finances, paperwork, and recruiting and retaining customers demand constant attention. Finally, coordination and planning beyond day-to-day activities are necessary, and fundamental questions about the company's direction and growth must be answered. Companies differ in the number of people assigned to each task, the numbers and types of tasks assigned to one person, and the use of noncompany personnel to do some of the work. For example, companies vary in the amount of loading, unloading, and vehicle maintenance they expect from their drivers. In unionized companies a contract spells out the division of labor as it applies to drivers, while in non-unionized companies owners either mandate or negotiate who does what.

The direct management of drivers is left mainly to the dispatcher. Dispatchers organize customers' orders into a delivery schedule that aims for the most efficient use of company equipment and personnel while satisfying customers and drivers. As the schedule is developed, often on the run, dispatchers assign loads and attempt to see that the schedule is met. Drivers and dispatchers often are at odds, because scheduling that is rational for the company does not always make sense to drivers. For example, after delivering a load, a driver may be sent well out of his way to pick up a return load that pays him little money, or he may be asked to stay put, without pay, until a return load is found. The dispatcher must please the owner while accommodating drivers enough to keep them cooperative about meeting work schedules. The more irregular the schedule, the greater the tension between these demands.

Truck drivers are difficult to supervise because they are away from the company and on the move. The expense of placing supervisors on trucks would put trucking at a severe cost disadvantage to its major competitor, the railroads (Wyckoff and Maister 1977, xlix). Further, trucking competes with railroads by promising fast, individually tailored service (xxvi–xxix), which requires a flexibility at odds with close supervision.

Given the impracticality of direct supervision, companies rely on indirect means. Before computerized and satellite tracking technology was widely available, which postdates the events in this book, some owners used one automated device: the tachograph. Tachographs record onto graph paper a truck's speed and mileage, the revolutions per minute at which the engine is operated, and the times the truck is started, operated, stopped, and shut off. Despite these measures, it is difficult to tell from a tachograph chart where the truck has been driven or its location during any particular time period (a driver might take a different route than the one he claimed), the level of skill with which the truck has been operated other than shifting and driving at the correct engine speed, or the veracity of a driver's explanations for recorded deviations (drivers can cover unauthorized breaks by claiming that equipment problems forced them to stop).

During the period covered by this book, state and federal laws governed the amount of time drivers could drive or be on duty, and drivers were expected to account for their time. In California, tachographs were allowed to track time as long as the truck operated within one hundred miles of its base terminal. Drivers not using tachographs and those beyond the hundred-mile limit were expected to keep a logbook. Logbooks are standardized forms on which drivers must account for every hour of every day they are employed as drivers. Four categories of duty status exist in the logbook: "off duty," "sleeper berth" (sleeping in a bed that is part of the truck), "driving," and "on duty (not driving)." An example of on duty but not driving is time spent loading and unloading. Drivers are limited by state and federal laws in the amount of time they can drive and be on duty in any twenty-four-hour period, in a seven- or eight-day period, and without a break. Drivers must also record in logbooks their points of origin and destination, daily mileage, the geographical location of all duty changes, and the bill of lading's identification numbers. Logbooks are easily faked, as indicated by popular epithets such as "comic book" or "lie book," and they have limited utility as a form of driver control.

While drivers are not at the mercy of an assembly line that determines their work pace, the truck's capabilities act as a pacing device and therefore as a form of machine-imposed control (see Edwards 1979). For example, modern trucks operating on flat roads and in fair weather typically can carry full loads at fifty-five miles an hour, and drivers would normally be expected to travel at least at fast where legal. But the control embedded in a truck's mechanical specifications is limited because of the many ways drivers can explain variations in their work pace. For example, a driver might justify driving below the truck's capabilities by claiming mechanical problems, traffic congestion, or dangerous weather conditions. Thus, rather than strictly determining the pace at which work is carried out, the mechanical capabilities of a truck constitute work-pace parameters within which the driver exercises control.

When work is difficult to supervise, compensation can act both as a control and as an incentive to perform (Stinchcombe 1983, 254). In trucking, the forms of compensation vary widely. Drivers may be paid by the hour or by miles driven, a set percentage of what the company charges to haul a load (in my experience, from 24–34 percent), a salary, a set fee per load, or some combination of these methods. Unionized companies usually pay hourly wages to drivers who do local pickup and delivery and mileage wages to their long-distance ("over-the-road") drivers. Three of the eight companies I worked for paid drivers a percentage, two paid a flat rate per haul, two paid by the hour, and one paid by mileage.

Trucking tends to be sensitive to economic fluctuations, especially small companies, because they usually specialize in one area of the industry. In my experience, it was not unusual to work steadily for sixty-five to ninety hours a week and then suddenly plunge to zero to fifteen hours a week. Evidence of these swings can be seen in what is perhaps the most common aphorism among drivers at such companies, "Get it while the gettin's good."

Compounding the problem of business cycles is the inability or unwillingness of customers to give trucking companies much advance notice about their needs. As a consequence, most of my employers found it a continual problem to develop schedules that would keep their equipment in use, keep unpaid mileage down, or both. The problem of use inclines owners to expect fewer trucks and drivers to do a greater amount of work. This kind of expectation may be common to most businesses, but without the burden of overtime pay, effective government regulation of employees' hours, or an organized work force that demanded adherence to the legal limits on working hours, these owners were free to exploit their inclination.

The companies in this book, AgriHaul, SandHaul, and PetroHaul, were alike in terms of size, nonunion work forces, specialized hauling, division of labor, and a highly competitive environment. On the other hand, each company had unique organizational problems and owners with different inclinations, which produced differences in how work was organized and drivers motivated. Once customers were recruited, the central problems for each company were how to organize work efficiently and how to get drivers to perform in a way that would generate profit.

AgriHaul

Like the other two companies, AgriHaul transported commodities that could be loaded by pouring them into a trailer and unloaded by letting them flow out. The company had many customers and hauled a wide variety of materials and products. Customers' needs for the materials handled by AgriHaul were, in many cases, markedly affected by seasonal fluctuations, general economic cycles, and acts of nature. A poultry disease, for example, once brought the demand for poultry feeds to a near standstill, and weather conditions affected the availability of agricultural products. The scheduling of loading and unloading varied greatly among customers—some were open twenty-four hours, seven days, while others were accessible for only a few hours a week. About 20 percent of AgriHaul's customers required the services of a specialized trailer that cost them more than delivery by a standard trailer.

Most outbound loads were hauled two hundred to five hundred miles from the yard to customers scattered throughout California and occasionally in Nevada and Arizona. Given these distances and the prevailing rates customers were charged, AgriHaul's owner sought backhauls (return loads) rather than have trucks return empty. Since these distances could be covered in a less than a day, AgriHaul did not have much time to set up a backhaul once it accepted an order for an outbound load. Thus, the company had to invest considerable effort in finding and coordinating both outbound and inbound loads.

Compounding the problems of scheduling were the contingencies associated with loading and unloading. For example, a driver hauling fish meal that takes one hour to load might arrive at the shipper's plant and find no trucks or five trucks ahead of him, hence a loading time of one to six hours. If the meal is especially greasy it will pack more tightly during transit and perhaps double or triple unloading time. Unloading could be further delayed by other trucks waiting to unload or the receiver's equipment breaking down.

Scheduling also was disrupted by truck breakdowns, accidents, delays caused by police or other regulatory officials, and weather conditions.

To summarize, AgriHaul had to serve many customers spread over a relatively wide area and located at distances that often did not allow the driver to return to the yard within a time period that could be reasonably considered a single shift. These customers had to be served under conditions that made scheduling unpredictable and subject to frequent modification. Thus, AgriHaul had to get the most possible use from its equipment without time for much advance planning and for customers whose needs precluded evenly paced demands on drivers' efforts. Given its many customers, various combinations of routes and loads, and unpredictability in loading and unloading times, AgriHaul found it particularly difficult to supervise drivers or hold them to performance norms.

For these reasons, AgriHaul did not use shifts. Instead, nearly every truck was permanently assigned to a single driver. Trucks were equipped with sleeper compartments that allowed drivers to legally log their sleeping time in a truck and to sleep comfortably. Drivers often worked seventy to ninety hours a week and sometimes more, though work could dip to twenty hours a week during the winter. They were expected to be highly flexible in their availability for work and willing to exert themselves fully when necessary.

The unpredictability of scheduling at AgriHaul reduced the opportunities to use load assignments as rewards for seniority or favored drivers. Instead, loads were assigned by a combination of economy (the most profitable way to get a truck from point A to point B and back to A), organizational needs (the coordination of a day's loads), and ad hoc bargains by which dispatchers assigned desirable loads in return for expenditures of high driver effort. In addition, loads sometimes were assigned on a first-come, first-served basis, for example, when allotting backhauls to a group of outbound drivers in the process of unloading. Within these considerations, the dispatcher made some effort to rotate loads among drivers. Typically, a driver received one assignment at a time; after completing that assignment, he would call the dispatcher for the next one. When drivers were given both an outbound and inbound load, the inbound assignment often was changed before the load could be picked up.

AgriHaul drivers had a great deal of freedom in completing their assignments. In almost every case the driver was told only what load he was to haul, the time it ought to arrive (as specific as "as soon as possible" or "nine A.M.," or as general as "tomorrow"), and whatever facts might make delivery smoother. It was up to the driver to determine a route, though the dispatcher or owner might suggest routes if the driver was not familiar with a particular run. Drivers also had considerable discretion over starting times. For example, a driver could depart many hours before the hour necessary for a timely delivery, perhaps intending to sleep on arrival or party along the way with other drivers at a favorite bar or café; or he could take the truck home, sleep there, and leave at the last possible minute.

Drivers were almost never accountable for their time. When late arrivals seemed clearly undue and had relatively serious repercussions (if the customer's production was interrupted, say, or the driver had to stay overnight to wait for a loading or unloading crew) drivers were asked to explain. Even in these cases, however, such questioning, though often angry, rarely descended into a detailed grilling, and it was difficult for the owner or dispatcher to determine if the driver was telling the truth.

Given the minimal supervision it could exercise over drivers and the difficulty of determining acceptable individual output, AgriHaul formally motivated drivers by using what amounted to a simple piece rate system, a predictable solution for an employer in this position (Stinchcombe 1983). Drivers were paid 27 percent of the company's price for hauling a load. Originally, drivers had no way of knowing what a load paid, but eventually the owner succumbed to pressure from the drivers and provided them with the unit price (per one hundred pounds) for each load; drivers then could multiply this rate by the load's weight and compute what it should pay them. (But, even after they were given the load price list, drivers were unaware of a ready means to confirm these prices and relied on the owner to be truthful.) In addition to percentage pay, drivers ostensibly received five dollars an hour once loading or unloading exceeded two hours, but large claims often were not fully paid. Finally, there was no guaranteed minimum daily or hourly pay.

The use of piece rates at AgriHaul differed in several ways from that usually found in factory production (Roy 1952; Braverman 1974; Burawoy 1979; Lamphere 1979; Shapiro-Perl 1979).[4] First, whereas piece rates in factories sometimes function as a bonus for excess production by an hourly worker, Agri-Haul's piece rate was not a bonus. Second, unlike factory production, the many contingencies associated with AgriHaul's hauling assignments made it difficult to establish precise productivity norms. In the absence of productivity norms and bonuses, there were no means or reasons for drivers to alter their claims of production (by stockpiling excess production, for example; see Burawoy 1979, 58). Neither could management reduce a driver's pay by subtracting from his bonus the amount supposedly lost by the company when he produced at a lower than minimum rate (Shapiro-Perl 1979, 295).

Another difference between piecework at AgriHaul and at factories where managerial calculations led to nearly identical hourly rates for most jobs (Shapiro-Perl 1979, 290) was that AgriHaul's rates differed by as much as 50 percent for different jobs when calculated in terms of hourly pay.

The greatest difference from most accounts of factory piecework (Roy 1952; Haraszti 1978; Lamphere 1979; Shapiro-Perl 1979) was the near-absence of rate cutting; certainly, rate cutting was never used as an obvious managerial strategy for reducing drivers' wages. AgriHaul's owner appeared indifferent to the ability of drivers to earn on some hauls a rate that at times exceeded by several dollars the hourly rate paid to union freight drivers. Rates were almost never reduced, and in the three cases of rate cutting I witnessed, the rates had not been high to begin with, so it was not the "fat" rates that were cut. The owner explained these cuts as necessary in the face of competitors' attempts to take high-volume accounts from AgriHaul that often provided stable alternatives, albeit low-paying ones, to back-hauling empty.

One reason for AgriHaul's restraint in matters of pay was that state PUC rules specified that within companies drivers engaged in the same type of hauling had to be paid in a consistent manner. Thus, for example, the owner could not pay hourly rates for high-paying hauls and percentage rates for low-paying loads or a fluctuating percentage based on the price of the load. However, the owner could claim that competition forced him to cut rates, whether or not that indeed was the case.

All AgriHaul trucks were equipped with tachographs, but

drivers were not required to use them. Instead, tachographs served simply as sturdy clocks, fitting symbols of the motivational power of piece rates. Drivers were required to keep logbooks only to satisfy state and federal laws; management knew that logs were routinely falsified and bore only a marginal resemblance to the drivers' actual workday. Usually this knowledge was implicit; however, in my early days with the company a dispatcher offered me tips on falsifying logbook accounts.

SandHaul

SandHaul hauled only a few materials within a single class of commodities. Demand for the products it hauled, other than a small amount of construction materials, was relatively constant and not particularly subject to seasonal changes, acts of nature, or national business cycles.

The bulk of SandHaul's accounts were with six large industrial customers clustered within 50 miles of SandHaul's yard; and SandHaul transported materials to these plants from suppliers located within 150 miles of the yard. Customers ordered a high volume of material daily. Since many loading sites and about half the customers were accessible twenty-four hours, five to seven days a week, SandHaul was able to divide work almost evenly between day and night shifts and keep most of its trucks in continual operation.

SandHaul's business consisted of bringing raw materials from outlying, often rural, areas to urban manufacturers. Its trucks rarely hauled outbound loads, because in these rural areas there was little demand for the products it was able to carry in its specialized trailers, and inbound loads alone were sufficient to generate a profit. In organizing for profit, SandHaul thus did not have the problems of AgriHaul in finding and coordinating loads.

But, like AgriHaul, SandHaul had uncertainties associated with loading and unloading. In particular, two suppliers of raw materials and two customers were notorious for loading and unloading delays. And like other trucking companies, SandHaul's scheduling was affected by equipment breakdowns, accidents, police and regulators, and weather conditions.

To summarize, SandHaul served only a few large customers clustered near its yard. Hauling took place around the clock and at distances short enough for drivers to regularly return to the yard and thus work in shifts. Finally, the volume and regularity of customers' orders and the lack of a need for inbound loads enabled SandHaul to construct a relatively stable schedule.

In contrast to AgriHaul, SandHaul was able to achieve a routine that made it more important for drivers to work steadily than to mix Herculean, normal, and inconsequential effort (during slow periods at AgriHaul, a driver could take as long as he wanted to complete his assignment; at such times I visited friends or relatives who lived along my routes). Nonetheless, drivers could not be supervised directly, and work completion times were unpredictable to a degree that rendered their averages fairly useless as a means for holding drivers accountable.

In SandHaul's shift system, at the end of an assignment, typically a period of ten to fourteen hours, drivers returned their trucks to the yard, where other drivers would take over. Drivers were expected to be flexible in regard to starting and finishing times, because irregularities, though diminished by the routine, still existed.

The ability to plan in advance made it possible for SandHaul to assign two or three loads to each driver in a way that kept unpaid time and equipment use to a minimum and took roughly twelve hours. Once assigned, these loads were not often changed, although a final load might be canceled if the driver was running very late. In this manner, the company was able to maintain a day shift that ended between 10 A.M. and 2 P.M. and a night shift that ended between 11 P.M. and 4 A.M.. Without load coordination problems of AgriHaul's magnitude, SandHaul rotated assignments more or less evenly among the drivers, with marginal consideration for seniority and—if drivers' complaints are a fair measure—no favoritism.

SandHaul drivers were free to choose their routes and delivery sequences, but this freedom was often moot because of the few loading and unloading sites and the nature of load assignments. For example, if a driver was assigned load A, then he almost always also was assigned load B, and under most conditions it made sense first to deliver load A. For the most part, the drivers' flexibility allowed them to adapt to the sort of contingencies no amount of routine can eliminate, such as accidents or weather conditions that call for alternate routes.

SandHaul drivers were paid a percentage of the price charged by the owner for each load they hauled, 25–31 percent, depending on seniority. This form of pay was identical to AgriHaul's, though the percentages differed. It was not a bonus, there was no guaranteed minimum pay, rate variations as large as 50 percent existed, and the ability of drivers to "make-out" (Burawoy 1979) did not lead to any detectable rate cutting. Like AgriHaul, SandHaul paid five dollars an hour for excess "standing time," but here it became effective after one hour. The major difference between piecework at SandHaul as compared to AgriHaul or a factory was that working fast at SandHaul did not result in more than normal production. When SandHaul drivers completed their assignments, their shifts ended; they did not have the opportunity to do more work.

SandHaul differed from every other small, highly competitive trucking company I knew of in that it demanded observance of the fifty-five miles an hour speed limit and used tachographs to enforce this rule, even though most California Highway Patrol officers allow trucks to travel fifty-nine in a fifty-five miles-an-hour zone without citing them for speeding. A driver with eighteen years of experience in this sector was incredulous on hearing of SandHaul's use of tachographs: "I've never heard of shit like that." In effect, SandHaul's owner had constructed an incentive system that encouraged drivers to work as fast as possible and then checked this inclination by monitoring speed. The owner's explanation for using tachographs was fuel economy. Given customers' predictable demands, SandHaul's owner strove to establish a steady level of effort that would both meet schedule needs and effect operational economies. In this way, SandHaul mirrored Edwards's (1979) description of core corporations that, in their exercise of bureaucratic control, "survive on their ability to organize the routine, normal efforts of workers, not on their ability to elicit peak performances . . . [unlike the] entrepreneurial firm [that] often depends on exceptional efforts. . . . Instead it seeks to raise as high as possible the minimal standards for acceptable performance" (146).

PetroHaul

PetroHaul operated a fleet of tank trucks that hauled petroleum products, about half of which was gasoline. Other products included crude oil, diesel fuel, naptha, and jet fuel.

PetroHaul served more customers than SandHaul (approximately twenty) but fewer than AgriHaul, ranging from a single independent gas station to multinational oil corporations. Day-to-day customer demand was almost as steady as at SandHaul, and most products could be loaded and delivered twenty to twenty-four hours a day. The demand for petroleum products, however, was seasonal and responsive to broad economic forces; demand once diminished so suddenly that in the span of a few days three of the most recently hired drivers, including me, went from working sixty to seventy-five hours a week to being temporarily laid off. Predictably, drivers at PetroHaul, as at AgriHaul, believed they ought to "get it while the gettin's good." Adding to this unpredictability, some customers, especially gasoline retailers, typically gave short notice about their needs. Thus, when business was good, day-to-day demand was relatively constant, but scheduling could be frantic and very short-term.

Most customers were clustered within 50 miles of the yard, and the products PetroHaul brought them were loaded at plants within 150 miles of the yard. Gasoline, diesel fuel, and jet fuel hauling were particularly localized, with about 75 percent of the loading and delivery taking place within a 40-mile radius of the yard. PetroHaul's customers, unlike those at SandHaul, had multiple delivery sites. For example, one gasoline retailer had thirty-eight stations. Thus, PetroHaul drivers, like those at AgriHaul, hauled to many more delivery sites than drivers at SandHaul.

As at SandHaul, the nature of PetroHaul's hauling usually dictated that trucks returned empty after delivering a load. But, given PetroHaul's many loading and delivery sites, loads could be sequenced to reduce empty mileage. Thus, PetroHaul did not approach the problems of AgriHaul in finding and coordinating loads, but the dispatcher paid more attention to loading sequences than at SandHaul.

In summary, PetroHaul served a moderate number of customers of varying size, most clustered near PetroHaul's yard, who ordered from suppliers located near enough that drivers were able to return to the yard within one shift. The relatively high volume of business (except during seasonal and national economic downturns) and smooth load coordination promised relatively stable scheduling, but this stability was countered somewhat by customers' short notices and erratic needs.

In order to operate its trucks around the clock, PetroHaul organized drivers into two shifts, each as close to fifteen hours as possible, reducing to the legal minimum the number of shift changes. Two drivers were permanently assigned to each truck; as soon as one driver ended his shift, he was replaced by his partner. Unlike SandHaul, where the drivers were organized into day and night shifts that changed at approximately the same times each day, shift changes at PetroHaul were tied to partners and took place twenty-four hours. As at the other companies, drivers were expected to be flexible about starting and finishing times that were never entirely predictable. Drivers also needed to be flexible in the sense that fifteen-hour shifts are badly out of sync with normal home life and human biological cycles.

Hauling at PetroHaul was divided into "clean" (gasoline, jet fuel) and "dirty" (crude oil). This division reflected the need to have a clean trailer before loading gasoline or jet fuel, the greater messiness of crude oil, and differences in loading and unloading procedures that made contact with the product more likely with oil than with gasoline or jet fuel. Different loading and unloading requirements meant that most drivers hauled either only clean or only dirty products. A few "swing" drivers hauled both categories, and some products, such as naptha and diesel fuel, were hauled by all drivers.

PetroHaul was usually able to assign full work loads to drivers at the beginning of a shift, though sometimes these were altered in order to serve a customer's immediate needs. Once or twice a week gasoline drivers were asked to do a particular load first because that customer was in urgent need. And about once every one to two weeks a driver could expect to be asked to make a higher than normal effort in order to meet a scheduling difficulty.

Drivers almost always had the freedom to select their routes. Gasoline drivers, who typically delivered to many more locations than oil drivers, were free to plan delivery sequences unless a load needed immediate delivery. For oil haulers, load sequencing usually was not an issue, because they hauled to fewer sites and often repeated the same load.

Given the absence of load coordination problems as severe as those of AgriHaul, PetroHaul was more likely to use seniority and favoritism as considerations in load assignments. However, assignments were less an issue at PetroHaul than at AgriHaul and SandHaul, because drivers were not paid a percentage of the gross, and hauls therefore were not rated by how well they paid. In addition, loads did not differ as greatly as at AgriHaul in terms of nonmonetary characteristics important to drivers such as ease, distance, cleanliness, and route. Clean hauls varied more than dirty hauls in ease of unloading, distance hauled, and safety (some delivery sites put drivers at relatively high risk for mugging and robbery) and thus were the most likely to involve seniority and favoritism when assignments were made. For example, the highest seniority driver was given a disproportionate share of popular coastal hauls, and on several occasions I saw another senior driver who was a friend of the dispatcher get to pick the gasoline orders he wanted. Nonetheless, the often last-minute placement of orders and immediate needs of customers, coupled with around-the-clock rather than set shift changes, reduced the dispatcher's opportunity to show favoritism or reward seniority. This limitation was evident in the near-total absence of claims by drivers alleging favoritism.

Unlike drivers at the other two companies, PetroHaul drivers were paid an hourly wage ($10.20 in 1981) rather than one based on output. The payment of hourly wages was possible here because the company thought it could measure a driver's productivity (Stinchcombe 1983, 180). Informal but clear quotas were used; drivers typically received the number of assignments they were expected to complete in a fifteen-hour shift if all went well. Problems inevitably arose, and assignments were not always completed, but even these variations were somewhat patterned. For example, gasoline drivers usually were able to complete five local hauls, but oil drivers more often than not fell short of the six deliveries always assigned for one customer. The failure to meet a quota was common enough to warrant a label: "kickback," that is, an assigned load that had to be "kicked back" to the dispatcher for reassignment. The meeting of quotas thus was somewhat erratic, though drivers usually met them.

Depending on the assignment, a driver's failure to meet a quota provoked little or no response. Sometimes the dispatcher would express minor irritation, because this failure forced him to make scheduling changes. But I heard of no instance of the general manager or owner reprimanding a driver for failing to meet a quota. The only times the general manager and owner expressed annoyance over an unmet quota was when they themselves were dispatching and the failure upset the schedule they had put together.

Tachographs appeared to underpin PetroHaul's quotas. In theory this instrument ought to reveal why a quota was not met. In practice, the owner and manger appeared to use the tachograph only to keep track of payable versus nonpayable hours (more than two breaks or breaks over twenty minutes long were not payable) and to satisfy the state requirement for drivers to log their hours. Drivers were free to drive any speed they desired, and, with a few exceptions, I never knew of a driver having to explain tachograph information other than when overly long breaks were questioned. The exceptions were: (1) when an engine blew up, the driver told me the owner and general manager had checked his chart to see if he had ascended a mountain grade too fast; (2) in order to anticipate problems stemming from an accident, the owner and general manager checked the driver's chart to see if his hours were legal; and (3) a chart revealed that a driver ended his shift after twelve rather than fifteen hours, and he was reprimanded. What is notable about these exceptions to management's usual lack of concern with the full range of tachograph data is that two of the three instances were provoked by unusual occurrences (an engine blowing, an accident) rather than by common daily activities.

PetroHaul's owner had an incentive system somewhat the opposite that at SandHaul. At SandHaul, the form of payment encouraged drivers to work fast in order to get off as early as possible, but they were restrained by a tachograph-enforced speed limit of fifty-five. PetroHaul drivers had no limits on their pace of work, but hourly pay and fifteen-hour shifts meant that they gained little or nothing by hurrying. Given that PetroHaul drivers were easily able to explain delays that appeared on their tachographs, they might be expected to exert comparatively little effort.

Trucking companies, in their competition with one another and with railroads (almost all the products carried by SandHaul and AgriHaul, and most "dirty" products at PetroHaul, were loaded and unloaded near or on rail spurs), need to offer fast, flexible, and reliable service. A key to such service and to profits at the three companies in this book is sequencing orders to meet customers' needs while also keeping empty mileage low or keeping drivers deployed in shifts. Load sequencing was a constant and major problem for AgriHaul, something of a problem for Petro-Haul, and mostly resolved at SandHaul.

In attending to customers' needs and the requisites of profit, considerable demands were made of drivers. They were called upon to work long, odd, and sometimes erratic hours. At Petro-Haul and, in particular, AgriHaul, scheduling conflicts and urgent deliveries led to variations in the effort asked of drivers.

Truck driving is not amenable to any economic method of direct supervision. In addition, the many contingencies associated with truck transportation—especially in these companies, where the same truck and driver handle a load from pickup to delivery, as opposed to the trucker who drives preloaded trucks between company terminals—make it difficult to establish production quotas that could serve to control drivers. The three companies met the problem of supervising and motivating drivers in different ways. AgriHaul relied on a simple form of piecework akin to a feudal rent (see Stinchcombe 1983 on *metayage*); drivers were accountable for very little other than getting the job done. SandHaul used the same form of piecework but simultaneously employed tachographs to keep driver effort within bounds that would at once meet scheduling needs and effect operational economies. In addition, SandHaul's drivers were constrained by a comparatively strict routine. PetroHaul thought it possible and useful to establish production quotas; drivers were paid by the hour, and quotas were combined with tachographs seemingly to ensure that drivers worked hard and were paid for only the time they actually worked. PetroHaul's owner and management showed a surprising lack of concern, however, when quotas were not met, and what concern existed had more to do with the disruption of orderly work schedules than with profit.

While the tachograph, logbook, quota, and mechanical capabilities of trucks give owners and managers some control over drivers, the unpredictable nature of trucking and the lack of direct supervision allow drivers considerable control over their own activities. How they exercise this control is the subject of Chapter 3.

CHAPTER 3

Drivers at Work

WHY DID THE TRUCK drivers in this book work so hard? Coercion? Financial incentives? Some would say so (Goldthorpe et al. 1968; Braverman 1974; Dubin 1976). To make better sense of drivers' behavior, I believe one needs to look at the logic inherent in the method of paying drivers, given a company's organization of work; and at how work is distributed, for the assignment of hauls and the order in which drivers are dispatched can affect a driver's income, rate of pay, length of shift, enjoyment of work, opportunities to see family and friends, and self-esteem.

SandHaul: Piecework, Routine, and Internal Competition

SandHaul drivers were paid according to their output, and their shifts normally ended when they completed an assignment.[1] In no case was the rate on a load lowered, and, in the one instance of such a rumor, blame was affixed to a competitor who was attempting to take over that haul. Since rates were not likely to be slashed and shifts ended when assignments were completed, drivers saw as reasonable the completion of work in as little time as possible. This inclination was strengthened by the long and tiring shifts; drivers wanted to finish quickly so as to have time for socializing, sleeping, and other interests.

The night shift at SandHaul, which is the shift I worked, serviced three customers and was organized into five assignments. Generally, assignments could be completed in ten to fourteen hours, and drivers usually worked until completing their assignments. Single-haul assignments were always completed regardless of how long they took, unless the customer was unable to unload the truck. When a driver was running late on a multiple-load assignment, however, such as the delivery of three short, local loads, he was often instructed to cancel his last load to return the truck to the yard in time for the day-shift driver to use it. Since three of the five assignments involved multiple loads and drivers were paid for completed loads, most drivers on any night's shift were concerned with finishing their assignments.

With thirteen drivers to perform the night shift's five hauls, drivers often were given the same assignment. In addition, drivers with differing assignments might share a loading or delivery site. The result was that any one driver was usually going somewhere that other SandHaul drivers were also going. Given the drivers' desire to finish quickly, overlapping loads proved a source of conflict, because SandHaul drivers saw each other as potential delays. For example, if two drivers were headed for the same destination, the driver who arrived second would probably have to wait for the first driver to load or unload—a wait that could last from thirty minutes to many hours (one SandHaul driver liked to tell about a breakdown at a shipper's plant that occurred just as he finished loading and caused the SandHaul driver behind him to wait twelve hours before being loaded). Delays were likely to grow exponentially. For example, Jack and I were given the same assignment and Jack arrived at the shipper's plant several minutes ahead of me; as a consequence, I had to wait thirty minutes for him to load before I could load. By the time I reached our shared destination, thirty minutes later than I would have had I not had to wait behind Jack, three non-SandHaul trucks had arrived after Jack. Since each truck took forty-five minutes to unload and Jack was fifteen minutes shy of being unloaded, the original thirty-minute delay had grown to two and one-half hours. Had it not been for Jack, I would have unloaded in forty-five minutes rather than three and one-quarter hours; for the added wait I added $11.50 to a bimonthly gross paycheck of approximately $1,200 ($5 an hour after the first hour). It was a trade-off drivers despise.

SandHaul's owner, Will, who had recently taken over the company from his father, became the sole dispatcher shortly after I was hired, and in this role he had three basic tasks each day: assign loads to drivers, dispatch the drivers according to some sort of sequence, and see to it that customers' needs were met. The first two tasks were issues with drivers. Because loads varied in desirability according to pay, ease of pickup and delivery, traffic encountered, starting time, cleanliness, and aesthetic pleasures associated with the terrain, drivers preferred some loads to others.[2]

Sequencing was an issue, because the order in which drivers were put to work affected the amount of time it took to complete a job, quitting time (for most drivers, the earlier the better), rate of pay (the sooner a driver started, the fewer delays he was likely to encounter, and thus the higher his rate of pay), and net pay (the sooner a driver started, the more likely he was to complete his assignments and earn full pay, but the less likely he was to accumulate standing time). All drivers also wanted to start as early as possible, because doing so affected these considerations favorably. Unionized companies, to the best of my knowledge, solve distribution and sequencing problems by the strict application of seniority rules, but nonunion companies inevitably take into account other factors.

Regarding distribution of assignments, Will paid scant attention to seniority and instead went to some lengths to rotate the load assignments evenly among the drivers. But, seniority was rewarded in that the senior drivers were given the highest paying assignment early in the week, which guaranteed they would have this haul even during weeks when the customer ordered less than normal tonnage. The idea behind load rotation was to give drivers equal incomes and variety; both the owner and drivers thought this reasonable and fair. I never heard a driver say that load assignments ought to be determined by seniority.

Seniority was supposedly the main consideration in solving the second problem, constructing a dispatch sequence. The general rule was that drivers should be put to work in order of seniority. Although the least senior drivers sometimes complained about their late starting times (1:30 P.M to 3 P.M.), no driver argued for abandoning seniority as the major determinant. Will generally followed this rule when dispatching the two drivers with the most seniority (they had been employees significantly longer than the other night-shift drivers, and there were fewer conflicting demands at the beginning of shift changes), but he often ignored it with regard to the other drivers.

In addition to using seniority to establish a dispatch sequence, Will reserved the right to assign priority to any load on any given day and, consequently, to ignore seniority if necessary. Thus if driver A had more seniority than driver B, but driver B was hauling a load that needed to be moved as soon as possible, driver B would be dispatched first. All SandHaul drivers told me they felt this was fair when done consistently, as it had been under the previous dispatcher, but Will was not consistent.

Will also ignored seniority and behaved unpredictably regarding the need to switch trailers between tractors. About twice a week, the tractor assigned to a night-shift driver did not have the appropriate trailers attached, so the driver had to unhook the current trailers and attach the needed set, a five- to ten-minute operation. At unpredictable intervals, Will defined trailer swapping as unnecessary equipment wear, took the truck from the driver due it by virtue of his seniority, and gave it to a lower-seniority driver who could use the current trailers. All the drivers, with the exception of one "company man," believed trailer swapping to be an unreasonable consideration in dispatching drivers, because the equipment wear was slight and what savings were realized came at the expense of the displaced driver.

Dispatch worked like this: the day-shift drivers usually delivered their final loads and arrived back at the yard between 10 A.M. and 2 P.M.; at this time their trucks became available to night-shift drivers. Between 9:30 A.M. and 11 A.M. each day, a night-shift driver was supposed to call the office for his assignment. He might be told to come to the yard, but all but the most senior drivers were usually told to wait for a summons from the office, because no trucks were yet available.

After hearing from a day-shift driver that he was unloaded and on his way back to the yard, the owner would designate that truck to a night-shift driver and call that driver to the yard. (A day-shift driver was given his orders in the afternoon or evening and then awaited notification from the night-shift driver assigned to his truck that the truck was available.) Supposedly, drivers would be summoned and given a truck in order of seniority unless a lower-seniority driver's assignment had priority that day. The waiting time for a summons varied from a few minutes to four hours, depending on the delays experienced by the day-shift drivers and the night-shift driver's seniority. A driver who was on call did not have to stay home; he could make arrangements either to telephone later or to be in the yard by a specified time, but doing this typically meant forfeiting seniority rights in that day's dispatch sequence.

Upon being summoned, the driver had about thirty to forty-five minutes to get to the yard if he intended to be there when his assigned truck arrived. Once in the yard, the driver might find that the owner had changed his truck assignment to reduce trailer swapping, a change that was likely to alter the dispatch sequence.

Dispatching drivers according to seniority was overridden in one more way. For reasons having to do with the time it took for a day-shift driver to return to the yard, the readiness of the night-shift driver to leave home when summoned, how soon after the day-shift driver's call the owner or secretary notified the night-shift driver, and the night-shift driver's commuting time, a truck sometimes beat the driver assigned to it to the yard. In at least half such cases the truck was given to the highest-seniority driver in the yard upon its arrival even when the driver who had been summoned was due to arrive within the next five to fifteen minutes. In a variation of this procedure, when several day-shift drivers finished at about the same time, a like number of night-shift drivers would be summoned without specific truck assignments; instead, these drivers would be assigned trucks on a first-come, first-served basis. And at times Will would not even summon the appropriate driver if another driver was in the yard.

Will was inconsistent in the value he placed on seniority. Sometimes he appeared to have no regard for it. For example, twice he told me and a higher-seniority driver whom he disliked to "fight it out between yourselves" to see who got the next available truck. But, in most situations he subscribed to seniority in either word or action. He seemed to endorse seniority as long as it did not interfere with his needs or whims. His view, however, was not simply that of a tyrant: for the most part, he appeared to feel that the effects of ignoring seniority were trivial. On several occasions, he explained his decision to ignore seniority by saying that the dispatch sequence was of little consequence to drivers. Moreover, he felt that his decisions served a greater good. When I was a new employee, he told me, "What we do [dispatching] may not always look like it makes sense, but we have the big picture in here. Just trust us that we're doing the best for everyone." Given the exponential growth of delays in an already-long shift and the poor payment for them, the effects of ignoring seniority were not seen as trivial by the aggrieved driver. Likewise, given Will's unpredictable allegiance to seniority, the drivers did not trust him to dispatch fairly.

Generally, then, starting times were arrived at as follows: the two drivers with the most seniority were dispatched first regardless of their assignments, while the remaining drivers were dispatched according to seniority, but with major qualifications based on load importance and trailer availability. Although seniority was attenuated, officially it was the rationale behind sequencing. However, in his willingness to dispatch drivers who were present in the yard rather than wait for the higher-seniority driver who had been summoned, Will offered drivers the opportunity to circumvent seniority.

All drivers endorsed seniority verbally as the basic principle in ordering the dispatch sequence. All but two drivers were adamant in their opposition to overt attempts to usurp seniority, as evidenced by their labeling this act "snaking" and offending drivers "snakes." Yet, besides the two drivers who were more than willing to take advantage of the opportunity to ignore seniority in dispatch sequencing, all drivers were willing to do so on occasion.

Whatever a driver's seniority, he shared with most piecework drivers the desire to finish work assignments, to complete them as fast as possible, and to complete them as early as possible— an obsession with time heightened at SandHaul by the relatively short hauls. For example, a thirty-minute loading delay means much more to a driver who loads three times a shift than to a driver who loads twice a week in the course of a four-thousand mile roundtrip. The concern of drivers with time was evident in their precise accounts: for example, they commonly talked in terms of "thirty-two minutes" as opposed to "half an hour" or "thirty minutes."

Sid: Tomorrow I'm going in to see Will and see what's going on. The only thing I can figure is that yesterday they tried to call me at 10:30 [A.M.] and I wasn't home. I got home at 10:45 and called in and they said, "We've been trying to call you and we couldn't get ahold of you so we called Judas out." That pissed me off, because Judas ended up going to [Plant 5] ahead of me and holding me up. It took that asshole an hour and a half to dump and forty-eight minutes to back out [as opposed to informal norms of fifty-five and twenty minutes, respectively]. I sat [where he could see me] and read a whole magazine while he backed out.

Each workday, the night-shift driver awoke with two immediate considerations: to start work as early as possible and ahead of as many fellow drivers as possible. These goals implied a two-part strategy: protecting his rightful spot in the dispatch sequence and, depending on the circumstances, advancing his dispatch position. Success in both increased the possibility of completing the assignment, completing it in as little time as possible, and finishing relatively early, all ends fervently desired.

According to driver norms, there were legitimate and illegitimate ways to start as early and ahead of as many drivers as possible. The overriding dispatch rule among drivers was that seniority rights should be observed, which was legitimized by the owner's use, albeit haphazardly, of seniority as a dispatch criterion. Legitimate strategies therefore recognized seniority rights and included calling the office early, being ready to leave home as soon as summoned, and living close to the yard to reduce commuting time after being summoned. By these means a driver was likely to be in the yard when his assigned truck arrived and thus in position to depart ahead of higher-seniority drivers who were less prompt. And such strategies were legitimate because no one expected a summoned driver to wait for a yet-to-arrive higher-seniority driver.

Illegitimate strategies (as indicated by drivers' use of the term "snaking" and other uncomplimentary expressions) circumvented seniority: the most common means was to go to the yard before being summoned, in order to be available immediately if a truck arrived ahead of the night-shift driver assigned to drive it. On a shift of thirteen drivers, two drivers used this method regularly.

A gray area was the source of considerable controversy

among drivers. To protect their rightful position in the dispatch sequence, all drivers came on occasion (and some regularly) to the yard before being summoned. In addition, two drivers claimed to prefer spending their waiting time in the yard to waiting at home. Drivers who defended their positions or socialized in this manner appeared to be trying to advance their dispatch positions illegitimately, because it was difficult to be certain of their motives, whether or not the owner took advantage of their presence and dispatched them ahead of higher-seniority drivers.

As soon as the night-shift driver knew his assignment, if not sooner, he began to make time projections.

> *Ringo:* So I got up this morning and started thinking about what they'd have me hauling today. I already hauled Capo, ash, and sand this week so I figured I was due for ore. Then I started thinking who else might be hauling ore, and I figured that I could be the first one [of the ore haulers] to go out since Sid and Leon [higher-seniority drivers] had already hauled ore this week. So right away I got ready to jam to the yard, and I was right. As soon as I called they wanted me to come on in.

Considerable conflict between drivers arose from their common goals of starting work early, working quickly, and completing assignments, coupled with their potential to delay one another and the opportunities for drivers to circumvent seniority in being dispatched, all common circumstances in nonunion companies that pay piece rates. As Ringo indicated, a driver's first work-related thought each day concerned whom he would be competing with and, by implication, who might attempt to snake him. Ringo's words show him protecting himself and measuring opportunities by figuring who were his most direct competitors (those hauling ore), their seniority (the likely dispatch sequence), and his possible starting time. I found this conflict quite stressful. Frequently a knot formed in my stomach as soon as I learned my assignment and began wondering what time I would be going out and who might try to snake me. With such thoughts in mind, I made preparations that would enable me to leave at a moment's notice, such as planning a meal that could be scooped up and eaten as I drove to the yard.

The dispatcher's summons rang like the starting shot of a race. Drivers described their reactions as, "[The office] called and I hauled ass," or "As soon as they buzzed me, I jammed," or "Jack, I wasted no time getting here after they called." For me, the drive to work was filled with thoughts of snakes and possible delays. I drove as fast as the law allowed and resented anyone who got in my way. As I neared the yard I watched for fellow drivers heading for it. When we spotted each other, we jockeyed for the lead position without appearing to do so. We both knew it was okay to arrive at the yard ahead of a higher-seniority driver and reap the rewards as long as our arrival appeared due only to circumstance.

At the yard, drivers surveyed the parking area to see if the car of a lesser-seniority driver was there.

> *Barney:* As soon as I got to the yard and saw that son-of-a-bitch's car, I figured he was in here trying to snake me again.

Even before parking their cars, drivers almost always went to the office; no one wanted to risk having another driver check in while they were parking. If more than one truck was available, the earlier arrival also was likely to get the better truck, that is, a faster one with a more powerful engine, a tachograph that underestimated actual speed, or trailers with low wind resistance; a lighter one (the lighter the truck, the more material that could be hauled and therefore the greater the earnings); or one that afforded the most prestige and luxury.

As drivers waited for their trucks to arrive, competition and tension among them were clear. For example, when two drivers met in the yard at the beginning of a shift, the common salutation was, "Hi, what are you doing today?" as opposed to, "Hi, how are you doing today?" It was something of a joke among drivers to mock this salutation by saying it in a monotone and as rapidly as possible, with no pause between the greeting and the question. To heighten the effect, a driver might then sarcastically ask how the other was doing. Drivers wanted to know one another's assignments in order to devise the most advantageous work strategies. For example, if I were hauling from points B to C and knew who was hauling from A to C, I might decide that I had a chance to beat that driver to point C if I pushed my truck speed slightly beyond the limit usually permitted by the owner.

Before a night-shift driver could depart in an incoming truck, that truck had to be serviced by its day-shift driver. A night-shift driver in a particular hurry might bargain with the day-shift driver to speed his servicing by, for example, forgoing minor repairs. He also might ask the day-shift driver of a competitor's truck to slow down his servicing by, for example, adding unnecessary oil or asking a mechanic to repair a minor problem.

According to federal and state law, company policy, and common sense, a truck should be inspected whenever a driver first puts it into operation. Given their desire to leave the yard as soon as possible and protect themselves from competitors, and the fact that they were not paid while waiting for their assigned truck to be repaired (unless it broke down on the road), drivers performed hurried and often inadequate inspections. Although the typical inspection form has more than twenty items that are supposed to be checked, at least half of the drivers inspected only for flat tires before leaving the yard. The owner complained about poor inspections only when a driver was caught making a gross error such as leaving the yard with a flat tire, blatant evidence of the absence of even a perfunctory inspection.

Once dispatched and on the road, drivers looked for routes that cut driving time. The savvy driver had options for dealing with foreseeable driving delays and was able to improvise when faced with unexpected traffic obstructions. Moreover, the driver had to be on the lookout for truckers who would advance their own positions at his expense, although passing fellow SandHaul drivers was legitimate in only three instances: when drivers were headed to different destinations; when both were headed to the same destination, but the truck to be passed was not able to maintain a reasonable speed; and when a higher-seniority driver trailed a lower-seniority driver on their way from the yard to a shared first pick-up, because the senior driver should have departed the yard first and should rightfully be in the lead. Drivers wanted to prevent the latter two instances, even though legitimate, because doing so would save time. All other instances of passing were illegitimate (snaking); though always a possibility, on-the-road snaking was such a brazen act that it happened much less often than in the yard, where intent could be disguised.

Of greater concern was the ever-present possibility of being passed by another company's drivers on the way to a common destination (all SandHaul's customers were also serviced by other trucking companies), because they were not held to a speed of fifty-five and few informal norms restricted such moves. Drivers complained constantly about delays resulting from being passed by non-SandHaul competitors and were almost fanatical about finding whatever speed leeway existed in both the tachograph and SandHaul's owner. Drivers hoped for a tachograph that erred by recording slower than actual truck speed.

> *Tim:* Whenever I return to the yard, I drive the truck at exactly fifty-five miles an hour. That way I can check the chart when I get to the yard, and I'll know just how far it's off [i.e., does the chart show the truck as having been driven at fifty-five? higher than fifty-five? lower than fifty-five?]. Then next time I drive that truck I'll know just how far I can go over fifty-five.

Others took note of Will's willingness to grant at least a one-mile-an-hour leeway.

> *Barney:* Let me check my chart. [Disappointed] Ya, it's right on [shows correct speed]. But you know what? I think fifty-five on the speedometer is actually about fifty-seven, so if you go fifty-six you'll be moving right along.

The amount of leeway granted by the owner was a topic on which some consensus existed.

> *Judas:* It seems like you can go fifty-six to fifty-seven on the chart without Will saying anything, as long as you aren't in the doghouse for something. I think if you're tight with him, like Leon is, you can go even faster.

However, agreement on the amount of leeway was not universal.

> *John:* Some of the guys have told me, "To hell with the chart. Run the truck up fast and then bring it on down [to fifty-five]. Just don't be constantly hauling ass." But I like to drive it steady so I just nip at the edges [of the limit as he sees it].

Tachograph variations (tachographs can lose their calibration; transmission repairs may alter the gearing and hence the accuracy of recorded speeds) and the owner's unpredictability in enforcing a speed of fifty-five insured endless discussions about beating the speed limit.

Because of the constant threat of being passed by another

truck, SandHaul drivers on the road took either no breaks or one short break, a fact that I observed that was confirmed by their tachograph charts. Stories made the rounds about the risks of taking a break.

> *Jack:* I stopped for a hamburger, and a Rapp truck passed me up. Then I saw the dude later, stopped on Desert Road. He saw me and jumped into his truck and tried to take off in front of me, you know? That fucker didn't pass me, but he sure tried. He chased me all the way in [to their common destination]. I hit seventy sometimes. Hell, I didn't want to sit behind him twenty-five to forty-five minutes while he loaded. I wonder how I'm going to ex-plain my chart [speeding] to Will, especially after he sees that I stopped for a hamburger? I'm not stopping for hamburgers any-more.

I recorded my own experience:

> *Field note:* At K-Junction, I stopped to wash the windows and get a snack, less than a five-minute break. Once at Plant 5, it became apparent that an Allcerdo truck had beaten me there by about one minute. I sorely regretted the stop at K-Junction and had an extra hour [while the Allcerdo truck unloaded ahead of me] to mull over that decision.

One night-shift driver, Barney, was an exception in that he took comparatively long, twenty- to sixty-minute breaks, be-cause he stopped at truck stops, while all other drivers stopped only at food-to-go establishments. Barney was disliked for these stops; because of overlapping loads and a domino effect, they often added to the unloading time of other drivers. Drivers were particularly annoyed by Barney's penchant for ending breaks in time to arrive at the unloading site a few minutes ahead of a driver who had loaded behind him. Instead of being unloaded when the second driver arrived, Barney would be only beginning to unload, delaying the other driver thirty to ninety minutes, not counting later delays as a result.

Barney was not seen by other drivers as lazy or exhibiting a preference for sit-down dining. Instead, his behavior was ex-plained by most as a desire to play an idealized trucker role that includes eating with fellow drivers at truck stops. Also, they thought he liked to show off the truck he was driving. Some drivers suggested he was hiring prostitutes at the truck stops.

Alan: That fuckin' Barney likes to play the big-time driver. He thinks truck stops are cool, and he's in hog heaven when he gets to cruise the 76 [a truck stop] in a shiny Petercar. He probably drives around the place three times before he parks. Leon said Barney buys pussy down there. I wouldn't doubt it; he was messing around with those whores over by [Plant 6]. I don't know if the ugly fucker needs his horn trimmed or if he just likes to be a big-strap driver (a driver who accentuates the work's macho overtones).

Warren: The guy lives at home with his parents, no woman in her right mind is going to give him the time of day, so what has he got going for himself? He'd rather hang out at the yard than be at home. His big thrill is to show off in his truck. I don't give a damn, except that the prick leaves [ends his break] just in time to unload right ahead of you.

Behind his back, Barney was severely criticized for his behavior. To his face, drivers teased and mocked him for his breaks. Barney never gave up these breaks, but they occurred no more than once every two weeks. Thus, while the company had no prohibition against breaks or limits on break duration, an informal norm was constructed and upheld by the drivers. Breaks were legitimate (though often risky and foolish) as long as they did not delay other drivers. In effect, only the last drivers out of the yard could take a long break without delaying another driver, but if they did so they were likely to anger their day-shift counterparts by the unnecessarily late return of their trucks. Since SandHaul used tachographs, such suspicions could be confirmed. Thus, without a word from management, almost all drivers took only few and short breaks.

Encountering a competitor on the road could trigger dangerous highway battles for position that might result in considerable anger. A SandHaul driver told me about his encounters with a particularly hated owner-operator who was leased to Sand-Haul and, as an owner-operator, not restrained by a tachograph.

Vince: Don't ever give that son of a bitch a break. He'll fuck you every chance he gets. He passed us [day-shift drivers] all the time. He'll go into the [illegal] lane to pass you; he's passed guys on the right-hand shoulder! Once he passed me on a blind curve. . . . If I'm on a road where I can help it, I won't let him pass.

Even if a pass was legitimate and safe, drivers were offended and took it personally.

> *Judas:* It must have been that goddamn kid [an Allcerdo driver].
> That fucker passed me the other day like I was standing still and
> then laughed all the way here.

To defend against would-be passers drivers learn blocking techniques; the most refined make the blocking appear unintentional, for purposely blocking another company's driver or a fellow driver who has the right to pass is considered bad form. As another defense, SandHaul drivers lied about their locations while talking on the company radio, so that other SandHaul drivers on their way to the same destination would not make extraordinary efforts to arrive first.

In order to "make time" all drivers ascended hills at the truck's maximum capability without blowing up the engine. In addition, I saw several night-shift drivers descend a steep mountain pass at unsafe speeds. The risk in such descents is that a truck will lose most or all braking power before reaching the bottom of the hill (the brakes may even ignite) and will gain so much speed that control becomes impossible.

One might assume that if neither the yard nor the road was free from cutthroat activity, relaxation might be possible at pickup and delivery points. There was some truth to this: it was almost unheard of for one SandHaul driver to make an open attempt to pass another at a loading or unloading site. Yet other opportunities existed in these places for drivers to advance themselves at each other's expense. For example, a driver could strike a deal with a plant employee to have his truck loaded or unloaded ahead of others in the queue, then present himself as the innocent beneficiary of good fortune in the form of an urgent need for his product. A similar tactic involved convincing a loader to overload or underload another driver's truck; while the victim was removing excess product or returning for more, the perpetrator could assume the lead fair and square. This tactic was more successfully bargained for, because it was a common error, easily accomplished, and impossible to prove intentional.

A more common attempt to cut loading and unloading time was to speed up the mechanical devices used for these procedures. The frequency of such attempts, drivers' intense desire to finish quickly, and the resulting dismay among plant personnel can be seen in this SandHaul driver's account:

> *Leon:* The other day I was at [Plant 1] and talking to Sam [who oversaw the unloading of trucks]. The truck on the pit emptied and drove on out, and it was my turn. I kept talking to Sam and this Allcerdo driver came up to me and said, "Why don't you pull up [onto the pit]?" I said, "What difference does it make? The pit is full. [It would take fifteen minutes to empty before he could begin unloading into it.] So the guy went back to his truck, and Sam told me, "Goddamn, I'm sure glad to hear you say that. These guys come in here, and they are in a big rush, and they want me to open it up [increase the unloading rate of plant machinery] and they drive me nuts. . . . I don't know why they don't just calm down.

At the least, drivers expect loading and unloading to be as efficient as the plant's norms allow. To this end, drivers employ both aggressive and passive strategies.

> *Judas:* What I do is act real dumb. Like when the first trailer is loaded, but no one comes out to start loading the pull [second] trailer. Instead of going in there and telling them to get off their fat asses and load me, I act dumb and tell them that the big yellow light came on, and I heard something [the loading equipment shutting off], and I don't know if that means something is wrong so I thought I better come in and tell them. They always come out after that and get me going.

This driver realizes it is not a good idea to anger plant personnel because of the problems and delays they can cause him. A loader, for example, can slow down the loading rate, under- or overload, spill large amounts of product on the trailer, decide to clean out a silo or perform other routine maintenance, load trucks out of order, hold up paperwork, or simply disappear, all to the detriment of the driver in a hurry.

While most drivers tried to speed up machinery by persuading its operators, some drivers acted on their own. Among SandHaul drivers, Alan was the most likely to operate machinery on his own, and his lack of judgment and restraint in these matters led to equipment breakdowns and sanctions by displeased customers. Alan's actions also delayed and angered other drivers, some of whom thought he ought to be fired.

At one plant, drivers loaded their trucks by operating the equipment themselves; here I witnessed a variety of rather marvelously choreographed routines aimed at shaving seconds from loading times. Several drivers could tell me their fastest self-loading time down to the half minute.

While waiting to unload, some drivers chose to sleep but did so with, almost literally, one eye open. If the sleeping driver was not aware of the unloading driver's departure, much time could be wasted. SandHaul drivers expected other SandHaul drivers who had finished unloading to awaken them, but some were untrustworthy, and others refused to awake those they disliked. In addition, fatigue and haste meant that even a friend could honestly forget to do this favor. Since the reasons for failing to awaken a fellow driver ranged from forgetfulness to revenge, and because driver relationships were tenuous (today's friend could be tomorrow's competitor, depending on the schedule), it was not clear who could be counted upon. The result was a driver who slept with considerable caution.

The likelihood of hostile interactions was greater among drivers from different companies. At a loading site frequented by drivers of competing companies, a loader described the following incident:

> *Andy:* A Rapp [Company] driver tried to pull in front of a Matta driver last week. That [Matta] dude will kick their ass. He got ready to hit the fucker, and a foreman walked around the corner so he just patted him on the back real hard and kept saying, "You're a good guy, aren't you?" He was really shaking the shit out of that kid.

While a driver might be subjected only occasionally to other drivers making obtrusive attempts to pass him at a plant, it happens enough for a basic distrust to form.

> *Field note:* At Plant 4 there was a long line of trucks waiting to load so Barney, Warren, and I parked and went into town to eat. By the time we returned, Rick had arrived. He said, "I pulled your truck up, Barney, because I was afraid that the Bowen truck might try to pull ahead of you."

This distrust, competitiveness, and hostility extends to truckers who share only the road and not destinations. Popular conceptions of trucking as an occupational subculture whose

members share mostly harmonious relationships with one another ignore these tensions.

> *Field note:* As I exited the state roadside scale a Frito Lay truck be-
> hind and next to me in the empty truck lane began racing me to
> the exit lane. I was clearly ahead of him and had the right of way,
> especially since I was loaded. At first I thought he would back off,
> but ultimately I was forced to slam on my brakes to avoid a colli-
> sion.

One of the SandHaul drivers told of a similar incident.

> *Leon:* I was coming up on [a truck stop] and had a good run at [the
> mountain] when all of a sudden this jackass in a flatrack [tractor
> pulling a flatbed trailer] looks me right in the eye and pulls out in
> front of me. Cars were coming the other way so I couldn't get
> around the son of a bitch before losing all my speed. If I could have
> caught up with him I would have stomped his ass. . . . But, you
> know, that kind of shit happens all the time. These drivers aren't
> any better than the idiots in cars.

Once unloaded and returning to the yard, SandHaul drivers
could relax somewhat, but this was not the end of possible competition. If a driver saw another SandHaul driver also returning
to the yard, a race was likely: being second at the fuel pumps or
wash rack could add ten to sixty minutes to a shift.

At the yard, drivers sometimes tried to snake one another on
the way to the service island subtly enough to avoid a confrontation. More revealing of the pervasiveness of competition between
drivers was the pretense of overt snaking while approaching the
service island. The instigator might choose to appear totally serious or to frame the act in buffoonery. In either case the pre-
tender was quick to unmask, allowing his victim to fire a round
of good-natured threats: "You do that to me, boy, and I'd have to
beat your ass into the ground." Everyone would then laugh.

In sum, the work world of SandHaul drivers was intensely
competitive and marked by hostility. Drivers worked fast and
steadily. Whatever their relationships beyond the company
gates, on-duty SandHaul drivers saw one another as competitors, even enemies.

> *Dave:* I have some shit on Ringo. I don't like going to the office,
> but, if this stuff [circumventing seniority] keeps up, I'll go in there
> and burn his ass. Ringo better watch it.

> *Deuce:* He tried to pick a fight with me. . . . He's not worth it, that asshole. If he wants to go around the block and mix it up that's fine. . . . That fuckin' Warren. I think he's the one who fucked with my car, but I'm not really sure. . . . If they fuck with my new car, and I find out who it is, I'll kill 'em. . . . Al has been mad at me ever since I went out ahead of him once and he had to wait three hours behind me at [Plant 4]. Plus I had 205 [a desirable truck originally assigned to Al].

> *Warren:* You gotta watch that Dave. He'll snake your ass in a minute.

Given SandHaul's organization of work, it is not surprising that Dave and Ringo were friendly enough to visit one another at their respective homes, and that Warren and Dave were best friends. A work world that could twist friendship into such animosity and distrust makes such comments as the following wholly understandable:

> *Barney:* This is killing me, you know? My nerves can't take this shit. You race up north. Then it's a big hurry to get loaded, and all their [the shipper's] fuckin' around up there drives you nuts. Then you race down here and try to keep from getting sacked [passed by another driver going to the same destination]. And all the way down you are hoping like hell twenty other assholes aren't here unloading. And if that isn't enough, I worry about something going wrong on the truck. Hey, blow a front tire, and it could be all over. My doctor says I worry too much, but I think I gotta find something else to do. My stomach isn't going to last on this job.

AgriHaul: Piece Rates and Low Predictability

Like drivers at SandHaul, AgriHaul drivers were paid for output: more loads, larger loads, and loads that cost customers relatively more to ship meant more money for the driver. Unlike SandHaul drivers, AgriHaul drivers could acquire additional loads by working fast (at SandHaul the point was to complete assignments). AgriHaul drivers typically received one load at a time; as soon as a load was completed, they were eligible for another. In addition, by working fast an outbound driver could better position himself to get the highest-paying backhaul. Finally, if working fast did not yield more work, it at least shortened the workday.

Loading and unloading destinations overlapped; depending on the season, 25–75 percent of the time more than one Agri-Haul driver was headed to the same destination. Drivers wanted as few other drivers ahead of them as possible, because fewer drivers meant faster loading and unloading (loading and unloading took generally forty-five to ninety minutes a truck, and longer periods were not uncommon). As at SandHaul, another reason for drivers to avoid loading and unloading delays was the low compensatory pay (five dollars an hour, about half of what drivers considered their normal hourly earnings) that began only after two hours had passed. Thus, AgriHaul drivers, like those at SandHaul, saw in one another the potential for costly delays.

Load size was the one determinant of income that was subject, within limits, to direct and exclusive control by the Agri-Haul driver. At shipping companies that loaded trucks while they sat on a scale, it was a simple matter to specify the amount of material desired. Two considerations limited a driver's autonomy in making this decision: some shippers refused to exceed the legal limit, and AgriHaul's owner wanted load weights no more than one ton under or over the legal maximum (lesser amounts cost him more money than he felt acceptable; greater amounts strained the equipment and increased the chance that, if detected, the truck would be detained until the excess weight was removed). In principle, a driver had good economic reasons for observing these limits. Though bigger loads paid drivers more, the upper limit made sense because overloads greater than one ton were subject to progressively severe fines, normally payable by the driver, and could result in the truck's detention.

Decisions about load sizes depended, however, on more than added income or penalties for gross excess. About 90 percent of AgriHaul's customer's were unable to load trucks while they sat on a scale. Instead, as a conveyer belt poured material into the trailer, the driver had to decide when the limit was reached. Many trailers had small chains attached to their frames that would touch an axle when a near-legal maximum weight had been reached, because the suspension gave way under the weight of a load; but this method was far from accurate. Once the driver thought he had enough material, he drove to a scale, weighed the truck, and decided if he would accept, trim, or add

to his load. Depending on the scale's location, the loading process, the presence of other drivers, and the material hauled,
each addition or subtraction could take ten to thirty minutes.

Sometimes large overloads were deemed reasonable because
the chances of getting caught were minimal or it was not worth
taking the extra time to unload. In other cases, drivers did not
think they would be able to seal or even shut the trailer's unloading gates after opening them to trim excess product. Un-
sealed gates leaked in transit; uncloseable gates necessitated
emptying the entire trailer and reloading, a time-consuming
task that angered most shippers. Finally, trimming a load always meant running the risk of removing too much product and
having to either reload or forgo the income it would have
brought.

Drivers felt often that loads lighter than the owner's minimum were in their best interests, because it took too long to
return for more material. Even when material could be added
quickly, doing so involved the risk of overloading, a common error. Altogether, it was easy to spend an hour or more, at no wage
cost to the owner, attempting to stay within a ton of the legal
maximum.

A final loading consideration involved the presence of other
AgriHaul drivers: since AgriHaul drivers frequently loaded together, they had the potential for delaying one another in their
quests for ideal-sized loads. For example, drivers wanting to add
more material had the right to bump the truck currently being
loaded. One AgriHaul driver could thus delay another either by
bumping or by refusing to be bumped until at least one trailer
was loaded.

In sum, drivers desired more loads, quick deliveries, loads
expensive for customers to ship, and, within reason, maximum-
weight loads. In pursuing these goals, drivers were more at conflict with one another than with the owner, a conundrum often
ignored in the literature on work.

AgriHaul's dispatcher, in assigning loads to drivers, had five
basic tasks each day: (1) assign the most efficient sequence of
loads possible to minimize unpaid ("deadhead") mileage, (2) minimize layover time, the period drivers who were out of town had
to wait before being assigned a backhaul, (3) try to distribute
good and bad assignments evenly, (4) satisfy customers' de-

mands for timely deliveries, and (5) satisfy legal contractual needs that stipulated time limits for moving certain amounts of material.

A typical dispatch sequence worked like this: between Friday night and Monday morning, a driver was given his assignment for Monday. On Monday about half of the drivers hauled locally, while the others made out-of-town deliveries. The driver hauling locally usually finished between 4 P.M. and 9 P.M., at which time he called the dispatcher for further instructions. Except when business was slow, the driver was likely to be given an out-of-town delivery, three to twelve hours away, due Tuesday morning. As already noted, it was not uncommon for other AgriHaul drivers to be given the same assignment. The driver would then pick up his load and could either go off duty or depart that night.

Upon delivery Tuesday morning, the driver called the dispatcher to get a backhaul. Since each morning roughly one-half of the drivers were making out-of-town deliveries, many to areas near one another, drivers were in line for backhauls coming out of the same area. These loads varied in desirability, and the best loads usually went to the earliest callers.

After the backhaul was delivered, either Tuesday night or Wednesday morning, the cycle would be repeated: haul locally Wednesday; load Wednesday night for out of town, deliver Thursday morning; backhaul Thursday.

The owner and drivers viewed the relative importance of the dispatcher's tasks differently. The owner most wanted to minimize unpaid mileage, satisfy customers, and meet the legal requirements of his contracts. While he did not want trucks sitting any longer than necessary, layover times of one to six hours after an outbound morning delivery usually cost him nothing. Drivers were not paid during these periods and, once assigned a backhaul, were likely to make up for lost time by sleeping less.

Drivers wanted the least possible layover time and unpaid mileage, for which they earned nothing. They also wanted loads distributed fairly, which in effect meant an equitable distribution of money, rate of pay, dirty work, long hauls, aesthetically pleasing routes, and fun. Meeting customers' needs for timely deliveries was not a great concern of drivers, who felt they worked hard and saw tardiness as a function of the dispatcher's incompetence or of unavoidable delays. Likewise, drivers were not concerned about or even aware of contractual obligations that sometimes determined dispatching decisions.

As noted earlier, since AgriHaul customers' needs were varied and erratic, it was impossible to distribute loads among drivers in the precise manner that characterized SandHaul. However, drivers felt they were treated fairly if they received a fair share of out-of-town loads, because these paid more and were more pleasurable to haul. The dispatcher accommodated drivers by trying to assign an out-of-town load to each driver every other day, a strategy that for the most part matched management's needs. Judging by the lack of sustained complaints, drivers believed loads were being fairly distributed. Seniority had no formal weight in dispatch decisions.

Because of differences in the organization of work, AgriHaul drivers were not as frantic as SandHaul drivers, neither as obsessed with time nor as intensely competitive with one another. AgriHaul drivers each had their own truck; starting times were not a daily issue; their assignments were less likely to overlap; longer hauls made delays less important, because a thirty-minute delay is a much greater portion of a two-to-three-hour haul than of an eight-hour haul; and they neither saw one another daily nor began work at approximately the same time each day, except Mondays.

Nonetheless, the differences between SandHaul and AgriHaul drivers were only matters of degree. Piecework imposed a similar logic and led to similar driver behaviors at both companies. AgriHaul drivers were very concerned with time, they were angered by delays, and they competed with one another and non-AgriHaul drivers. AgriHaul drivers worked fast, for long periods of time without a break, and for as many as one hundred hours in a week, and more if working seven days.

When an AgriHaul driver hauled locally, he wanted to finish as early as possible because then he could load earlier for an out-of-town haul or go off duty sooner. By loading as early as possible for an out-of-town load, the driver had more time to make the delivery and therefore more time to stop at home, eat at a café, socialize, or sleep. Moreover, the earlier he loaded, the more likely he would unload ahead of fellow drivers headed to the same destination, thus upping his chances for getting a desirable backhaul. And the earlier he unloaded, the more time he had to backhaul and, again, to eat, socialize, sleep, or visit home.

If a driver's assignment was likely to be duplicated by other AgriHaul drivers, he would ask the dispatcher for the names of others hauling the same load, their current position, and an estimate of their time of arrival for loading. Knowing with whom he was competing, the driver could devise a strategy that would allow him to unload first and possibly also stop to eat, sleep, or socialize. For example, if I loaded directly ahead of Joe, I knew I could take only a short break, because Joe always drove directly to the unloading site without stopping. If I loaded behind Lou, I knew I had a good chance to pass him, because he was likely to go home first.

At least once a week, the driver was told that the load he was assigned needed to be delivered as soon as possible. In effect, the dispatcher or owner asked the driver to work as fast as possible and with as few breaks as possible. Usually this request involved a long haul, and implicit in the request was that the driver forgo sleep. In such circumstances, the driver negotiated for a reward, typically a desirable backhaul (such as a short, late-starting local haul that would allow a leisurely morning at home) or time off in the near future. On one occasion, two drivers were allowed to take their wives with them for an all-expenses-paid weekend in a nice hotel. Always, exceptional high effort was seen by drivers as earning credit that could be drawn on when they were not inclined to expend such effort. For example, several times a year a driver, including myself, would refuse to work anymore, usually because of exhaustion or encroachment on weekend off-duty time; on many occasions I heard drivers assert this right by citing past instances of exceptional effort.

When a driver arrived at the loading site, his goal was to take on as much material as was reasonable in as short a time as possible. In deciding what was reasonable, drivers considered the amount of time and exertion involved, income to be derived from extra effort, the owner's wishes, the consequences of delay, and the delays that additional effort might cause a friend or foe waiting to load. One means used by drivers to earn more money yet avoid exceeding legal maximums for either total weight or weight per axle was to overload the truck, leave the shipper's plant, and surreptitiously dump the excess before encountering a state scale. This was of course illegal and could not be done if the customer also weighed the truck. Given all such considerations, at least once a week I hauled a load that weighed less than the owner specified. He was more likely to complain about this violation of company policy than any other, yet in my case he did so no more than a few times a year, and then in the form of a mild gripe. No one was punished for deficient loads. At least twice a week I hauled and saw other drivers haul loads that exceeded the legal maximum though not the owner's upper limit.

Once a driver was on the road and headed for an out-of-town delivery, his goal was to unload as soon as and ahead of as many other drivers as possible, which did not always mean he had to hurry. For example, he might be hauling the only load going to a particular customer located seven hours away. If he finished loading at 8 P.M. and the customer would not accept deliveries until 8 A.M., he had five hours to spend as he wished while still managing to unload as early as possible. But even in these situations, a driver who wanted to eat, sleep, or visit his family had little time to waste.

On the road, AgriHaul drivers sought the shortest and fastest routes, made alternative plans to deal with possible delays (say, alternate routes if a road was closed because of snow), and guarded against being passed by any drivers headed for the same destination. As a matter of practice, all AgriHaul drivers exceeded the official state speed limit of fifty-five; all also occasionally exceeded the unofficial limit of fifty-nine to sixty, and several did so regularly. In the mountains, all drivers descended long, steep, dangerous grades as fast as they believed possible without endangering themselves, and all did so at a rate that exceeded the rule of thumb for such descents: go down the mountain in the same gear you went up (some claim even this is too fast; see *Go West Trucking*, December 1985, 21). Trucks equipped for fast mountain ascents or descents were prized.

Seniority held no sway in ordering the on-the-road or loading and unloading site behaviors of AgriHaul drivers, who generally subscribed to an ethic based on first come, first served. Competition between drivers was regulated, however, by informal, driver-constructed rules. As at SandHaul, there were legitimate and illegitimate forms of passing fellow AgriHaul drivers when on the road. Passing was legitimate in three instances: when drivers were headed to different destinations, when one driver took a shorter route than another, and when the truck to be passed was not able to maintain a reasonable speed. Reasonable speed was an issue because out-of-town AgriHaul drivers crossed mountains up to four times a day; the drivers of trucks that, because of variations in engine power, weight, and braking capability, could ascend or descend mountain grades faster than others were not obligated to wait for slower trucks. On flat terrain it was illegitimate to pass a fellow driver who was going the speed limit of fifty-nine to sixty and headed to the same destination. The reason for this informal rule was clear: determining who would unload first by engaging in a head-to-head race subjected the drivers to speeding tickets and an uncomfortable level of competition.

Three other rules governed on-the-road encounters between AgriHaul drivers. First, if a driver saw another AgriHaul driver sleeping by the roadside, that driver should be awakened. Unless a prior agreement had been negotiated, the sleeping driver would follow the driver who stopped for him if they were headed for the same destination. Second, when one driver stopped to join another at a café or bar, the latter was expected to follow the former when they departed. However, if the first driver wanted to stay longer than the second driver, the latter was free to depart. Finally, when drivers headed for the same destination and, traveling together, stopped to take a break, no driver was supposed to use the break to advance his position by either refusing to stop or not maintaining the same order when the break was over.

AgriHaul drivers did not forgo on-the-road breaks as much as SandHaul drivers did, for several reasons. Sometimes a driver could see that a break would not interfere with his goal to load or deliver as quickly as possible. In addition, AgriHaul drivers hauled over greater distances and found breaks more necessary than was the case at SandHaul. Finally, AgriHaul drivers sometimes headed to the same destination in convoys and could take a simultaneous break that did not endanger anyone's unloading position.

In the common instances, however, when taking a break meant risking being passed by drivers on their way to the same destination, losing a desirable backhaul or quick turnaround, angering a customer, or diminishing the chance to visit home, drivers were likely to forgo breaks. And, as at SandHaul, it was considered poor form for a driver to take a break that could foreseeably delay another AgriHaul driver.

At AgriHaul's loading and unloading sites, as at SandHaul's, open attempts to pass another driver constituted gross violations of etiquette, but covert attempts were not rare. Deals were struck with plant personnel that allowed one driver to usurp another's place while appearing to be nothing more than the beneficiary of good fortune. Loaders could be convinced to overload or underload another driver's truck to delay the victim. Drivers also pressed plant personnel or took it upon themselves to speed up loading and unloading machinery. Where drivers loaded themselves, they did so with great haste.

In sum, AgriHaul drivers worked fast, worked for long periods without a break, and worked for many hours a week. In pursuing their work-related goals they came into conflict with other drivers and, occasionally, the owner. But unlike SandHaul drivers, AgriHaul drivers were not locked into near-unbearable competition with one another.

PetroHaul: Hourly Pay and High Productivity

In a fundamentally capitalist system, the worker sells his potential for labor to a capitalist in whose interest it is to extract, according to Marx (1977), "the greatest possible daily expenditure of labor power . . . that can be rendered fluent in a day" (265). Of this exchange, Edwards (1979) says, "In a situation where workers do not control their own labor process and cannot make their work a creative experience, any exertion beyond the minimum needed to avert boredom will not be in the workers' interest" (12).

One way capitalists deal with the conflict inherent in their contracts with laborers is to link pay directly to output (the piecework system), thereby supposedly aligning labor's interests with those of capital. Payment by piece rate may be almost impossible, however, where the division of labor has made it almost impossible to measure individual productivity (Stinch-combe 1983, 180). In other cases, piecework may be undesirable, from the capitalist's point of view, because it generates more problems than it resolves (Edwards 1979; Rose 1985).

Hourly pay removes the need to measure individual output and does away with conflicts associated with piecework, such as those that arise from rate reductions when more productive machinery is introduced. Hourly wages are typically accompanied by direct supervision, at least among lower-status workers without career incentives (Stinchcombe 1983). The worker is paid a set amount per hour, and it is up to the capitalist to ensure that the worker's labor power is translated into enough labor to produce a profit. Miklós Haraszti (1978), in a comparison of piecework with hourly wages, describes the logic of hourly pay from the worker's point of view (though the setting is a Hungarian tractor factory, management's goals matched those of the prototypical capitalist: translating labor power into the most labor possible at the lowest possible cost).

> There is little chance of [the hourly worker] getting bogged down in details and coming to see part of his work as "paid" and part as "unpaid," or to see some of his jobs as "good" and others as "bad." He does not envisage that astute tricks or individual effort might turn the system to his advantage. . . . Coercion, dependence, and obedience—the very essence of paid labor—are quite clear to him, however well paid he happens to be. Whenever he possibly can, he reduces his suffering. When he works faster, or infringes on technical regulations, he doesn't do so, like a piece-rate worker, to produce more. On the contrary, when he feels that his output is more than is being asked of him, he slows down. (56–57)

In the conduct of work, hourly pay appears to provide little motivation for workers, especially in the absence of career incentives. Once a contract is struck between hourly workers and the capitalist, it seems logical for workers to expend as little effort as possible beyond that necessary to keep their jobs and stave off boredom. To get the desired amount of labor from hourly workers, especially those without career incentives, capitalists have been thought to rely on coercion, usually in the form of supervision and technical control (Braverman 1974, 180; Marx 1977; Edwards 1979).

Since PetroHaul drivers were paid an hourly wage and did

not have the sort of career incentives thought to motivate higher-status workers, it seems reasonable to expect more tension between the owner and drivers regarding the wage-effort bargain than at SandHaul or AgriHaul. Unlike drivers at Sand-Haul and AgriHaul, PetroHaul drivers were guaranteed a fixed wage as long as they were on duty, regardless of work done. Where SandHaul and AgriHaul drivers had great incentives to work fast and without breaks, PetroHaul drivers would seem to have incentives to loaf.

PetroHaul's dispatcher, in assigning loads to drivers, had two basic tasks each day: assign the most efficient sequence of loads possible, and satisfy customers' demands for timely deliveries. The dispatcher needed also to distribute good and bad assignments equitably, but, since pay was not an issue here, drivers were less concerned with this matter than were drivers at Sand-Haul and AgriHaul.

A typical dispatch sequence worked as follows: off-duty drivers were summoned to work by their partners approximately an hour before they thought the shift change would occur. Ideally, the summoned driver would be in the yard when his partner arrived in their truck. Once in the yard, the summoned driver learned of his assignment by checking with the dispatcher, or at night by retrieving from the dispatch board an envelope containing the paperwork for his hauls. Assignments were understood to constitute approximately fifteen hours of work and included up to eight hauls, but sometimes the dispatcher had to assign loads one at a time.

Since shifts were supposed to last fifteen hours and varied from thirteen to nineteen hours, a normal week (roughly Monday–Friday and totaling sixty hours) was composed of four shifts. The mismatch between these shifts and the twenty-four-hour day meant that drivers' starting times varied greatly from day to day. For example, given fifteen-hour shifts, shift changeovers of thirty minutes, and a first shift that began on Monday at 8 A.M., a driver's remaining shifts would begin on Tuesday at 3 P.M., Wednesday at 10 P.M., and Friday at 5 A.M.

PetroHaul drivers' assessments of loads as good or bad differed from SandHaul drivers', because hourly pay removed the economic component. The one exception was that certain assignments almost guaranteed a shift longer than fifteen hours, an outcome that some drivers valued as a means of earning "extra" income. Otherwise, PetroHaul drivers rated loads in much the same manner as did SandHaul and AgriHaul drivers. Long hauls were almost always preferred over short hauls, because they were more interesting, less trouble, and opportunities for on-the-road socializing with fellow drivers. A final preference for longer hauls is difficult to explain or document, but it may be the most powerful: open-road hauling feels less fettered and is more consistent with the idealized image of a truck driver. A cross-country driver once told me, "Delivery boys run around the city; drivers are out on the road." The most popular oil assignment, one that every oil driver said he most hoped for, was a single delivery that totaled almost seven hundred miles. Likewise, the most popular gasoline hauls were the longest.

Oil hauls were also judged on their cleanliness. A "dirty" haul was one with a high chance that the surface of one's *truck* would be fouled by oil while loading; drivers expressed considerable dislike for these assignments.

Since oil hauling could be divided into local and out-of-town, clean and dirty, the worst assignments were local dirty loads, and the best assignments were out-of-town clean loads. Oil drivers wanted good and bad loads to be evenly distributed; I heard no claims that distribution should be based on seniority. Judging from the lack of sustained complaints, oil drivers felt that loads were equitably distributed. However, the lone Hispanic driver was given far more than his fair share of a particularly monotonous local (but clean) assignment. The driver claimed to like this haul, but, if he was telling the truth, he was the only one who felt this way.

Gasoline hauling was mostly local, though each day several loads were hauled to beach cities 125 miles away. Thus, while gasoline drivers liked hauling the longer loads and wanted their fair share, they saw their work as local hauling and were not as concerned as the oil drivers with getting longer hauls. Several drivers noted that the great variety in delivery sites helped compensate for gasoline hauling's shorter runs. In addition, when PetroHaul undertook large movements of crude oil over longer distances, each gasoline driver could expect to be given this assignment at least once a week; they were not restricted to local delivery.

Gasoline hauls were also distinguished according to ease of delivery: good hauls were those delivered to stations involving routes with less traffic and easy access, while bad hauls involved heavy traffic and difficult, sometimes strenuous, maneuvering for unloading. Some bad hauls were compounded by unloading problems such as the need to add hose or to run the hose uphill, which increased the likelihood of a spill.

Finally, gasoline delivery sites varied in safety; poor African American and Hispanic neighborhoods were considered unsafe at night. Surprisingly, drivers did not use this condition to label a load bad. To be sure, most drivers disliked deliveries they considered unsafe, but no one seemed to think such loads were worth counting in their determinations of equitable treatment. The dispatcher tried to assign such deliveries during daylight hours, though I found myself assigned night deliveries of unsafe loads once every week or two.

In sum, PetroHaul drivers did not care as much about the distribution of loads as did SandHaul and AgriHaul drivers, because load distribution had little effect on their incomes. Since all of a driver's time was paid, PetroHaul drivers' interests clashed less with the dispatcher's and owner's needs than was the case at SandHaul or AgriHaul. For example, AgriHaul drivers greatly resented layover time, and SandHaul drivers hated being dispatched to the same location in bunches, but PetroHaul drivers, while belittling these sorts of inefficiencies, did not suffer as a consequence. This is not to say, however, that PetroHaul drivers were unconcerned with load distribution: the company's general manager felt it necessary to issue a memo stating that drivers' assignment envelopes should not be opened by anyone other than the drivers to whom they were addressed. He was attempting to end the drivers' nighttime practice of opening one another's envelopes to check the equitability of assignment distribution.

Given the questionable motivational power of hourly wages, one might expect the PetroHaul driver to fit Fredrick Taylor's description of the average worker who, "devote[s] a considerable part of his time to studying just how slowly he can work and still convince his employer that he is going at a good pace" (quoted by Braverman 1974, 98). In fact, given the impossibility of direct supervision, the reliance on technical supervision (the tachograph) that was far from infallible, the low level of day-to-day coercion, and the lack of consequences for not meeting quotas, one might expect PetroHaul drivers not even to bother deceiving the owner about the intensity of their labor, because they had no need to work hard. This was not the case.

PetroHaul drivers worked fast, rarely took more than an hour for breaks per fifteen-hour shift, and typically thirty minutes or less, and attempted to meet the quotas. Drivers bragged about how fast they could complete a trip, how long they could work without a break, and the speed with which they could unload. The importance to drivers of meeting quotas was evident when a large customer switched from gasoline to gasohol. A driver who previously went to only one refinery to pick up a load of gasoline now had to load the gasoline at an oil refinery and then go to an alcohol plant to complete the mix. Having to load at two plants took more time, and drivers expressed concern over their frequent inability to meet the five-load quota. For example, Donnie asked me how many gasohol loads I usually managed to haul per shift; when I told him three to four, he said, "Oh good, I was beginning to wonder if I was some sort of fuck-up or what, because I've been averaging only three or four loads." It is important to remember that drivers were not punished for failing to meet the quota.

While inquiries such as Donnie's might be seen as an attempt to establish a consensus among drivers that would lead to a new rate and the need for less effort, they were never phrased this way. Instead, the consensus sought seemed to be based on a calculus quite favorable to the owner: in effect, drivers asked, "How much can be accomplished by a competent driver who works very hard?"

Lending credence to such a standard were drivers' venomous complaints about the general manager's abilities as a dispatcher. On the dispatcher's day off the general manager dispatched, and he was much more likely than the dispatcher to give local drivers one load at a time and tell them to call or drive to the yard after each delivery for further assignments. Dispatching in such a manner reduced drivers' ability to plan and was inconvenient, but the drivers' major gripe was lowered productivity, typically one less load delivered per shift. One driver was so upset by this sort of dispatching that each week he threatened to call in sick when the general manager was due to dispatch, a threat that on at least one occasion he claimed to have made good.

Some of the tactics used by drivers to speed their work also flew in the face of what seemed to be their best interests. Most of the drivers I followed while traveling an interstate highway or local freeway at times exceeded the unofficial speed limit of fifty-nine to sixty. Some exceeded the limit almost constantly, often at gross levels (sixty-five to seventy-plus) and did so at night when it is difficult to spot police. The oil drivers I knew to have made the single-load, seven hundred–mile haul, which included loading and unloading, bragged about how fast they could complete it; two claimed times of fifteen hours to my seventeen, even though I loaded and unloaded as fast as I could, drove at fifty-nine to sixty, and limited my break time to thirty minutes. The paradox here is that speeding had the effect of reducing pay while inviting expensive citations by the police, and accumulating several of these could result in license suspension. Speeding also was especially dangerous in the type of trucks PetroHaul operated, truck-and-trailer tankers, which are particularly top-heavy (*Los Angeles Times*, March 5, 1982, sec. 5, p. 1).

The only quota that provoked indifference in PetroHaul drivers, judging from the absence of bragging and comparisons of quota completion rates, was one that, because of the haul's unpredictability, was not an accurate reflection of what was likely to be accomplished. If all went well on this haul, a driver could haul eight loads per shift. But loading and unloading contingencies over which drivers had little control resulted in day-to-day variations of up to four loads below the quota. Thus, though the dispatcher always gave drivers enough paperwork for eight loads, no one expected eight loads to be delivered.

The only instances I observed of drivers attempting to avoid work while "on the clock" involved this same short, repetitive haul.[3] All but one driver expressed a dislike for this haul, because it was boring and required too much loading and unloading. Two drivers told me they tried to time their arrival at the refinery to coincide with the refinery's gauging time—a one-hour period during which loading was not allowed. By arriving during gauging time (7 A.M. to 8 A.M.), drivers could rest or sleep while getting paid. Thus only a few PetroHaul drivers talked about trying to avoid work and did so on only a few occasions and in regard to a particularly hated haul that lacked a predictable quota.

The major difference between the intensity with which Petro-Haul drivers worked compared to drivers at SandHaul and Agri-Haul was that PetroHaul drivers were not greatly upset at delays beyond their control. Drivers at AgriHaul and SandHaul exhibited what Haraszti (1978) calls "the nerves," a symptom of piecework that he describes in various ways: "Desperate, in a cold sweat, with a trembling stomach, I try hard to get a grip on myself under the pressure of working conditions and my personal preoccupations" (23); "I have this vision of a taxi meter which, with a curt click, clocks up a mounting cost, minute by minute" (31); "'Nerves' get most acute when work is 'bad' [i.e., too low a piece rate]. . . . At such moments, the more sensitive workers are unapproachable: they explode at a single word" (50). Although SandHaul and AgriHaul drivers were not as severely afflicted by "the nerves" as were Haraszti and his co-workers, they worried about and were notably upset by any event that either translated into unpaid time or effectively lowered their rate of pay. PetroHaul drivers, on the other hand, were not terribly upset by delays. This is not to say that PetroHaul drivers were indifferent to them; they complained about delays and generally attempted to prevent or circumvent them. The difference was that events out of the PetroHaul driver's control did not send him into a frenzy or eat at him from within.

Thus, contrary to what one would predict from the experiences of work theorists and participant-observers such as Haraszti (1978) and Burawoy (1979), hourly pay did not make PetroHaul's drivers noticeably less productive than the piecework drivers at SandHaul and AgriHaul. PetroHaul drivers worked with great industry and attempted to meet quotas for all but one haul. At the same time, though SandHaul and AgriHaul drivers worked industriously, they occasionally slacked off when the haul paid poorly (typically considering the day a lost cause) or, in the case of AgriHaul, when they were exhausted.

The high effort of PetroHaul drivers begs for an explanation and casts doubt on piecework as the only reason for the equivalent effort among SandHaul and AgriHaul drivers. Given hourly pay coupled with low coercion and supervision, why did Petro-Haul drivers work so hard? Did factors other than piecework contribute to the industriousness of SandHaul and AgriHaul drivers? Driver-owner conflict sheds more light on the motivations of drivers, for drivers' interests were revealed in those aspects of their work they were willing or unwilling to fight over. What do owners want of drivers? What do drivers want of owners? When do their respective interests clash, and what forms do these conflicts take? These questions are the topics of Chapter 4.

Easy access, plentiful parking, and inexpensive meals and rooms make this hotel/casino south of Las Vegas popular with truckers

Trucker filling out logbook

Crossing the Mojave desert on Interstate 15

Escape ramp designed to stop trucks whose brakes have failed as they come down a long, steep mountain grade

Truck burning, apparently as a result of its brakes igniting as it descended a deceptively steep grade

Long-wheelbase Peterbilt tractor pulling a 48-foot refrigerated trailer ("semi"). The combination of this truck's make, model, specifications, and accessories makes it highly desirable among truck drivers

An example of a "truck-and-trailer"; this unit hauls livestock and is waiting to unload cattle

Odd sights are not uncommon in truck stops. Here, someone equipped a Cadillac to carry a car on its roof while towing a second vehicle

Unloading a chemical fertilizer. The hopper trailer sits over a pit on a railroad siding

Driver clearing the unloading hose of gasoline that remains after the trailer has emptied

"Double bottom-dump" unloads gravel at an asphalt plant

Loading gasoline

Boxes of frozen foods assembled on pallets, a lift ramp, and a pallet jack make unloading quick and easy. In contrast, "fingerprinting" (loading/unloading by hand) a fully loaded trailer is arduous and time-consuming work

Repairing equipment while unloading—a common situation for long-haul drivers

Wash racks open twenty-four hours are common in areas with a high volume of truck traffic

To meet both business and legal requirements, truckers often weigh their trucks—both individual axles or sets of axles and the truck as a whole

Snow- and ice-covered roads add to trucking's dangers. Here we are crossing mountains in Montana after delivering fresh produce in Calgary and reloading peat in Edmonton

CHAPTER 4

Conflict between Drivers and Owners

*A*T ALL THREE companies, conditions seemed ripe for conflict between drivers and owners. Much was asked of drivers. They often worked sixty to seventy-five hours a week, more at Agri-Haul, often many consecutive hours with only short or no breaks. Starting and quitting times constantly changed, and work shifts were at odds with both family routines and biological cycles based on day and night. Drivers ran afoul of various laws in the performance of their duties and consequently were subject to legal penalties. The work involved danger, and gasoline hauling at PetroHaul was particularly hazardous. Each company required unpaid work, such as waiting time in the yard, and at two companies some work went unpaid almost daily and in significant amounts.

In return, drivers made "good" money, but more because they worked long hours than because they were well paid.[1] And these long workdays were not compensated with an overtime differential; had they been, each PetroHaul driver, for example, would have earned approximately $5,000 to $7,500 more a year. No company guaranteed drivers a minimum daily pay after being summoned to work, sick pay was nonexistent, and one company had no paid holidays. All three provided good health insurance, but only two had pension plans, and these were modest. At no company were seniority rights codified, and there were no protections from dismissal beyond those mandated by state and federal law.

In addition to the demands made of drivers, the method of payment at SandHaul and AgriHaul, piecework, is thought to provoke discord. "Piecework systems have been described as creating 'hot-house conditions' . . . for the development of informal bargaining, and a system where wages depend directly on output might be expected to be particularly prone to attempts to negotiate loose rates" (Edwards and Scullion 1982, 169). Shapiro-Perl (1979) characterizes piecework as "a battlefront between workers and management . . . every day, workers challenge management's manipulations of the piecework system and develop their own strategies of resistance, though they may not fully realize the implications of their actions" (288).

Further, the form of piecework at SandHaul and AgriHaul, percentage pay, reveals both the owners' and drivers' shares of company income, which would appear to lay the system open to more charges of unfairness than do hourly pay or salaries, which mask this split.

Prominent forms of resistance by workers to their employers include bargaining over appropriate effort, foot-dragging (Hodson 1991, 64), sabotage, and various forms of withdrawal: absenteeism, quitting, and strikes. But it is a mistake to assume that participation in one of these actions of itself signals conflict between workers and their employers. For example, longshoremen who operate the cranes used to unload ships sometimes engage in acts that could be seen as sabotage but that in reality are directed against peripheral workers who slow them down (Finlay 1988, 132–133). Further, when these tactics are directed against an employer, the impulse may not be rooted, as is often assumed, in the employer's attempt to extract more labor or productivity from workers. For example, Juravich (1985) found that much of the strife between workers and supervisors at the company where he worked arose from management decisions that interfered with workers' attempts to be more productive, a situation also identified by Edwards and Scullion (1982, 2) and Hodson (1991). Thus, the ways workers exert control over their activities must be examined within their social context if they are to be understood. Workplace conflict is a struggle for control of not only the labor process but also the meaning of the work and, by implication, the worth of those doing it.

Effort Bargaining

How hard an employee is expected to work is rarely spelled out when a worker is hired. Instead, appropriate effort is determined at the point of production, and combinations of coercion and incentives used to motivate workers. Many observers of work believe that workers, often collectively, respond to these forces with their own agenda (Mayo 1933; Roy 1952; Shapiro-Perl 1979); putting forth as little effort as possible is thought to be high on this agenda and a major source of employer-worker contention. Systems such as piecework that attempt to establish a concrete link between effort and rewards are, as noted, thought to make conflict between employers and workers even worse.

At SandHaul, AgriHaul, and the two other piecework companies that employed me, there was no bargaining over rates. Other than a few half-hearted complaints by SandHaul drivers about having to work for a year before earning the top rate, drivers *never* questioned the percentage by which their share of the gross income was determined. Likewise, the rates customers were charged, the second element determining drivers' wages, were not a point of contention. At both SandHaul and AgriHaul there were grumblings about "cheap" hauls, but drivers did not seriously pressure the owners to raise these rates.

Several reasons for the absence of conflict over piece rates are apparent. As noted, the owners engaged in little, if any, rate cutting. When a rate was cut, it almost always was to acquire a competitor's haul, so drivers experienced cuts as either a lost haul or a new source of income. Thus they were not provoked, and the concerns associated with rate busting were absent. In addition, customers' rates appeared to be set by the market, not by the owners, and drivers understood their companies to be engaged in fierce rate bidding.[2]

> *Gene:* Gypos like Northmen, Allcerdo, and Rapp are coming in and cutting the rates on everybody. I said something about it to Ernie [AgriHaul's owner], and he said, "Give them six months and they'll be out of business." I told him I didn't see how they were making any money, and he said, "They aren't."

By pointing to market forces, the owner could easily counter any suggestion that customer rates ought to be higher or should not be cut. And these forces were not at all abstract to drivers, who themselves constantly competed with drivers from other companies for advantages such as quicker loading and unloading times.

Another reason for the absence of conflict over piece rates is that working for a percentage of the gross did not involve bonuses for specified rates of production. For example, when Burawoy's (1979, 58) fellow machinists at Allied Corporation produced more than their quotas, they stashed excess production in a kitty that could be turned in later when they underproduced. Drivers had no need to manipulate accounts of their production.

Finally, drivers saw the owners as, for the most part, impartial in distributing work and precise in computing earnings, which helped divert criticism (see Edwards and Scullion 1982, 173–174).

The only collective action I observed regarding piece rates occurred when AgriHaul drivers demanded that paychecks include a load-by-load accounting of driver's earnings. Drivers wanted to know how much customers were charged to be sure they were being paid all the money due them. The owner resisted, claiming that he did not want this information to fall into the hands of competitors. Once he acquiesced, all conflict over rates ended. What this event reveals is that drivers were more concerned with playing the game fairly than with the game itself. While a few AgriHaul drivers wanted an independent confirmation of customers' rates, the others settled for the owner's unconfirmed figures. Thus, conflict ended when consistent rather than independently validated calculations of pay became possible.

At PetroHaul, I observed no instances of individual resistance to work quotas, and certainly there was no collective resistance. This lack of action is particularly interesting in the case of gasohol deliveries. Because gasohol was a new product for PetroHaul and required loading at two plants rather than one, neither the owner nor the drivers were certain how many loads could be done in a shift. The process of answering this question gave me an excellent opportunity to observe attempts by drivers to construct an informal quota. What I observed contradicted the predictions of most theories of work: a near-absence of conflict. Management conveyed an expectation for five loads per shift, the gasoline-only quota, by giving drivers the paperwork for five loads. However, management then undercut this goal by openly wondering if it was realistic. Drivers declined to take advantage of management's doubts or the many opportunities at the alcohol plant to delay loading.[3] Instead, they loaded as fast as possible and tried to equal the gasoline-only quota.

I saw this acceptance of a new quota replicated among oil drivers when they began working on a massive shipment of crude oil. The owner set a goal of two loads per shift for this relatively long haul simply by giving the drivers paperwork for two loads, and drivers tried their best to meet it. The consequences for drivers of not delivering two loads were minimal: by delivering two loads a driver stood to work slightly more than fifteen hours and thus make a few dollars more; failure to meet this goal at worst meant slightly less than a fifteen-hour shift and the loss of a few dollars.

It would be wrong to suppose that drivers did not resist PetroHaul's quotas because they found them reasonable. For example, I heard a gasoline driver at a large unionized company describe as "absolutely ridiculous" PetroHaul's expectation of averaging one gasoline delivery every three hours.

While owners and drivers at all companies bargained over effort, the subject and frequency of explicit bargains varied considerably. At SandHaul, where the routinization of work was the greatest, there was not much daily bargaining over expenditures of effort; the amount of effort needed to complete any assignment was predictable and accepted by both sides. Sometimes, however, the owner needed a few day-shift drivers to begin their shifts by certain times, and thus certain night shift drivers had to finish quickly and return to the yard without delay. Occasionally, loads had to be delivered before cutoff times. These concerns were translated into bargaining chips for night-shift drivers who wished to gain earlier starting times or better equipment such as a more powerful truck.

But bargaining at SandHaul was more frequent than the work would suggest and, compared to AgriHaul, more often initiated by drivers. Night-shift drivers consistently tried to get earlier starting times and the best trucks. Most often they seemed to bargain with their commitment to doing a good job and, by implication, to the company. For example, drivers might tell Will, the owner, "Give me the truck I want, and I'll probably be able to get the load there on time if I stay with it." Even though cutoff times were rarely a problem for the night shift, the driver's offer suggested to Will a no-nonsense approach to work. Since these deals cost the owner virtually nothing, pleased drivers, and put the driver slightly in his debt, he usually went along.

More explicit bargaining revolved around weekend work and equipment maintenance. Drivers were asked to volunteer when there was weekend work. In return, Will tried to accommodate drivers' particular needs. For example, night-shift drivers who had to work on Saturday usually asked to keep the truck and trailers they used Friday night in order to save a return trip to the yard. When there were too few volunteers, drivers were told to work, although a driver could usually plan to have a Saturday off by working the two preceding Saturdays. If asked to volunteer, the driver would then point to his past performance and more or less demand the day off; I knew of no instances where this tactic failed. Obviously, this means of gaining control presented little threat to the owner and was not a collective action.

The other common form of effort bargaining revolved around truck maintenance. Almost every day-shift driver took good care of his truck's appearance, though he was not paid directly to do this.[4] Drivers with clean trucks were always enraged by night-shift drivers who left their trucks dirty. Day-shift drivers expected the owner to reprimand the culprits and perhaps force them to wash the trucks. One fussy day-shift driver submitted to the owner a list specifying which night-shift drivers were permitted to drive his truck, and he was successful for several weeks in having his wishes enforced. Day-shift drivers angered by trucks left dirty told Will they would stop caring for their equipment.

> *Al* [to Will]: If you can't get these clowns [certain night-shift drivers] to start leaving my truck the way I left it, then there is no point in me spending all my time cleaning the son of a bitch. I'll just become like them and not give a shit. Why should I waste my time?

Another driver, Clint, backed up similar threats by refusing to clean his truck. To make his point even more forcefully, Clint once dismounted his truck, walked up to the front bumper, and kicked off a ten-dollar custom light that he owned and had mounted, a powerful symbolic act; he then drove his truck for several days with the light dangling by its wires. The owner finally agreed to admonish the offending night-shift drivers.

Day-shift drivers also bargained to have the shop perform maintenance that was more important to them than to the owner, such as tune-ups and air conditioner repairs. Drivers negotiated with Will by citing their high-quality performances and suggesting that they would continue at this level.

> *Al* [bargaining for an engine tune-up]: Hey, I get up there early, don't mess around and get loaded right away, and what do I get? Every asshole in the world is passing me, because that pig [his truck] won't run worth a shit. If the truck isn't going to run, why should I bother?

The significance of these bargains and the ensuing conflict is that they present weak challenges to the owner's control, and no challenge to the structure of work and concomitant rewards. For example, in arguing about dirty trucks, drivers do not directly address the major issue: washing them without receiving any obvious monetary compensation. Day-shift drivers were less bothered by this chore, because they felt the trucks were theirs, and they reaped ego rewards from their appearance. Night-shift drivers liked driving the best-appearing trucks but had less incentive to wash trucks not permanently assigned to them. The result was that the conflict inherent in a piecework system that does not clearly differentiate between paid and unpaid time took the form of conflict between drivers. In addition, most bargaining at SandHaul was initiated by drivers and not by the owner, a circumstance that both reflected and reinforced the drivers' inferior position.

PetroHaul drivers, like those at SandHaul, also experienced tensions over the maintenance of trucks. Relief drivers who left trucks dirty angered the permanent drivers, who took their complaints to the owner or managers. Two driving teams gave the dispatcher lists of relief drivers permitted to drive their trucks, and he attempted to honor their requests. The drivers felt, and management appeared to agree, that they put forth exceptional efforts to maintain their trucks' appearance and that these efforts should be rewarded. Unlike SandHaul, paid versus unpaid time was not an issue; the cleaning expected of relief drivers could usually be done while loading or unloading. Also, about once a month drivers were paid to take their trucks to a wash rack and have them cleaned. Thus, bargaining over truck maintenance at PetroHaul involved the effort levels of drivers during their normal, paid, on-duty hours. As at SandHaul, the bargaining at PetroHaul over maintenance barely challenged the owner's control and did no harm to his other interests, as is apparent in the response of the two teams who submitted lists of approved relief drivers: if an approved driver was not available, the teams worked the weekend to prevent unapproved drivers from taking their trucks.

Bargains over the daily amount of effort were more common at PetroHaul than at SandHaul, because PetroHaul drivers were more likely to be asked to haul loads in need of quick delivery. When the dispatcher or owner made such a request, he offered little in return other than goodwill. However, goodwill could be exchanged for immediate favors, such as a load to a desirable site, and it contributed to a favorable relationship that later could be traded on.

At AgriHaul, bargains over the level of effort asked of a driver were common. Typically the assignment of a load included an indication of the effort level the dispatcher felt necessary; for example, the dispatcher might say, "They need that load first thing in the morning, and if you can get it off early enough, I can probably get you [good paying] almonds coming back." As noted earlier, drivers wanted something in return for exceptional effort: favorite requests included good-paying backhauls and extra time at home after delivering the backhaul. Sometimes the load itself was the reward. For example, the dispatcher might tell a driver that a desirable haul (good pay, easy to load, attractive route) is available if it can be picked up and delivered by a certain time. In such instances, not meeting the deadline usually meant a loss of time and money for the driver, so he had little incentive to take the load unless he intended to expend the needed effort. Drivers usually tried their best to meet delivery needs.

But drivers did not always acquiesce to the dispatcher's requests. Sometimes they were too exhausted to do what was needed. Direct confrontations over this issue were not uncommon. For example, one tactic effectively used by several drivers, including myself, was to say something like, "Asking me to deliver it by then is the same as asking me to take amphetamines, because you know that's the only way I can do it. Are you telling me I have to take pills to do my job?" Backed into this corner, the owner and dispatcher invariably relented. Drivers sometimes were more direct and simply cited exhaustion and said no to a request for exceptional effort. They occasionally refused to work anymore, period. For example, on a job where we were staying in a motel and making a daily, summertime round-trip of eight hundred miles across a desert—some of us in trucks without functioning air conditioners—the dispatcher at the yard begged three of us to close out the week by hauling one more load each, even though we had already told him we would not be able to. We agreed, but after we had delivered those loads, he again begged, then demanded, that we haul another load on Saturday. We refused and told him that we were returning to the yard. When we got back, the dispatcher was curt, but we were not punished, threatened, or given bad loads in the coming week.

Finally, drivers would not respond to pleas for exceptional effort when they felt such pleas were too frequent or unwarranted. For example, a driver might make an exceptional effort only to be told by the customer that no great need for the product existed. Likewise, when it seemed that every load was "hot" (to be delivered as soon as possible), drivers retaliated by driving at their normal rate and refusing to forgo breaks or sleep.

Effort bargains at AgriHaul thus involved considerable conflict: drivers directly challenged the owner's control over intensity and length of effort; these challenges were often partially collective (a group of drivers, all with "hot" loads and on their way to a shared destination, might agree to ignore the dispatcher's or owner's wishes) and received widespread peer support. Drivers agreed there were limits to what could be expected of them, that AgriHaul commonly asked for effort beyond these limits, and that drivers had the right to refuse.

One might see these challenges as a victory for drivers, but they did not pose much of a threat to the owner's control. First, Ernie, the owner, was wise enough to know he had to lose some of these confrontations. Certainly he had an interest in not having his trucks crashed and drivers seriously injured or killed, so it was to his advantage to listen to a driver who claimed to be exhausted. Further, he knew that he asked for more than was always possible, so refusals were inevitable. By asking more of drivers than was achievable, by pushing them to their limits and then acquiescing to their demands for relief, Ernie appeared to be a fair man who would listen to reason; paradoxically, this strategy enhanced drivers' feelings of control over the labor process. Finally, in striking effort bargains, drivers appeared to share with one another and with Ernie a sense of what constituted reasonable and unreasonable demands and responses.

Foot-Dragging and Sabotage

Foot-dragging, the purposeful reduction of effort by workers, is the most problematic form of resistance because it is the most subjective. What looks like loafing to the employer or outsider may seem like a hard day's work to the one doing it. Consider the truck driver who described his day to Friedman (1982, 46). He picked up three loads of freight that, combined, appeared to fill the trailer. The first pickup weighed seven thousand pounds; heavy items were loaded with a forklift, while the driver placed lighter items on carts. At his next pickup, which took forty-five minutes, a forklift brought one-hundred-fifty-pound cartons into the trailer and these the driver handstacked. This was heavy work. The driver then drove fifteen to twenty minutes to his final pickup and spent 30 minutes loading appliances with a pallet jack. He then returned to the yard. During the day, the driver went to his bank and took four breaks totaling approximately two hours, though only three breaks totaling one hour were authorized. The driver also appeared to have punched out thirty minutes short of the eight hours for which he was paid. Had the employer known the extent of the driver's breaks, he almost certainly would have thought the driver was loafing. Even Friedman's own colleagues often agreed with this assessment when he described the day's events to them. The driver characterized the day as "easy" but noted periods when he worked quite hard. For Friedman, this pattern of work constituted a "highly efficient rhythm" whereby drivers deal with work tensions by laboring intensely and then slacking off. While drivers at the three companies studied here probably would agree that this sort of rhythm can be highly productive, most would see Friedman's driver as a unionized loafer. Ultimately, the determination of proper effort is a value judgement (Hughes 1958) that in practice is almost always negotiated at the point of production. I define foot-dragging here as a purposeful reduction in effort to a level below what drivers hold as reasonable.

As might be predicted for piecework systems that do not cut rates when production is high or otherwise limit the advantages of high effort (Burawoy 1979), drivers at SandHaul and AgriHaul did not often loaf. Drivers saw themselves usually as working hard or working very hard. There were, however, three occasions when drivers could be expected to foot-drag: when business was slow, when the day's entire assignment consisted of poor-paying loads, or when being off duty was preferable to hauling a load. In the first two cases, AgriHaul's owner almost never cared about drivers dawdling because it cost him little if anything. Likewise, SandHaul's owner said nothing as long as the delays did not cause whoever was assigned that truck for the following shift to be late. The third case, avoiding hauls, was a source of some conflict.

To dodge bad hauls and hauls they were too exhausted to undertake, drivers positioned themselves so that they could not pick up the load by the time it was needed, or so that someone else would make themselves available first and thus be given that assignment. The easiest strategy was to stretch out the time delivering the load that preceded the undesirable haul. In a variation on this tactic, drivers hid from the dispatcher after unloading by not calling in until they believed the undesirable loads were no longer feasible. This sort of foot-dragging was limited in two ways: drivers often did not know what loads to expect next, and they usually preferred a bad load to no load. At Sand-Haul such foot-dragging was far less common than at AgriHaul, because SandHaul drivers had more routinized schedules, more consistent hauls (few that were really good or really bad), and schedules that rarely required drivers to haul one load and then contact the dispatcher for their next assignment.

Drivers at AgriHaul and SandHaul also somewhat regularly tried to leave work earlier than was scheduled. Rather than sneaking out in these instances, drivers almost always employed subterfuge with the owner or dispatcher. For example, most AgriHaul drivers hated having to haul a local load late on Friday afternoon, because it infringed on their weekend off-duty time, and they saw the added pay as insignificant. To avoid these hauls, the drivers either delayed calling the dispatcher un-

til it was too late to pick up the load or returned to the yard
without first calling the dispatcher, claiming that they thought
there was no more work to be done. SandHaul drivers sometimes lingered over deliveries until it was too late to do their final
assigned load and then tried to convince the owner to have them
return to the yard rather than haul a different load. Drivers occasionally also exaggerated mechanical problems with their
trucks to persuade the owner or dispatcher to return them to
the yard.

At PetroHaul, I saw little evidence of foot-dragging. At times I
was worn down by the fifteen-hour shifts and worked rather
slowly; I assume others did the same. Still, we all typically tried
to meet the informal quotas. Early departures generally were not
possible because of the expectation to work fifteen hours. But if
a driver wanted to get off a bit early, he might be able to create
the opportunity by foot-dragging or working especially fast so
that he unloaded near enough to the shift's normal end that too
little time remained to haul another load.

Only at AgriHaul did foot-dragging erupt into open conflict,
but even here it was not much of an issue. Some of the conflict
remained between drivers, as when a driver resented being
stuck with undesirable loads that another driver had side-
stepped. However, all the drivers avoided loads at one time or
another, and it was almost always impossible for the victim to
know for certain that a particular driver had caused him to be
stuck with such a load.

The foot-dragging that most involved AgriHaul's owner was
directed at getting off work early on Fridays. By the end of the
week, drivers were tired and felt that their many hours of work
had, in effect, amounted to sufficient discharge of their obligations to the company, especially when additional work added little income. Given this perspective, they were not hesitant to
force the issue. And whereas attempts at SandHaul to end shifts
early were isolated, did not engender wide support, and could
result in a driver being labeled "stupid" or "lazy," AgriHaul
drivers supported one another's efforts to avoid Friday afternoon
local loads and always applauded stories about successfully
confronting the owner or outwitting the dispatcher.

Perhaps surprisingly, AgriHaul's owner and dispatchers were
not terribly upset by this resistance and, though they might
complain, never punished a driver beyond making him haul the

load he was trying to avoid. I believe they failed to react because they were engaged in continuous effort bargains with drivers and were willing—indeed, needed—to grant concessions. And drivers expected concessions; they felt that their high level of effort was something they could call upon if leaving early provoked a confrontation. However, this willingness to engage in direct confrontation in order to go home early should not be overestimated; it was virtually unheard of Monday through Thursday.

While foot-dragging was uncommon in my experience with trucking, sabotage was even more rare. In contrast to the unionized truckers studied by Friedman (1982), I was not aware of one instance at any of the three companies of drivers retaliating against an owner or manager by purposely destroying equipment. Stories existed of intentional equipment abuse, as opposed to destruction, but these were infrequent. Moreover, the abuse was typically minor and not intended to disable equipment, and it usually arose out of frustrations with the work or equipment rather than with management. Such abuse was often directed against the equipment itself; I suspect that most people who use tools or work with machines find themselves occasionally angry at the object and wanting to punish it.

> *Bobby:* I had to bullshit around half the day getting loaded, because those idiots [the shipper] haven't got it together, and then I had to take that hot, hard-shifting, pig through the desert. . . . I got so mad I finally put my foot on the damn stick [shift lever] and just crammed the son of a bitch into gear a few times. It's dumb, but I felt better.

In similar instances I have found myself vaguely angry at an owner for having such an unpleasant truck and foisting it on me, but at the same time the owner seemed usually to be doing only what had to be done. In a few instances at AgriHaul I witnessed equipment abuse directed against management by drivers who were either exhausted or angry at being slighted. Such abuse always was short-lived.

A much more common abuse of machinery centered on drivers' attempts to increase output or minimize the amount of time it took to complete a job. As noted earlier, it was not uncommon for drivers at all companies to climb or descend mountain grades at the limits of their trucks' capabilities. Taylor and

Walton (1971) call this behavior "utilitarian sabotage" (sabotage that facilitates the work process) and distinguish it from sabotage aimed at challenging managerial control, such as stopping an assembly line.

Utilitarian sabotage is common enough in trucking to have earned slang terms: for example, "Mexican overdrive" denotes putting the transmission in neutral so that a truck can coast down a grade faster than its gearing would otherwise allow, which promotes excess transmission wear. Drivers sometimes use "the funny gear" in a popular thirteen-speed transmission to climb hills faster by not having to shift into low range, but that gear is not designed for the strain of climbing. Other abuses include exceeding limits on water temperature, combustion temperature, and revolutions per minute; not letting the turbo cool before shutting off an engine or after ascending a long grade followed by a quick descent; and by forgoing needed oil or water. Some drivers secretly alter their trucks' fuel pumps to increase the engine's horsepower, a practice known as "jacking up." A jacked-up pump is likely to cost the owner by cutting fuel mileage, lowering the engine's life expectancy, and putting more wear on the drivetrain and drive tires.

Another form of sabotage involves sacrificing quality to output within a fixed time period or taking less time to do a fixed amount of work. AgriHaul drivers, for example, hauled a variety of commodities, many of which should not be mixed. After hauling a load, drivers had to decide whether or not to clean their trailer before reloading. On one hand, for example, the feedlot operator would throw a fit if he saw caustic soda in his meat-meal, and the roofing tiles maker was always enraged by seeing feed mixed in with the decorative pebbles he had ordered. On the other hand, cleaning the trailers might delay the driver just enough for a competing driver to assume the lead or for a good backhaul to be lost. Likewise, when PetroHaul drivers loaded gasohol, a mix of gasoline and alcohol that required loading at two plants, they saved time by putting all the alcohol into one or two compartments of gasoline rather than into every compartment so that each had the correct blend. Since different compartments might be unloaded into different storage tanks, the gasoline-to-alcohol ratio that reached customers' automobiles could vary considerably.

Whatever the variant, all forms of utilitarian sabotage present, at most, only weak challenges to the owners' and managers' control of the labor process. Indeed, utilitarian sabotage basically coincides with the owners' desire for high production and the dispatchers' desire for driver behavior that makes scheduling easier.

Finally, a few incidents looked like sabotage directed against the company. A fifth wheel, the device that locks a trailer to a tractor, was twice surreptitiously unhooked, causing the tractor to pull away from its trailers and the connecting lines to break; once the trailer dropped onto the ground. I also knew of air tanks being opened and brakes set so that a truck was either unable to stop or unable to move. Once a front tire was slit. In each case, however, the sabotage was directed against the truck's driver and not the company owner. Furthermore, there was little support among drivers for sabotage serious enough to disable a truck or put anyone in danger. Almost all drivers voiced doubts or outright condemnations of such sabotage, even when it was directed at the most hated drivers. (One limit on sabotage I discuss below was that both drivers and owners viewed the ability to operate a truck without damaging it as an indicator of a driver's skill; given the desire to appear skillful, drivers were not quick to damage their own or one another's equipment.)

It is not theoretically useful to label as sabotage all instances of abuse and destruction of machinery, or of intentional low-quality work. At the three trucking companies nearly all sabotage was utilitarian and so represented only minor challenges to managerial control. While utilitarian sabotage indicates some disagreement between drivers and owners regarding aspects of managerial control, it also constitutes an implicit endorsement of the system as a whole. It is an attempt to "make out" in a system rather than to change it.

Withdrawal: Absenteeism, Quitting, and Strikes

A driver's failure to report for work could significantly hurt owners. Though the owners spend no money on sick pay, absences usually idled trucks (a capital investment of $40,000–$135,000 per truck, excluding associated fixed costs such as insurance and licenses) and caused loads to be lost or delayed. In a pinch, owners sometimes enlisted a company mechanic as a driver, but this tactic often caused delays in the shop. Despite its potential for harm, no trucking company owner identified absenteeism as a problem: there were no memos, verbal communications, or sanctions related to absenteeism, nor were absent drivers questioned or expected to produce medical verification of illness. The reason for this seeming lack of concern by owners was that absenteeism was almost nonexistent.

At SandHaul, which appeared to have no more or no fewer absences than the other two companies but where it was easiest to note them, absences were such rare events that they stirred discussion among the drivers. At SandHaul and PetroHaul I only once heard a driver say that he took the day off simply to avoid work. On one other occasion, a PetroHaul driver said he stayed home to avoid a substitute dispatcher's inept scheduling; however, he worked on the weekend to compensate for his absence. I never heard an AgriHaul driver claim to have stayed home to avoid work. Absenteeism, especially of the sort that owners find unjustifiable, was so rare that no slang terms existed for this practice (compare "taking a ringer," Edwards and Scullion 1982, 124).

When a driver was known to be absent, fellow drivers at all companies expressed concern over his health or guessed at important personal affairs that might have caused his absence; these assumptions indicate an underlying belief that absence was brought on by events beyond the driver's control. Only once did I hear a driver speculate that another's absence was an instance of "goofing off."

More common than absences, though not frequent, were threats by drivers to take a day off to avoid work or get even with the owner or dispatcher. As noted, I observed only one instance where the threat was carried out.

In sum, what little absenteeism there was rarely reflected driver-owner conflict.

Like absenteeism, quitting is frequently thought to indicate conflict within an organization and to demonstrate hostility toward the employer (Watson 1980, 239). High turnover is thought to diminish productivity and therefore to create problems (Special Task Force 1973, 11; Hirszowicz 1981, 43).

The two basic measures of labor turnover, the quit rate (the proportion of workers quitting in a year) and work-force stability (the proportion of long term workers), do not necessarily correlate and must be used with care. For example, a firm that offers good core jobs but bad entry-level jobs could have both high turnover and high stability.

At all three companies, quitting was as common as absenteeism was rare. Of the twenty-nine drivers at SandHaul in December 1982, eleven (38 percent) quit by December 1985. This figure is conservative in that it does not take into account the many drivers who joined and left the company during this period. Within eight months at PetroHaul, five of twenty-three drivers quit (nine drivers were assigned to haul for a large oil company, and I do not know their status). I estimate AgriHaul's quit rate to be about 20–25 percent. As another indicator of turnover at AgriHaul, I would have been the driver fourth highest in seniority within five years of employment, although fifteen drivers were ahead of me when I began working there.

Despite high turnover, each company appeared to have a stable, if small, core of workers. When I left SandHaul, eight of the drivers (28 percent) had worked there for more than five years, a proportion that increases to 38 percent if newly added driving positions are ignored. PetroHaul is more difficult to assess because of its brief existence. When I left, however, eleven drivers (48 percent) had been there more than two years; of the nine I spoke to about their plans, seven gave no indication of an intent to leave. Of the drivers I worked with at AgriHaul (in effect, I am holding constant subsequent work-force expansion), ten (27 percent) either stayed with AgriHaul until retirement, had more than ten years of seniority as of 1986, bought their own trucks and leased them to AgriHaul for a total employment of at least ten years, or were men in their fifties who had intended to stay until retirement but were forced out by work injuries.

Can we assume that the turnover and stability rates at SandHaul, AgriHaul, and PetroHaul indicate widespread job dissatisfaction among drivers (Pfeffer 1979) and are important expressions of conflict? No. The decision by drivers to quit their companies did not necessarily express discontent with management. And when discontent with management was an issue, it was not necessarily over exploitative features of employment.

None of the five drivers who quit PetroHaul cited profound unhappiness with company policy or with the owner as the reason. Two were ex-union drivers who saw working at PetroHaul as a temporary stop on their way back to a union job (they told me this almost as soon as they were hired). Neither was unhappy with PetroHaul in particular and one said that PetroHaul was as good as nonunion companies come. These drivers simply preferred union to nonunion work because of advantages in pay, the pension, and workers' rights. Both left PetroHaul for union jobs within five months of being hired. Another ex-union driver took a job with PetroHaul because it was the best he could find after losing his union job; he left PetroHaul upon securing employment with an almost-identical company much closer to his home. The fourth driver left for a job similar to the one he had at PetroHaul but with an even smaller company where he expected to have greater autonomy and longer hauls. The fifth driver left to haul construction materials because he decided hauling gasoline was too dangerous. None of the drivers who left were with PetroHaul for more than eighteen months.

Of the three PetroHaul drivers who *talked* the most about quitting, two were fond of the owner and their jobs. For example, one of these drivers told me, "Roy [the owner] is a damn fine man, and I like working for him." One, however, wanted to be an owner-operator, and another wanted to return to long-distance hauling. The third was unhappy with PetroHaul, but his unhappiness was more with nonunion driving and being an employee. He said that PetroHaul was a good nonunion company but that a driver with a clean record and a couple of years of tanker experience could move to a better, union job. However, he planned to become an owner-operator.

In sum, quitting at PetroHaul typically was not an expression of direct conflict between drivers and the owner or managers. Discontents had more to do with nonunionized trucking in general—mainly lower pay, too many hours, or inferior pensions— than with PetroHaul in particular. For its type, PetroHaul was rated favorably by drivers. Furthermore, PetroHaul prided itself on hiring first-rate drivers; if management's assertions about hiring only the best were true, PetroHaul's drivers occupied a relatively strong labor market position. In addition, work at PetroHaul, more than at the other companies, put drivers into direct contact with union and excellent nonunion jobs. Thus, PetroHaul drivers, more than those at SandHaul and AgriHaul, knew of good jobs and had the credentials and characteristics to acquire them. Most drivers saw quitting less an escape than as a career advancement or accommodation to changed needs. Quitting did not stir resentment against management in the drivers who remained. And the owner and managers gave no indication that quitting was a problem.

Quitting at SandHaul was a different matter. It involved core-group drivers (drivers with more than five years of seniority), it signified a conscious retaliation against the owner, and it stirred resentment among those who remained. Will, SandHaul's owner, thus defined quitting as a problem.

During the time I worked at SandHaul, no driver quit, though these drivers were among the most dissatisfied I had ever known. There was little mystery about why they stayed, however: the United States was in the midst of a recession (depression, according to some), and decent trucking jobs were hard to find. Many drivers told me that there were few good jobs available. One of the few satisfied drivers commented on another driver's dissatisfaction.

> *Pete:* If he doesn't like [his job], he should go someplace else, if he can find a place that will even take applications. These days you are lucky just to be working; there are a lot of guys who aren't.

My experience in the job market confirmed their impressions. In addition, SandHaul drivers were well aware of the many applicants for their jobs.

Shortly after I left SandHaul, Will reorganized driver deployment in a manner similar to PetroHaul's: every night-shift driver was paired with a day-shift driver, and together they operated the same truck in shifts (the day-shift/night-shift dichotomy was maintained). I assumed this pattern would greatly reduce both driver unhappiness and drivers' desire to leave, because it promised to eliminate much of the conflict between drivers (snaking and truck-cleaning issues). However, a large number of driver defections took place after this reorganization, and all but one of the departing drivers cited displeasure with Will as the reason for quitting.

At first I thought these departures were reactions to managerial style rather than to changes in the labor process, as Edwards and Scullion (1982) suggest. While Will's disregard of seniority by pushing drivers to arrive at the yard sooner than necessary made night-shift drivers work longer and thus affected the labor process, this problem was resolved when driver deployment was reorganized. In addition, seniority was not a dispatch consideration for day-shift drivers, yet seven of those quitting were day-shift drivers, and six cited displeasure with Will as the reason. The problem seemed to be Will's personality: drivers described him as "unpredictable" and "chickenshit." However, closer examination revealed that quitting had more to do with control than with personality. From the drivers' point of view, this struggle was at least as much about the valuation of their worth and control over the labor process as about the owner's nature.

As SandHaul's owner, Will put great stock in running an efficient operation; efficiency was valued for its own sake even beyond the requirements of profit. For example, Will's disregard of seniority in dispatching night-shift drivers may have sped the completion of night-shift work, but the results of earlier completions did not often enable him to take on more work or decrease his wage bill; in fact, since his methods caused drivers to bunch up, he likely increased his standing-time costs. The earlier arrival of night-shift trucks typically meant that they sat longer in the yard before their day-shift drivers took them out.[5]

In pursuing efficiency, Will made it clear that he saw his authority as absolute and that all he owed drivers was their pay. What looked liked an unpredictable personality was most often his drawing the line over some issue he read as either a challenge to his right to use employees as he wished or a driver's assertion that employees had the right to expect something beyond wages. For example, he might comply one day with a driver's request not to send his truck out until he had time to wash it, and a week later respond to the same request from the same driver by asserting that drivers had no say in this sort of matter.

Given the absence of a formal employment contract, formal rewards for seniority, or even a specific hourly wage at all but PetroHaul, the companies I worked for got the work done and rewarded drivers through a variety of informal deals beyond pay. For example, a senior or particularly hard-working driver might be granted more autonomy or have his truck customized at the owner's expense. Like the owners of AgriHaul and Petro-Haul, Will made informal deals. His reputation as "unpredictable" and "chickenshit" arose out of his capricious interpretations of the deals he made or had inherited when his father turned the company over to him, a capriciousness that demonstrated his authority and served his immediate needs.

Comparing SandHaul with AgriHaul illuminates the differences in the way owners treat informal deals. To better advertise the company, AgriHaul's owner, Ernie, once purchased mudflaps imprinted with the company's name. One of the road drivers, L.G., who was a particularly hard worker, thought these flaps were ugly and consequently mounted them backwards, with the company's name facing the tire and the blank side facing out. Ernie complained directly to L.G. about this waste of his money, but he did not make him remount the flaps. Soon, several other road drivers mounted their flaps backwards and, again, the owner let them have their way. As small an issue as this may seem, these drivers had always been fussy about their mudflaps; they preferred long, heavy, unworn flaps and kept them looking clean by regularly coating them with tire blacking compound. In effect, control over flaps and the truck's appearance, in general, belonged to the drivers, and the owner let the deal stand. Such a response by Will is impossible to imagine; he would have seen this issue as a power struggle that he had to win.

In short, Will reneged on deals, both his own and those he inherited after he took over the company, and thus renegotiated, mostly by fiat, what Edwards and Scullion (1982) call "the frontier of control"; many drivers responded by leaving. Given the importance of informal deals at SandHaul, and the fact that higher-seniority drivers are more likely to be affected by changes in these deals (because they have the most currency to trade with, a currency that was being deflated), it is no wonder that core-group drivers were heavily represented among those leaving. In this light, the departure of Sid, a top-seniority driver who was quite skilled and dependable and who seemingly left over $127 worth of truck chrome that the owner refused to buy, makes sense: Will had diminished his worth.

Of the drivers who remained at SandHaul almost all expressed support for the quitters and anger at Will for creating an untenable situation. In addition, Will, according to two drivers close to him, was distressed by the turnover rate, especially among core-group drivers. The driver second in seniority told me he had tried to explain the problem to Will at Will's request.

> *Leon:* I said to Will, "What did you think about Sid as a driver?" He said, "He was a great driver." So I said, "So why didn't you just give him his chrome, and he'd still be here?" And he said, "No driver is going to tell me what to do." So I just looked at him and shrugged. There you have it. The ignorant fucker. That's why I'm looking for another job.

At AgriHaul, quitting was common among drivers, but neither drivers nor management defined quitting as a problem; quitting rates were stable, drivers did not resent management because of the quitting of others, and management rarely tried to prevent a departure. Both drivers and management seemed to see quitting as a natural feature of a business in which long hours and much time away from home appeared inevitable.

To be sure, it wasn't unusual for drivers to quit in anger, but their anger was different from that of SandHaul's drivers. Few AgriHaul drivers accused the owner of being particularly unfair, petty, unpredictable, or otherwise hard to work for. Indeed, Ernie was generally liked, and at least some drivers were quite fond of him. For example, one driver who quit said, "You know, I actually like the bastard, but I have to move on." When an Agri-Haul driver quit out of anger, he typically defined himself as unsuited for or simply worn out by the long hours and short-term scheduling, conditions that imposed considerable strain on domestic life. In other words, though the anger might be personalized—the most common form was cursing the dispatcher—it was generally directed against the exigencies of the business and was not a consequence of battles for control. This response by AgriHaul drivers is akin to that of those workers Edwards and Scullion (1982) report as experiencing "sophisticated managerialism"; managers were able to define the labor process as inevitable and convince workers to blame themselves for a failure to adapt. In addition, as I did once, drivers sometimes quit when they felt that the dispatcher was not deploying them efficiently; it seemed our time was being wasted and we were not earning enough money for the hours we were putting in. Finally, drivers also quit simply to seek other kinds of hauling.

Quitting thus meant different things at different companies. At SandHaul it expressed conflict over the renegotiation of control and the valuation of drivers. At AgriHaul, quitting was typically a response to long work hours and domestic tensions caused by irregular scheduling, but drivers usually did not blame the owner or dispatchers. Quitting at PetroHaul seemed almost devoid of any expression of conflict; those who quit were not so much escaping as improving their situations: in the absence of internal labor markets, significant formal seniority rewards, and a wide range of hauls and equipment within a single company, drivers advance, change, or adapt their careers by changing companies. Thus, quitting at such companies can be seen as a means of furthering a career.

As for employee resistance in the form of strikes, no company was unionized, and there were none. AgriHaul experienced an unsuccessful attempt to unionize, which, however, suggests the presence of more conflict than I have so far depicted. But the impetus for unionization came from drivers from a unionized company purchased by AgriHaul, not from AgriHaul drivers. In the end, only three of AgriHaul's drivers voted for unionization.

AgriHaul's owner used both the carrot and the stick in resisting unionization: he let it be known informally that, in the event of unionization, he would consider reorganizing the company so that owner-operators rather than company drivers would operate his tractors. This threat was not taken lightly by the drivers, though some thought it a bluff and others were not totally opposed to the idea of buying and leasing to the owner the trucks they drove. However, most drivers had other reservations about the union; they wondered if it was crooked and what work would be like if unionized. In particular, they worried that the freedom to negotiate deals and organize work would evaporate under a host of work rules. Once Ernie agreed to itemize load charges on drivers' paychecks—in effect, once he agreed to play the piecework game correctly—resistance crumbled.

In summary, despite demanding working conditions, at the three companies there were low rates of absenteeism, sabotage aimed at halting production or punishing the owner, tardiness, and foot-dragging. Utilitarian sabotage was common as an accommodation more than as a challenge to work relations. Strikes were nonexistent and refusals to work were rare and never involved more than a few drivers at once. High turnover at all companies constituted salient driver-owner conflict only at SandHaul. At SandHaul and PetroHaul, routinization and the acceptance by drivers of quotas made bargains over the daily expenditure of effort typically implicit and low-key affairs; explicit bargaining had more to do with issues peripheral to hauling loads and was initiated most often by the drivers. At AgriHaul, explicit effort bargains were more frequent, confrontational, and likely to be initiated by management. At all three companies, however, most of these bargains implied a general acceptance of work relations and posed little threat to the owners' control.

Only at SandHaul was conflict serious enough to be deemed a problem by the owner. Though he did not attempt to intensify the labor process, Will diminished the informal rewards related to seniority, clouded the connection between effort and informal rewards, infringed on off-duty time, and devalued drivers' sense of worth. Once SandHaul drivers found informal bargaining unpredictable and identified other jobs, many quit, engendering widespread support among the remaining drivers.

Actions such as absenteeism, quitting, and sabotage should not be viewed ipso facto as expressions of conflict between employees and their employers. For example, quitting at PetroHaul was marked by a lack of hostility and constituted career advancement, while at SandHaul quitting was an expression of great hostility, and at AgriHaul it was seen as a largely natural response to demands inherent in the nature of the business. As another example, the few instances of nonutilitarian sabotage were directed at fellow drivers, not at owners.

Likewise, the assumption (Kerr et al. 1960) that some forms of workplace conflict are individual (quitting, absenteeism) while other forms are collective (strikes) is called into question. Quitting at SandHaul had important collective elements: drivers endorsed quitting as a form of protest, praised those who quit, shared information about jobs available at other companies, in one instance quit as a group (three drivers went together from

SandHaul to another company), and held the owner responsible for the high turnover rate.

It is also apparent that piecework does not necessarily generate a high degree of conflict. Contributing to the absence of conflict over piece rates at SandHaul and AgriHaul were the lack of rate cutting; rates that translated into decent incomes; occasional raises in the rates charged customers; the owners' ability to point to the market as the determinant of customers' rates; enough variation in the rates for drivers occasionally to earn notably high wages; the generally equitable distribution among drivers of good and bad jobs; and the straightforward computation of pay that eliminated the rationale for drivers to "keep a kitty" (stockpile output), "chisel" (manipulate time records to maximize bonus pay), or "goldbrick" (refuse to exert extra effort because bonus pay is impossible to achieve).

Finally, conditions at these companies suggest that Burawoy (1979) is somewhat mistaken when he says that "anarchy in the market leads to despotism in the factory . . . in which coercion clearly prevails over consent" (194). All three companies operated in competitive markets, especially PetroHaul, yet explicit coercion—other than an occasional firing at SandHaul that most drivers agreed was just—appeared not much greater than that reported by Burawoy (1979) at Allied Corporation; as was the case there (67), the greatest amount of conflict occurred between workers.[6]

This lack of coercion and of hierarchical conflict similarly calls into question the notion that entrepreneurs in small firms control workers through a mix of coercion and inspiration (see "simple control" in Edwards 1979). Trucking company owners used little obvious coercion, instead relying on variations of pay, routinization of work, technical monitoring, driver autonomy, paternalism (AgriHaul's owner helped pay the funeral expenses for a loyal driver's father; SandHaul's owner sponsored and played on a company softball team), welfarism (health plans, pensions), job security, and bureaucracy.[7]

Likewise, the charisma of company owners is of limited use in explaining drivers' behavior. A few of the original drivers at each company were quite attached to their company's owner, but most drivers felt no great personal bond. The owners of these three profitable companies varied considerably: AgriHaul's owner, Ernie, was popular with drivers. SandHaul's owner, Will, was at once liked and disliked. (A SandHaul driver once said of Will, "Look at how he stood behind Lewis when Lewis had a drug problem. That showed class. So why is he such a jackass?") PetroHaul's owner, Roy, was neither particularly liked nor disliked by most drivers. Will interacted a great deal daily with drivers, Ernie interacted somewhat less than Will but still often, while Roy spoke to most drivers infrequently. While Ernie on occasion was able to inspire drivers to work harder—drivers joked about the his use of "Thata boy" to get more work out of them—I saw few such instances at SandHaul and PetroHaul. At any rate, inspiration seemed more the result of simple appreciation for a driver's effort than a product of charisma.

Conflictlike actions thus hold a variety of meanings for drivers and are not necessarily expressions of driver-owner conflict. And when drivers and owners engage in conflict it is not necessarily over control of the labor process. In particular, the high rate of quitting at SandHaul, though it concerned control, did not have much to do with the tasks and effort expected of drivers. It is true that the owner diminished the worth of seniority in negotiating informal deals, but these deals often were not specifically addressed to effort bargains. Will did not try to get drivers to work harder and did not redefine their duties, diminish their pay, impose greater discipline, or institute new work rules other than tampering with the informal relation between seniority and dispatch sequencing on the night shift—something he later resolved to the drivers' unanimous satisfaction. Conflict between Will and SandHaul's drivers mostly concerned noneconomic assessments of driving and drivers' work efforts.

The evidence from the three companies suggests that, while the labor process explains a great deal about drivers' workplace behavior, it is impossible fully to make sense of this behavior without understanding drivers' noneconomic needs. Studying the labor process does not tell us enough about the conflict at SandHaul, the surprisingly low levels of driver-owner conflict at AgriHaul, or the near absence of conflict a PetroHaul. Nor is it apparent in the labor process why PetroHaul drivers strove to finish assignments as fast as possible and later bragged about their successes even when exceptional effort resulted in less pay, nor why so little support could be drummed up among drivers for unionization.

While Burawoy (1979) incorrectly assumed that coercion is what makes employees in the competitive sector work as hard as they do, his explanation of workers' efforts in monopoly sector companies such as Allied Corporation recognizes the importance of noneconomic motivations. However, he draws these motivations narrowly and sees them only as reactions to the psychological deprivations suffered on the shop floor (82). The truck drivers at the three companies had a broader and deeper agenda then Burawoy suggests: work was a means to make sense of their lives and to develop and support positive self-images. Inherent in this process, and completely missing from Burawoy's analysis, is the issue of masculinity.

CHAPTER 5

Work Skills and Self-Esteem

*I*N ANSWER TO the question Who am I? men in modern societies are most likely to refer to their jobs. Employed men design an occupational self by combining social values regarding manhood and work, their expectations about their particular occupations, actual work experiences, esteem based on their work, and the prestige associated with individual occupations.

Truck drivers assess themselves through their jobs in two general ways: based on personal qualities suggested by the job (e.g., bravery as one who performs dangerous tasks), they decide what sort of man they are; based on notions of their skills, they decide what sort of driver they are. The various audiences that drivers come into contact with are crucial to drivers' understandings of themselves. These audiences provide points of comparison—for example, between trucking and factory work, or between the driving skills of truckers and those of motorists—and interact with drivers as the latter present and interpret images of themselves. To understand how drivers create occupational selves, we need to look not only at the work itself but also at the people they interact with as they work.

In the remaining chapters I examine the process by which a truck driver answers the question Who am I? beginning with the relationship between masculinity, occupational myths, and the problems a truck driver has in assessing his own skills, and then exploring the influence of several audiences on how he defines himself, including peers, owners, other workers, and highway audiences.

100

Masculinity, Work, and the Call of the Open Road

Most men today are expected to assume paying jobs, and earning money is a cornerstone of masculinity. At the least, employment in paid work removes men from the emasculated status of his unemployed fellows (Komarovsky 1962; Liebow 1966). Masculinity may also be validated or invalidated in varying degrees by the type and content of paid work. Men learn social scripts that describe masculinity, and the world of work is the major institutional arena for acting out this script. A man can be a man without having a family, but rarely without income-producing work. Since definitions of masculinity are closely linked to work (Tolson 1978) but lag behind changes in the work world (culture lag), opportunities vary for performing the masculine script. For example, on the basis of work alone, few would question the masculinity of the male steelworker, lumberjack, or electrician. On the other hand, the male clerk, office-machine service worker, accountant, and fast-food worker are in jobs that offer no particular claim to masculinity other than being paid work. While it is true that the accountant's relatively high pay makes him a more satisfactory provider, the work itself is not generally seen as particularly masculine. The male telephone operator, nurse, and day-care-center teacher have jobs that are identified as women's work and so impugn their masculinity. Given the social and psychological consequences for individuals, particularly men, of conformance or nonconformance to sex roles (Pleck 1983, 147), traditional measures of work satisfaction used in studies of men's work should have taken into account the fit between jobs and male role expectations.

One way to understand the norms governing men's roles is to differentiate between traditional and modern versions. According to Pleck's and Pleck's (1980) reading of dominant culture in the United States, traditional men are supposed to be physically strong and aggressive. The traditional man also should be emotionally cool, with the exception of certain impulsive emotions such as anger that are tolerated, especially when directed at other men. On the other hand, the modern man validates his masculinity by using his brains to increase his income and his organizational power. While the modern man is supposed to be emotionally cool at work, he should be able to have a full emotional life with a woman. Whereas the traditional conception of masculinity holds individualism in high esteem, the modern conception puts considerable emphasis on being a good team player.

. We are in a period where the modern definition of masculinity is eclipsing the traditional definition, but images of the traditional man still provide a powerful model for men's behavior (Pleck, 1983, 139–142). One could argue that the ideal modern man is the traditional man with more brains and smoother social skills.

Different definitions of masculinity appear to be related to variations in class (Tolson 1978, 28–31): the model of the traditional man corresponds closely to the hard physical labor of the sort performed by blue-collar workers; the model of the modern man describes the ideal corporate white-collar worker. Given the relation of these definitions to class, it appears likely that the impact of each model and the opportunities to conform to it are differentially distributed by class. Male blue-collar workers, as compared to male executives, are likely to have more opportunities to demonstrate physical strength and fewer opportunities to display brain power (see Braverman 1974). Nonetheless, it is reasonable to assume that men of all classes share some notions concerning masculinity (Tolson 1978, 31), and that these notions may be represented by cultural icons.

Our sense of the past, as constructed through the work of historians, writers, and artists, until recently has been largely concerned with the activities of men (see Pleck and Pleck 1980). The male construction of history has helped create and sustain conceptions of national character intimately bound to idealized notions of men's behavior. Cultural icons that take human form provide us with mostly male models that combine men's idealized behavior with traits supposed to represent the national character. For example, John Wayne, by virtue of the cinematic roles he played, appears to represent for many people all that they admire (or loathe) about both traditional masculinity and the supposed national character of the United States. In this sense, cultural icons are allegories addressed to all a society's members, but especially to men. In our society, male icons seem particularly to embody the tension between masculinity and social constraints. For example, Smith (1980, 160) described the

first generation of fictional western heroes as "symbols of anar-
chic freedom," and Etulain (1982, 425) notes the opposing attractions of domesticity and the frontier confronted by the
heroes of James Fenimore Cooper's novels.

Icons, of course, also take nonhuman forms, and it seems
reasonable to suggest that as the cross is to Christianity, the
road—including the trail and river—is to the United States.
Both icons sum up beliefs and represent experiences held to be
fundamental to the character of the people they represent,
though the cross is more encompassing. While the eagle serves
as the official symbol of the United States, it is the road to which
historic and artistic interpreters of national character are likely
to turn. From the writings of Cooper, nineteenth-century dime
novelists, Mark Twain, and Jack Kerouac to the history texts
used by our children; from Frederic Remington's paintings to
the songs of Willie Nelson; from the television dramas of *Route
66* and *Then Came Bronson* to the cinema's *Easy Rider*, John
Ford westerns, or even European cinematic portrayals of life in
the United States such as Wim Wenders's *Paris, Texas*, the road
represents qualities assumed to exist in the national character.

Prominent among the human figures transformed into cultural icons are men in endeavors or occupations associated with
the road, especially as it pointed west. A lineage of such men
has evolved beginning with Leatherstocking, the hunter of Cooper's novels. These characters were then followed by the "sons of
Leatherstocking" such as Kit Carson, trappers who moved beyond the Mississippi into the Far West and who were heroically
depicted by nineteenth-century dime novelists (Smith 1980).
The trappers were superseded by the cowboy, easily the most
romanticized historical figure of twentieth-century popular pre-
sentations (see *Film Center Gazette*, June 1983; Kehr 1984).

The depiction of these three figures has not been static; they
have been imbued with qualities reflecting the often class-based
values of those describing them and their audiences (Smith
1980). For example, the early depictions of the trapper presented him as a near savage, but within twenty years he embod-
ied the virtues of a Victorian gentleman (Smith 1980). The cowboy of U.S. films began as a virtuous fellow, but by the 1970s he
was something of a nihilistic anti-hero (*Film Center Gazette*,
June 1983). Though these characters change, they have a com-

mon denominator in their relation to the road and what it stands for: escape, adventure, possibilities, loosened social bonds, and the implied individualism, self-containment, daring, strength, and bravery of its travelers. In addition, all of these figures possess qualities of the traditional man, though some later cinematic versions of the cowboy cast his relationship with women in more modern terms (e.g., *Grey Fox*).

Not everyone regularly on the road shares in its mythic connotations. For the hunter, trapper, and cowboy the road is pictured as an end in itself, though these figures are presumed to be engaged in conquest or economic endeavors—noble pursuits, in Veblen's (1905) terms—that elevate them above the supposedly listless hobo. The iconographic status of these figures arose out of their embodiment of the road's mythic qualities, also assumed to exist in the national character. On the other hand, those for whom travel is mostly a means to an end, and therefore tangential to what they "do," do not evoke in the popular imagination the road's mythic overtones, especially if what they do is not masculine in the traditional sense. The traveling salesman thus has not joined the hunter, trapper, and cowboy in a common iconography, and the modern, highly mobile businessman does not appear as a descendent of this lineage.[1]

More than any current occupational category, truck drivers are associated with the road. Because being on the road is what they do, and because popular notions of truckers understand them to be on the road as an end in itself, truckers are seen as embodying the road's mythic connotations. For example, popular portrayals of truckers in movies (e.g., *White Line Fever*), television series (e.g., "Movin' On"), songs (e.g., "I Fought the Diesel and the Diesel Won"), and personal-interest newspaper and magazine accounts usually paint a picture of a man who is not simply doing a job, but who is doing this particular job because he has a certain wanderlust: the road is in his blood.

In addition, the truck driver appears to be the most literal descendent of the cowboy. The stereotypical truck driver looks more like a cowboy than do the members of any other common occupation. Of the fourteen advertisements featuring drivers in two issues of *Overdrive* (June 1980; March 1982), seven show drivers wearing clothes associated particularly with cowboys (see also Thomas 1979). The stereotypical driver also often talks with something of a Texas accent, which is often heard among those using CB radio, and is thought to be a lover of "cowboy music." For example, in 1986 I knew of three radio stations that aimed their programming at truck drivers, and all featured country and western music. Playing on this image, an advertisement in a magazine for truckers shows a radar detector mounted on a saddle (*Overdrive*, June 1980, 8). A country and western song, "Asphalt Cowboy," written by Clark Bentley and Lawton Williams, sums up this image.

> A faded pair of Levi's, sharp-pointed rubbed out boots,
> Fancy buckle on his belt, he's got that Texas look.
> He's a cowboy,
> He's a diesel-doggin', truck drivin' asphalt cowboy.

Like the imagined cowboy, the trucker appears to roam about the countryside, sometimes alone, sometimes joining other drivers for companionship, recreation, and convoys that might be compared to cattle drives.[2] For example, an article relating the author's impressions after a cross-country driving trip stated that "trucks . . . flock together . . . [and] their drivers belong to a sort of fraternity. They eat together, have special lounges in restaurants, share stories. . . . They own the road" (*Daily Northwestern*, October 2, 1985, 2). Drivers' slang embodies images of the cowboy: one term for a truck is "horse," boarding a truck often is called "climbing into the saddle," and "hitting the trail" is one way of describing departure. The national truck-driving competition until 1986 was called the National Truck Rodeo. And the most prestigious brand of truck, Peterbilt, has as its logo what appears to be the head of a longhorn steer.

The trucker's subculture itself excites a certain romanticized public interest because it is somewhat mysterious and deviant. The members of this subculture are nomadic, they have their own gathering sites, and these are at once public yet closed. They do much of their work at night, which can be understood as a frontier where one finds greater solitude and tranquility, a camaraderie with fellow night workers, the loosening of social rules, and more danger and outlawry, at least of the more public sort (Melbin 1978). Drugs, prostitutes, night people of all sorts, thieves, travelers and wanderers, and police are thought to be part of the trucker's life, if only in passing. In short, the trucker appears to be closer to the fringes of society than are the holders of many other common jobs.

Trucking's myth-imbued associations with the road in general and the cowboy in particular can be seen in popular reactions to trucking. Although many people are indifferent to this occupation, truck driving clearly has struck a chord in the national imagination. Movies, songs, books, two television series, advertisements, and popular magazines have all featured truck drivers who are, for the most part, cast in favorable, mythic, and even heroic terms. For example, the Brown and Williamson Tobacco Corporation committed $20 million to cigarette advertisements featuring a truck driver and explained their strategy:

> The [campaign is designed as a] contemporary symbol of tradition and heroism. . . . We were looking for the great American folk hero and romantic way of life. We believe he is the American truck driver. His trademark is an 18-wheeler and his way of life is tough, hard-driven, yet curiously romantic. The reason we chose the trucker and the truck was due to their romantic appeal and symbolism associated with power, independence and freedom. . . . He has a distinctive set of values and knows right from wrong. He is a down-to-earth guy who's willing to give up creature comforts for the open road. He's married or single, has strong inclinations to family, but also yearns for his personal freedom. He lives a tough life, peppered with certain amounts of danger. He is confident, tough, and masculine. (*Overdrive*, May 1981, 60)

Movie portrayals of truckers have starred male actors among the most popular at the time: Burt Reynolds, Kris Kristofferson, Sylvester Stallone, and Jan-Michael Vincent. Songs saluting truck drivers have occasionally crossed over from country to popular music charts and become hits, for example, C. W. McCall's "Convoy."

The association of truckers with cowboys and related myths was perhaps most obvious during the urban-cowboy craze of the late 1970s, a period that saw middle-class urbanites wearing cowboy clothing and patronizing simulated cowboy nightclubs. During this time, at least four truck driver movies appeared, CB radio became popular (Smith 1978), and truck drivers were prominently featured in all forms of popular media.

There is a flip side to the positive images of truck drivers that emphasize adventure, heroic qualities, and the more noble elements of traditional masculinity: truckers also are commonly depicted as crazed madmen with no regard for motorists, ignorant or stupid, sexual perverts, dirty and sloppy, and drug users. For example, a *Chicago Tribune* editorial on December 12, 1985, asked, "When was the last time you saw one of those 80,000-pound monsters obeying the speed limit. . . . Do you sometimes wonder whether the persons behind the wheel of those thundering semis got their license from a caramel popcorn box?" The editorial then related stories of accidents, including one in which a trucker hauling missiles was drunk and had fourteen previous traffic violations including nine speeding tickets. A letter to the editor in the August 6, 1985, *Tribune* told of truckers "running rampant on our highways like madmen." A spokesperson for the American Automobile Association said that their national travel survey indicated that motorists "perceive 18-wheelers as inconsiderate, unsafe, irresponsible, insatiable" (*Heavy Duty Trucking*, October 1985, 26), and a reporter in the *Daily Northwestern* (October 2, 1985, 2) imagined truck drivers "sharing their dirty magazines."

These negative images are apparent in the concern leaders of the trucking industry show for the public's perception of drivers. An editorial in *Heavy Duty Trucking* (June 1985) told of a documentary on truckers in which one driver said that motorists should stay off the road because they get in his way, another driver admitted driving past the ten-hour limit, and a third driver said he used drugs. The editorial quotes the head of the Bureau of Motor Carrier Safety, Ken Pierson, as saying that reporters are "taking the worst examples and calling them typical"; the editorial then laments the "bandit driver" and proposes counter-measures. In 1985, the American Trucking Association inaugurated a "multimillion dollar . . . campaign to strengthen the trucking industry's public image" (*Go West*, October 1985, 10); featured in the campaign were "America's Road Team . . . six drivers chosen for their records and ability to speak enthusiastically about the driving profession" (*Heavy Duty Trucking*, January 1986, 26). This attempt to rebuild the image of truckers led the American Trucking Association to change the name of the National Truck Rodeo to the National Driving Championship, because "rodeo" was thought to imply a reckless driver (*Heavy Duty Trucking*, October 1984, 64).

In sum, the images the public holds of truck drivers combine stereotypes associated with blue-collar work in general; direct but limited experiences with truck drivers, such as being tailgated or helped by a truck driver or seeing drivers in truck stops; and the mythic connotations of the road. These images range from the very positive, for example, knights of the highway, to the very negative, such as drug-impaired, irresponsible fools.

Truckers are not immune to popular images of their occupation. While the blue-collar background of most drivers explains much of why they ended up in a blue-collar occupation, many are drawn to trucking by positive images rooted in masculinity and myths of the road.[3] The work looks adventurous, self-directed, and even heroic, and the trucker personifies traditional notions of manliness. Supposedly, he is strong, tough, and fearless, and he will fight if crossed. He can handle huge machinery. He sits high above the ordinary motorist and provokes fear. He is his own boss, and he stands alone. Trucking thus provides recruits the opportunity to act out the script of the traditional man.

> *Norm:* You know how it is when you begin driving; it looks really good. You get to play macho-man sitting up there in your big rig.

> *Warren:* It should be easy for the owner to hire weekend drivers. For a lot of guys, it's a really big deal to drive one of these things. They can get out on the boulevard and be king of the road. Hell, I was that way. I couldn't wait to start driving.

> *Rusty:* Being a truck driver looked cool.

In sum, neophytes often possess strong notions about the work and who they expect to be as a driver.

Even if a neophyte has few such preconceptions, the possibilities are likely to become apparent soon after employment; other truckers will espouse these beliefs, and the actions of some members of the new driver's work-related audiences will be informed by them. For example, Al, the SandHaul driver who put the most time into customizing and cleaning his truck and who talked incessantly about trucks and driving, had originally wanted to be a farmer. When he was unable to enter farming, he began working in a factory. Five years later, he entered trucking after becoming dissatisfied with the amount of money he was making in his factory job, given his responsibilities as a foreman. I asked Al if he had always been greatly concerned with his truck.

> *Al:* Not when I started driving. Then I was mainly interested in just making some coin. Trucking looked like a way to make more money without having all the worries I had at [the factory]. But then you start learning what's going on and you begin caring. Like, my truck was *my* truck. That was me out on the road. And I saw other drivers in really nice-looking trucks, and I thought that that was the way I wanted people to see me. Plus, the guys here that took the best care of their trucks were the guys I had the most respect for.

In short, the new trucker, if he does not know it upon entering the occupation, soon learns that he can be a "somebody."

The opportunity to fulfill the prescription for the traditional man is common to many forms of blue-collar work, but its usefulness as a source of satisfaction appears to vary. For example, in the documentary film *Wrapped in Steel*, Edward Sadlowski, president of United Steel Workers, told of the attraction of steel mill male recruits to the brawny, sweaty, and otherwise traditionally manly images of the steelworker, but he added that within two weeks this image inevitably loses its appeal. I suggest that this loss stems from two sources, the limited satisfaction of defining oneself primarily as a strong and hard worker and the lack of a public audience before whom these qualities can be displayed.

A man's satisfactions in trucking, as compared to steel work and many other blue-collar occupations, appear to be longer lasting, because in trucking they are not as limited and they have greater reinforcement. Trucking offers a recruit the chance to be more than just a man; he can be a notable man. He can become "the last American cowboy," a "knight of the road," a "gypsy," an "outlaw." In addition, he can play these roles in public as opposed, for example, to the steelworker in the mill, the logger in the forest, or the machinist in the factory. Naive audiences, particularly motorists, can share with the trucker the positive mythic images that attracted him to his occupation and act toward him on the basis of these images. Most blue-collar occupations fail on one or both of these counts; they offer only the chance to be a traditional man, and their semipublic-to-pri-

vate performances leave the worker with an audience of only co-
workers not likely to respond in terms of the work's heroic qualities.

The Problem of Skill Assessment

While most truckers recognize and embrace the identification of
trucking with traditional masculinity, they are less sure about
how to demonstrate their work skills or to distinguish skill in
another driver.

In my estimation, two categories of skill reflect the experiences of workers. The first category, work skill, denotes the activities inherent in the task itself. For example, steering a truck
is a work skill for a truck driver. No matter what system truck
driving is organized under, steering is a necessary activity in the
performance of that role. The second category, job skill, encompasses activities not inherent in the task that come to be called
skills. Job skills are adaptations to the system in which the
work takes place, for example, industrial capitalism and its emphasis on profit, efficiency, and control. Job skills often have to
do with effort levels, cunning, and bravery. For example, when
workers attempt to meet quotas by working with great vigor, employing shortcuts, or risking danger, they are exercising job
skills.

Workers and employers appear to have somewhat different
understandings of the meaning of skill, and workers' definitions
are closer than employers' to activities inherent in the task
(work skills). Based on my observations, workers appear generally to wish to "do the work right," and their inclination is to
make this evaluation based on work skills. For example, machinists want to make high-quality gears that meet all specifications; telephone installers want their installations to be as devoid of visible wiring as possible; mechanics wish to diagnose
and correct the cause of an engine's misfiring; and truck drivers
want each gear shift to be perfectly synchronized.

Veblen (1905) posited an "instinct of workmanship . . . that
disposes men to look with favor upon productive efficiency and
whatever is of human use" (15). One need not accept Veblen's
depiction of workmanship as an instinct to accept its existence
as a widespread inclination. If humans seek esteem; if members

of industrial capitalist societies are defined largely in terms of paid work;[4] and if those who sell their labor find that a task's inherent activities (e.g., milling a gear) and products (e.g., a finished gear) are more immediate, concrete, creative, and therefore compelling measures of task performance than are measures derived from the exigencies of a capitalist enterprise, then an inclination toward quality work is likely to be widespread in such a society.

Employers claim a desire for quality work, but the demands of profit, organizational needs, and the wish to control their employees leads to a calculus that dilutes notions of skill based on qualities inherent in the task with notions of skill based on profit, administration, and control. The employer is likely to be concerned with greater output, lower costs, and smooth organizational functioning. The employer's needs and desires lead to a structuring of work wherein, for example, the machinist is rewarded for sacrificing quality in return for high output (Burawoy 1979); telephone installers are given a work load that does not allow time for high-quality installations, and my experience indicates that taking the time will mean that co-workers must complete their unmet assignments; and the mechanic is castigated by a supervisor for wasting time replacing parts needed to treat the cause rather than simply fixing the symptom. In short, employers are likely to put a greater emphasis than do workers on high output and organizational citizenship as measures of worker skill.

From the workers' point of view, work skills form a more satisfactory basis for self-esteem than do job skills, because work skills have to do with what is particular about a workers' activities in comparison to other workers and are less associated with the idea of exploitation. Occupations are distinguished by specific tasks and the needs to which those tasks are directed, whether it be a need for widgets, health, entertainment, or information. When modern workers ask Who am I? they are likely to answer in terms of these tasks and purposes, not in the more abstract notion of themselves as producers of capital. Workers also want to know where they stand in relation to others who perform the same purposeful bundle of tasks, which is to say that esteem is an issue. And cultural norms honor capable performances of any bundle of tasks, even if work systems make certain work skills largely irrelevant, such as those of the wood-carver, weaver, or self-contained mechanic (Harper 1987).

Job skills are inferior to work skills as measures of self because they are associated with exploitation. As Veblen (1905) made clear, to be in the employ of another is tinged with ignobility; commitment to employment is, therefore, always problematic. Whereas the exercise of work skills demonstrates a commitment to a particular bundle of tasks serving some need, the exercise of job skills, because they are adaptations to the employment relationship, may be taken as an indication of commitment to that ignoble relationship. Even job skills that are developed to increase the worker's advantage within a particular system of work—for example, "making out" (Burawoy 1979)—by the very nature of their exercise make apparent the exploitative nature of the employment relationship.

Modern professions are able to counter this problem of commitment to employment by providing members with a set of fictions that bestow honor on their work skills and services while downplaying the fact that the work is a livelihood. Professional ideologies are so powerful that professionals (for example, college professors) who demonstrate a lack of high commitment are suspect, even when such professionals are employees. On the other hand, employees in low-status occupations are not so able to call on ideologies that explain the presence of high commitment.[5] The highly committed low-status employee generally is suspect—the use of the pejorative "company man" is easier to imagine among truck drivers than among account executives and almost impossible to imagine among university professors, even though all three groups are in the employ of others and may be required to work approximately the same number of hours for the same amount of money. Thus, for low-status workers in particular, work skills and not job skills provide the most satisfactory measure of self.

The inclination of workers to judge themselves and one another by measures inherent in their tasks can be thwarted in jobs so rudimentary that little is required in the way of human talents or knowledge (Braverman 1974; Rubin 1976). Further, this inclination is likely to diminish when a company need not depend on quality work to insure a profit.[6]

Co-workers hold the potential to be the most meaningful

source of esteem. More than anyone else who understands the work, they are the ones with whom a worker is likely to have the most contact, they are likely to know more about the work than anyone else, and their judgments are most likely to center on intrinsic qualities of the work without reference to the short-term demands of profit or organizational exigencies.

Occupational esteem requires, first, agreed-upon standards that can be used to assess practitioners and, second, activity or output that is observable and can be assessed. For example, in Harper's (1987) study of a self-employed master mechanic, people brought Willie broken cars, farm machinery, tools, and appliances for repair. In making these repairs, Willie had a clear idea of the skills he brought to the enterprise, and customers could tell whether the repair was successful enough to restore the item to use. Further, many customers were sufficiently familiar with performing mechanical repairs, welding, and electronics to more fully appreciate Willie's skills. One consequence of these understandings was that, though Willie took all the time he felt appropriate to make a repair, his skills rarely were doubted and in fact were highly valued by most people who knew him.

Because in trucking work standards are not clear, much activity is unobservable, and output is not a product but a performance typically evaluated in terms of the absence or presence of undesirable events, esteem is a problem for drivers.

Driving Skills

A trucker's work skills can be separated into three types: driving, equipment operation, and mechanical. They can also be discerned at two levels, gross and refined. Driving means maneuvering the truck through space; the relationship is between the driver and the operating arena outside the cab. Equipment operation signifies what goes on between the truck and its driver when the truck is running; activities such as shifting, control of the engine, and braking constitute operating skills. Mechanical skills involve diagnosis, adjustment, and repair of the equipment.

The work of truck driving, at the gross skill level, consists of using a truck to move a load from one point to another. Learning how to perform this task is relatively easy and can be accomplished in a short period of time, at least by someone who has good command of automobile driving. I rode with an experienced driver for seven days, the first four as an observer and the final three as a driver. Although I had accumulated no more than eight hours and two hundred miles of actual driving experience, I was assigned my own truck.

More refined skills are necessary as other demands are made of the driver. Not only must he move a load between two points, he must be able to do so regularly and without often becoming lost, having an accident, or damaging the truck or its contents. Doing this task repeatedly means doing it in a wide range of weather and driving conditions and under varying amounts of physical stress. Time is also a major consideration; hauls must be completed within periods that require driving with some equipment strain and some disregard for safety. Furthermore, many drivers must learn to handle types of equipment and loads that vary considerably. For example, both a trailer filled with "swinging meat" (meat hung on hooks attached to the trailer's ceiling) and the truck-and-trailer combination popular in California for hauling gasoline are top-heavy and therefore easily overturned, while a bottom-dump sand trailer with its low center of gravity is almost impossible to upend; liquid loads in unbaffled tank trailers ("clean bores"), unless filling the trailer to capacity, slosh around and dramatically affect how a truck handles;[7] an empty truck is more likely to jackknife than a fully loaded truck when braking on wet pavement; traction on rain-slick or snow-covered roads varies by tire type; a semi must be swung wider than a set of doubles when negotiating a corner; and backing a truck-and-trailer requires turning the steering wheel in the opposite direction to that of a tractor-trailer to accomplish the same move.

Further, a driver responsible for loading and unloading has a good deal to learn. For example, flatbed haulers must learn how to secure a variety of loads so that the load does not end up on the roadway or cab; produce haulers must learn loading and temperature-maintenance techniques that will preserve the various perishables they carry; drivers of van trailers need to know how to plan the van's loading so that everything fits and the weight is legally distributed; and haulers of inflammables must know under what conditions it is dangerous to load.

In addition to the exigencies of driving, still more skills are required if a driver is to increase what I call "equipment operation" skills. The mark of operational skills is control over the truck as a piece of machinery. A skillful driver displays great control over the truck, so that safety and comfort levels for him and his codriver are high and mechanical wear and tear are low.

Finally, if drivers are to operate safely and efficiently they must be able to spot mechanical problems. Knowing how to make simple adjustments and repairs will also add to the driver's safety and income. A thorough knowledge of the truck as a piece of equipment takes considerable learning and is not commonly found among drivers, because of lack of time, training, incentives, and both the sheer bulk and technical demands of the knowledge to be mastered.[8]

It took several years of driving for me to feel that I was a skilled driver and, in my own estimate, about five years of experience to approximate the skill level one might associate with a craft journeyman in this area, one who can successfully manage such problems as those I have discussed.

Drivers' Uncertainty about Measures of Driving Skill

Despite some general ideas about proficiency, it is not clear to drivers what exactly constitutes skilled driving. They are often uncertain if there is an agreed-upon right way to perform much of their work and if other drivers' opinions on such matters are credible. This lack of certainty and credibility is evident in their bull sessions and in their reaction to a seemingly objective performance measurement, the tachograph.

Drivers at the three companies engaged in bull sessions about work almost daily; these discussions occurred in the yard as they waited to begin work, in or near the yard after work was finished (SandHaul day-shift drivers met daily, weather permitting, in a vacant lot next to a nearby liquor store), and at loading and unloading sites. In discussions of how best to do some aspect of their work, arguments and disagreements were more likely than consensus. For example, SandHaul drivers, who did a lot of mountain driving, argued frequently about how best to descend long, steep grades—not a trivial matter, because an error when driving a truck weighing almost eighty thousand pounds can quickly result in loss of braking power.

Beyond the frequency of such discussions, drivers raising these questions among themselves points to the problematic nature of driving skills, because raising such questions means taking a risk. All holders of operating licenses that imply licensees are fully qualified drivers are embarrassed to ask point-blank questions about driving. Since much of a driver's work is not visible, such questions are a primary means of disclosing the possibility that one is not the driver one is supposed to be. Compounding this risk is the threat to one's masculinity: in the car culture of California and, probably, of the western states, a man is supposed to be a competent driver. Men enter trucking thinking they are good drivers, and to admit to anything less risks a blow to their masculinity. Drivers nonetheless voice their concerns about how correctly or best to do their work, but they do so in ways that defuse the risks.

Drivers usually do not ask point-blank how best to handle a driving situation. Instead they tell a story about themselves handling such a situation and then wait for feedback, itself often initially in the form of a story. By telling a story rather than asking a question, the driver not only avoids an outright display of ignorance of other methods of driving but also, through lack of explicit standards, is in a position to defend what he did. Occasionally drivers ask outright questions regarding driving, but these almost always occur either when drivers are one-on-one or in a small group with an established pecking order—that is, in situations where, because of clear skill differences, the questioner feels comfortable in admitting his ignorance. For example, most SandHaul drivers had no experience with driving in snow, but freak weather conditions on several occasions forced them to negotiate a steep mountain pass covered with snow and ice. Only two drivers, including myself, were experienced in driving in these conditions, and some fellow drivers consulted us privately. In a highly unusual instance, four of these drivers jointly admitted their ignorance and fear and asked me to lead them over the pass. Notable about all of these admissions is that they arose only when there was an extreme situation in which a small mistake easily could lead to accident, injury, and even death. At the same time, the situation presented clear and known differences in experience. Without such provocations and obvious skill differences, drivers rarely admit to ignorance or to another's superiority in matters of driving.[9]

The form of such work-related stories gives further insight into the information-gathering and information-sharing functions of the stories and the uncertainty drivers have regarding skill. Rather than providing general accounts of how they performed some operation or handled a driving situation, drivers often give highly detailed descriptions. For example, instead of saying simply, "I came off the Grapevine and then . . . ," a Sand-Haul driver said, "I came off the Grapevine in fifth-over [a gear that allows the driver to go approximately twenty-five to thirty miles an hour] with my jake popping [using the added braking power of an engine compression brake] and laying in about five pounds [per square inch] of brake and then . . ." In this instance, even though the topic was not ostensibly how to descend from mountains, the speaker told his audience his formula for descending a steep, continuous, five-mile-long grade, given the combination of weight and auxiliary braking capability he had available. The combination of gear, brake pressure, and use of an engine brake also conveys to the audience the speaker's unwillingness to push the truck to capacity in this potentially dangerous situation.

In another example of information gathering, a driver, in the course of a story, said, "I was cruising along at fifty-nine in eighth-over at nineteen hundred rpm." In this case, the driver was, in effect, gently probing the audience for its reaction to his theory of gear selection, while leaving himself in a position to defend his choice and not admit ignorance. This driver was left uncertain in this very basic matter by engine design changes in the 1970s and 1980s that affect their usable rpm range and corresponding gear selections. In both examples, if an agreed-upon right way existed, the detail of the descriptions would be pointless.[10]

Judging the answers to one's query regarding work skills has its own problems, especially when the query is indirectly posed, because there are few indicators of which drivers are the most qualified to respond. Every driver has a license, there are no formal occupational grades, and most driving performance goes unobserved, factors that make it hard for drivers to judge skill levels and therefore the worth of the information provided. This is not to say that no drivers speak with assurance about their work skills; self-assurance varies according to combinations of experience, feedback from others, and personality. The point is that discussions of work skills can be characterized as tentative and problematic, and assertions regarding work skills are easily challenged.

An exception to the reluctance of drivers to ask direct questions about driving is their readiness to ask about loading and unloading. Three reasons explain this exception. First, the possession of a driver's license implies nothing about the loading or unloading process, beyond the ability to maneuver a trailer into its proper location. Second, load handling is, on the whole, more observable than driving: drivers more often are in a position to observe another's load handling than another's driving, which makes constructing standards and determining expertise easier. Finally, load handling does not have the same male role overtones as driving, and ignorance or lack of skill in load handling is not the blow to masculinity that it would be in driving. By the time a man in the western states is old enough to drive a truck, he is expected to know how to drive well; men are not expected, by virtue of their masculinity, to know how to load oil into a tank trailer, or produce into a refrigerated van.

Bull sessions, then, are used by drivers to elicit information about task performance, to seek reassurance for their individual methods of performing these tasks, and to assess their techniques in comparison to those of other drivers. These sessions also provide drivers the opportunity to present themselves as skilled workers. In all these cases, bull sessions highlight the lack of consensus regarding driving techniques and are a means of constructing work standards among drivers.

This lack of certainty about work performance is further underlined by the reaction of SandHaul drivers to a seemingly quantitative and readily visible (hence "objective") measure of their performance, the tachograph. This instrument plots truck speed, engine rpm, and time onto a round piece of graph paper (the "chart") to heighten management's control over driver performance: speed, length of stops, total hours worked, and engine speed can be monitored. The use and interpretation of each of these measures varies according to management's objectives.

The tachograph's utility to drivers in assessing their own performances is minimal. Excepting one type of engine abuse and without a very close and astute reading, charts reveal little about driving skills as I have defined them. Instead, charts record driving behaviors that are valued by management because they directly affect profit; in addition, tachographs increase the owner's control over drivers. For example, SandHaul installed tachographs to improve fuel mileage by reducing top speeds, but few drivers would call driving fifty-five rather than sixty miles an hour a driving skill. PetroHaul used tachographs to monitor length of time worked; again, no PetroHaul drivers would call taking a twenty-minute rather than a twenty-five-minute break a driving skill.

Despite the seeming irrelevance of charts in measuring driving skills, drivers at SandHaul used the charts as just such a measure. I frequently witnessed drivers showing their charts to other drivers and bragging about the flatness (therefore constancy) of the line charting truck speed. This graphic picture was not used as a measure by the owner, who said nothing about the line's contour. Nor did all drivers brag about their line contours; those most given to the practice were the less-experienced drivers. Even the more-experienced drivers, however, would inspect the charts of drivers they disdained; if that driver's chart showed a rather uneven truck-speed line, the chart would be shown to other drivers and the target driver ridiculed. The chart, then, could be used to bolster a prevailing prejudice. While there is some notion among drivers that a vehicle should be driven at a steady speed, doing so says little about a driver's total skills, and not doing so, because of the many impinging factors such as traffic, hills, weight of load, weather conditions, wind, and engine power, also says little about a driver's skills. In fact, a driver who was concerned about the flatness of his chart's speed line might operate the truck in an abusive or dangerous manner to achieve this end. The low correlation between a flat truck-speed line and driving skills is supported by the near-total lack of use or even mention of steady speed as an indicator of driving skill at companies that did not use tachographs, or those like PetroHaul where charts are not accessible to drivers.

Because drivers are affected by and react to uncertainty

about their skills, it is worth examining how this uncertainty comes about.

Sources of Drivers' Uncertainty about Assessing Driving Skills

Drivers are unsure about what constitutes skilled driving (including driving, operational, and mechanical skills, unless otherwise noted) as a result of single-mentor training, the short training period for new drivers, a lack of reliable information, and limited opportunities to observe driving skills.

During the time I drove trucks, most neophytes were trained by only one driver.[11] Entry into trucking typically came through a personal relationship between the novice and someone in the industry who either conducts or arranges for this training. Of SandHaul's twenty-eight drivers, twenty-five were trained by one driver; the others reported riding with two drivers. At the eight companies where I witnessed novices being taught to drive, no company made it a point to have the novice ride with more than one driver. The same held true at all but two of the companies when it came to teaching loading and unloading techniques to newly hired drivers unfamiliar with the company's specialties. Given the practices of these companies, it seems clear that little value was attached to exposing a novice to a variety of drivers. Since most novices move into solo jobs, this single-mentor training limits their exposure to the range of driving skills.

In addition to being trained by only one driver, most drivers during the time I drove did not go through an extended period of training before acquiring a license. First, states did not demand a level of skill requiring extensive training before a driver could be certified (*Heavy Duty Trucking*, October 1985, 64).[12] Nineteen states did not require a special license to drive a truck, and only twenty-seven required for such a license either a state driving test or certification of driving skills by an employer. In California, written tests for this license were more involved than for an automobile license but could be mastered quickly by reading pamphlets made available by the state. The two written tests covered much the same ground as the automobile license test, and I almost passed them despite having no experience with trucks and without having first read the pamphlets. In California, a novice did not need to take an official driving test to be granted a license.[13] Instead, some trucking companies had individuals with the authority to certify that a novice was sufficiently skilled to receive a license. I was certified after I had managed less than two hundred miles behind the wheel of a truck. Even had would-be truckers been required to take California's official driving test, they would have needed to demonstrate only a gross skill level.

The second reason for short driver-training periods is that economic incentives push both driver and employer to speed training: the sooner novices are driving, the sooner they will be making money. Furthermore, the novice is typically trained for a job that is immediately available from the mentor or an acquaintance of the mentor. In these cases, both the novice and the future employer may be anxious to begin employment. The companies willing to hire a novice are often those that do not offer enough to attract the more experienced and desirable drivers. According to one owner, most novices can offer a lesser company something that the experienced pool of recruits cannot—a clean driving record and, consequently, lower insurance premiums. Novices are also easier to exploit, because they have yet to learn drivers' interpretations of a fair effort bargain, and they feel both highly vulnerable to firing and indebted to those who gave them access to an occupation that is not easy to enter without personal connections. In short, both the novice and the company hiring the novice are often anxious to complete the training and begin paid work.

The third reason for short training periods is that drivers do not need high skill levels to get a job. Two major considerations inform the decision to hire: a driver's written record and references. The main features of the written record are experience, moving violations, and accidents. But a clean record is usually not enough to get a driving job. Although I have worked at eight companies, I have yet to meet a driver who entered trucking without some personal connection in the industry to refer him. No driver at SandHaul simply acquired a license and began knocking on the doors of employers; all knew someone in the industry who aided them. Typically, the novice has a mentor who trains him, directs him to potential employers, and provides a reference. Some mentors are also in a position to support a novice's exaggerated claims of experience because they are self-employed and can say that the novice was an employee. These written and personal skill indicators lessen the need for novices to possess a high level of skill.

A driver who wants to change companies also does not need a high skill level to land another job. Again, the written record and references are what most potential employers use as primary indicators of driving skill. While a positive correlation exists between skillful driving and a driver's written record and references, that correlation is not as high as often thought and can be confounded by other variables. In my own case, long periods of inactivity have helped me maintain an excellent citation and accident record. As another example, drivers at SandHaul accumulate few citations because their speed is strictly monitored by the company; they run regular routes and learn the habits of the police they are most likely to encounter; most of the hauling is outside the city (city driving is much more susceptible than open-road driving both to violation codes and to apprehension when they are not met); the company has excellent equipment and is not targeted by police; loads are always within legal weight limits; and the existence of two shifts lessens the strain on drivers.

If a driver can assemble a good written record and make some connections in the business, neither of which requires anyone to directly observe his skills, then he is employable. By the time a road test is given to a job applicant, it is often a perfunctory ritual covering at best only gross skills and intended to confirm what management believes it already knows. Of my eight employers, only two required thorough road tests administered by management. One company trained me, but no one in management gave me an actual road test. Instead, management relied on the word of the driver who had trained me and who, I later discovered, was considered skilled but neither truthful nor dependable. Three companies took recommendations of mutual friends in place of a road test. Aside from the thorough road tests already noted, two other companies gave tests, but these were administered by drivers, not management: one driver hated the owner and was not likely to care whether or not I was proficient, and the other driver had only one year of experience. In the case where the driver hated the owner, the driver was asked for his evaluation while I was standing next to him; de-

spite my inept shifting and rough braking of unfamiliar equipment, he told the owner, "He did just fine." In this case, more
than thirty drivers had applied for three jobs, but only three of
us were given a road test, and we three were hired. In sum, companies seem to select whom they will hire on the basis of an
applicant's paperwork and mutual acquaintances. The companies that hired me were anxious to hire; the road test, if administered, was often more a ritual than a trial.

The ability to find employment without demonstrating much
beyond gross skills can also be seen in employment advertisements. For example, on the basis of advertisements in April
1985 in Chicago's two major daily newspapers, the *Chicago Sun
Times* and the *Chicago Tribune*, five large, nonunion, relatively
low-paying companies made the use of advanced neophytes
their policy, as indicated by their stated willingness to hire those
with only six to twelve months of experience.[14]

The third reason for drivers' uncertainty about what constitutes skillful driving is a dearth of official information about
driving. These drivers do not belong to any formal driver organizations that provide information about driving skills. Likewise,
management rarely takes an active stance in terms of teaching
driving, operational, or mechanical skills. For example, I have
seen considerable changes in engine design and operation requirements—running an engine at low rpm ("lugging") used to
be a taboo, but more recent fuel-efficient designs require lugging
for economical operation—but only one of my employers made
even a marginal attempt to inform drivers of the needed changes
in operating techniques. At AgriHaul, the exception, no formal
meeting was held nor was printed information distributed; the
owner casually approached drivers when the opportunity presented itself and gave them a general idea of how to operate the
new engines. At SandHaul I asked the owner about the operating requirements of a new model engine he had just received,
and he replied, "Just drive them like you do the others." Based
on trade magazine articles, this reply was not entirely correct. At
AgriHaul, I became frustrated by the lack of information on how
to handle the then-new high-torque-rise engines, so I went to a
major truck dealership and asked their mechanics how to operate them; even they were not able to tell me the essential fact of
the engine's usable rpm range. Other than an occasional meet-

ing on the subject of driving safety—and these, drivers claim, are held to satisfy insurance policy requirements rather than to educate drivers—I have never seen management formally communicate with drivers about driving skills. When management does speak to drivers about driving performance, it is done individually and almost always centers on the driver's violation of a gross-level skill such as crashing the truck into something.

Trade journals occasionally provide information on driving skills, but I have never seen drivers reading, in possession of, or quoting from these publications. At any rate, trade journals are aimed at management, and their interests regarding drivers mostly concern how to extend control over them and insure driving habits that maximize profit. For example, the October 1985 issue of *Heavy Duty Trucking* devotes twenty-six pages to "Collaring the Bad Driver." Solutions include drug testing, personality testing, centralized license reporting, and computer monitoring.

Finally, drivers are uncertain about driving skills because they have little exposure to one another's driving. For the most part, all but the grossest skills are not open to observation except from within the cab, and most drivers drive unaccompanied by a codriver. It is not especially difficult to steer a truck on an open road, to shift the transmission enough times to reach cruising speed, to put on the brakes when there is a need to slow down, and to find a given destination. The failure to acquire these skills is readily observable.

More refined skills that demonstrate both a higher level of control over the vehicle under a wide variety of conditions and the ability to anticipate myriad driving situations as well as simply to navigate through traffic are subtle and not nearly as observable. For example, the ability to shift the transmission each time so that the gears do not grind and to do so while controlling the engine's speed to minimize drivetrain stress takes considerable practice and coordination; I would estimate that not more than 20 percent of the drivers I directly observed have mastered this process. In observing from another truck, however, at best all that can usually be told about shifting is whether the shift was completed or missed, or if the driver is exceptionally abusive in engaging gears. Observing from the side of the road so that the truck can be heard as well as seen, it is possible to determine if a driver synchronized a shift and, to some degree, what method he used, but it is not usually possible to assess drivetrain stress. Refined skills are nearly impossible to assess unless the observer is in the cab to see, hear, and feel all that occurs. Since driving is usually solo, most drivers have had little opportunity to make in-depth observations of other drivers' performances.[15]

The lack of contact drivers have with one another's skills is evident in an examination of the most damning moniker drivers saddle one another with, "cowboy," which refers to a driver who submits his truck to overly rough treatment. A cowboy typically is in a great hurry, even when hurrying is pointless, and in his rush he abuses his truck or ignores norms applicable to driving in a particular environment. For example, a driver would be labeled a cowboy if he drove into a truck stop without slowing down for the bump caused by the gutter and driveway, rapidly accelerated on his way to the fuel pumps, slammed on the brakes at the pumps, and immediately shut off the engine rather than letting it idle until the turbo cooled. This driver would have subjected his truck to needless wear and tear and violated norms governing speeds in settings such as truck stops and cafés. Since there is little to gain by hurrying in this situation, this display would be taken as indicating the trucker's poor driving and operational skills. The label "cowboy" applied in such circumstances engenders high consensus and, if assigned by co-workers, is difficult to shed.

"Cowboy" is also used to signify truckers who drive faster than road conditions warrant, grossly exceed speed limits, or otherwise display senseless haste. For example, a driver who passes other truckers in a heavy fog or who is traveling at seventy-five on an open highway and rapidly cutting in and out of traffic can be called a cowboy. Complications arise, however, in basing the label "cowboy" on these on-the-road indicators. First, given the variations in equipment, loads, road conditions, and skill, few hard and fast rules exist for driving in adverse situations. Also, a driver who passes others in rain or snow might be considered by some drivers to be more skillful and therefore able to drive faster without losing control. Drivers are thus likely to disagree about what constitutes prudent driving in any given set of circumstances. Further, speeding on the highway is less likely than off-the-road speeding to be taken as indicative of a driver's overall driving and operational skills, because highway speeding may be relatively rational. For example, the speeding driver may have a load of produce that needs to be delivered before the receiver closes for a rapidly approaching weekend if it is not to spoil. Truckers know that drivers who display inordinate hurry on the road may have good reason. Thus, when someone is labeled a cowboy based on his on-the-road performance, consensus is more problematic and the label less likely to become permanent than for off-the-road performances: "He is driving as if he were a cowboy." At the three companies in this book, the drivers considered cowboys by their co-workers did not earn this designation solely or even primarily by on-the-road performances.

Off-the-road driving performances create cowboys, not because they demand a display of skill beyond the rudimentary level (with the exception of backing a trailer, they do not), but because off the road is where co-workers are able to observe one another's driving, most often in the company yard, followed by either cafés or loading and unloading sites. Although drivers from the same company do get to observe one another on the road, at only at two of the eight companies that employed me were drivers from the same company likely to travel together at least once a week. Even then there is the difficulty of judging another's driving skills from a separate truck.

The cowboy driver, therefore, does not so much fail to display refined skills, which are difficult to observe, as to give off signs, such as driving too fast over bumps, that are thought to be incompatible with refined skills. Cowboy driving may indicate a lack of skills, but it may also indicate ignorance of the norms governing various settings (e.g., young drivers not frequently think hot-rodding in front of other drivers is stylish), disagreement or lack of concern with these norms, protest against the employer, or simply irritation or exhaustion. For example, at AgriHaul a fifty-nine-year-old driver with long service and considerable skill (I had accompanied him on several runs and was able directly to observe his driving) began slamming on his brakes when he arrived at a loading or unloading site, hot-rodding the engine, and occasionally running over curbs, all of which he explained by saying, "I don't give a shit anymore."

When cowboy driving is determined by on-the-road indicators, it is mostly a judgment of the prudence of another driver's speed, so it is again a limited assessment of a driver's skills. Since speeding and hurry are relative, often rational and situational, and evidence of skill as well as of poor judgment, the term "cowboy" applied in these settings is fraught with ambivalence.

The pedagogical usefulness of observing other drivers is limited. Even when refined skills are observable, the variability of loads and equipment undermine the usefulness of such observations. For example, as a novice I was preparing to haul my first load "over the hill," a steep, five-mile grade dangerous enough to warrant a truck escape ramp, in a retarderless (no engine brake) truck loaded to the legal maximum weight. An experienced driver told me what combination of gear, speed, brake pressure, and braking technique I should use and then said: "Drive your own gig. Don't watch the other guys, because you don't know how much weight they have on, how much brake they have, or even if they know what the hell they are doing." "Drive your own gig" is a philosophy that indicates the limitation of on-the-road observations as a basis for estimating driving techniques and skills.

The consequence for me of lack of contact with other drivers in the act of driving and the limited dissemination of information about driving skills became clear as soon as I took my first turn at the wheel after being hired by a cross-country trucking company that used driving teams. My new partner, an older driver, drove the first shift, and, within a few minutes after our departure, I knew his skills were markedly superior to mine. When he shifted, there was no perceptible movement of the truck; it neither lurched forward from too low an engine speed nor backward from too hard an acceleration. Using constant foot pressure on the throttle, he perfectly controlled engine rpm between shifts as opposed simply to removing his foot from the throttle and timing a shift, hoping that it would not grind, the method used by most of the drivers I have observed from within the cab. His every shift was synchronized, and deceleration from braking was almost imperceptible. I had no idea a truck could be driven with such precision. After I took the wheel my partner said nothing for about twenty minutes and then asked, in an obviously unhappy tone, "Who gave you your road test?" At the time of my hiring, I had driven full- and part-time over a period of three years, accumulating approximately 150,000 miles, almost entirely solo, and had been told I was a good driver, an assessment I shared.

Because of single-mentor tutoring, the short training periods, the lack of information, and the infrequent opportunities to drive with one another, truckers have little exposure to the range of driving skills and therefore little certainty about skills. This limits drivers' development of those skills, makes their occupation seem less skilled, and has two important consequences for drivers' workplace behavior and sense of self: it creates a void that is filled by the standards of nondriver groups, and it reduces the importance of co-workers as a source of esteem while enhancing the importance of other work-related groups.

If a driver is not certain about what constitutes skilled work and has little opportunity to demonstrate the skills he knows, how is he to know when he is doing well or how is he to experience the gratifications of a job well done? Most drivers incorporate the visible standards of work-related groups who can have an important and immediate consequence on a driver's life: owners/management and, to a lesser extent, police. In addition, drivers measure themselves by selectively interpreting the actions and reactions of less powerful work-related groups: company support personnel, motorists, employees of customers and shippers, and drivers encountered on the road. A common denominator in these responses is that they involve observable indicators. Finally, the problematic nature of esteem for drivers increases the importance of masculinity and occupational myths in self-assessment.

CHAPTER 6

What Owners Want from Drivers, What Drivers Want from Owners

Owners and their managers constitute a powerful audience before which drivers shape their performances. As with drivers' other audiences, this one has particular interests and expectations. In Chapter 5, I point out that owners and managers rarely encourage the development of driving skills: the mastery of the equipment in driving, operational, and mechanical terms. Instead, they set forth values that they treat as skills, and these are, for the most part, what I have termed "job skills": the aspects of driving that most directly enhance profit and contribute to the smooth running of business operations. For example, while sitting in his office and trying to solve organizational problems or attract new customers, the owner does not know and is not particularly concerned that one driver can consistently make a smooth shift into low range when pulling a 6 percent grade, while another in the same situation strains the drivetrain by using brute force to engage the gears. What concerns the owner and what he can observe are whether or not a load was delivered on time, the amount of time a load took, quantity hauled, gross damage to the truck or load, competence in paperwork, customer complaints, the driver's willingness to take on more work, and perhaps the driver's ability to make repairs (although drivers are expected to have only minimal repair skills).

The inferior status of driving skills (what I call "work skills") in the estimation of owners and managers did not mean that these skills were not valued. While the owners' priorities were profit and organizational needs, owners expressed the belief that drivers differed in driving skill levels, and they acted on this belief. PetroHaul had a certain esprit that centered on the owner's and management's contention that PetroHaul drivers were first-rate. AgriHaul selected a driver of the year and gave various awards for safe driving. While SandHaul's owner seemed to have less regard for driving skills than the other two owners, he awarded cash bonuses to drivers who avoided accidents and citations.[1] All three owners and their managers bestowed informal rewards such as a better truck and greater autonomy on those perceived as good drivers.

The opportunity to evaluate driving skills was limited, however, for owners as well as for drivers. Though all of the owners had been drivers, two did not appear to be particularly skilled drivers themselves (I rode with one owner and was told stories about the other two by veteran drivers). They, like most drivers, after only a brief introductory training had driven solo. Two owners thus did not understand the range of skills an expert driver could bring to the job. This was not the case at PetroHaul, whose owner was reputed to be a good driver and whose general manager was a highly skilled ex-driver with many years and a variety of partners in cross-country operations behind him. But even at PetroHaul, after my brief introduction was completed, I only once heard anything said directly about these skills. When most owners want to address the question of refined driving skills, they thus not only have difficulty in discerning them but also are not entirely sure what to talk about.

Given their rather poorly specified notion that some drivers possess more driving skills than others, and given the limited opportunities to observe these skills, when owners directed attention to driving skills beyond the demands of short-term profit and organizational harmony, they turned to indicators they associated with their notions of driving skill: cleanliness of a driver's assigned truck, the driver's appearance, the driver's ability to talk up his skills, the absence of mistakes and mishaps, truck repair frequency, and paperwork. Among these measures, only paperwork and the truck's appearance are the result of positive on-the-job work behaviors. The others, for example, a driver's appearance, have little to do with work, or indicate behaviors that are accomplishments only in the sense that something undesirable, such as destroying an engine, did not occur. Are such indicators of any use in determining refined driving skills?

It is not clear that personal appearance has anything to do with driving skills. The owners I worked for who most obviously showed a concern for drivers' appearances operated on the belief that beards and long hair indicated something undesirable about both a driver and his place of employment; the objection appeared rooted in a political bias more than in the owners' experiences with particular drivers.

Truck appearance was taken by the three owners as an indication of whether or not drivers take care in their work, and care was translated into skill. However, some drivers do not see truck cleanliness as important. In addition, since truck cleaning is almost always unpaid and much of it has to be done while off duty, a dirty truck may indicate the unwillingness to work without pay rather than indifferent workmanship. Finally, care does not necessarily translate into skill; skill requires knowledge, experience, and certain abilities. For example, in riding with three of the PetroHaul drivers who kept their trucks the cleanest, I saw that only one had superior driving skills. Conversely, the PetroHaul driver who put the least effort into caring for his truck demonstrated a high level of skill when I rode with him.

A driver's ability to talk up his skills indicates he knows something about what ought to be said, and a careful listener may gain some insight into the speaker's driving skills. However, a driver who has a good ear for drivers' talk can learn the language much faster than he can acquire the skills. This discrepancy was particularly evident at SandHaul, where Ringo, a brash neophyte, insisted on presenting himself as a seasoned trucker. His talk angered other drivers not only for its presumptions, but especially because it was difficult to cut him down to size simply through conversation. For example, one driver said about Ringo, "You'd think that guy had driven a million miles already. I try to tell him something, but what do I know? I've only driven eight years compared to his six months, but do you think he wants to hear it?" The inability of veteran drivers to counter Ringo's presentation of himself as a know-it-all trucker made clear the limitations of verbal presentation as an indicator of skill.

The occurrence of many mistakes and mishaps would seem to indicate lesser skills, but they may also indicate a driver who does not know how to prevent their detection. For example, the dispatcher at PetroHaul told me, after seeing scuff marks on all of my truck's curb-side tires, "You've got to watch that, Larry, they really frown on curbing tires." What I learned from his admonition was to remove signs of this error before returning to the yard. A driver who overheard the dispatcher's warning confirmed my impressions when, without solicitation, he told me his method for hiding such marks.

The smart driver learns to carry tools and certain replacement parts such as marker-light lenses, which are easily broken, that are useful for hiding evidence of mishaps. In an occupation where most work is not directly observable by management and co-workers, the ability to cover errors is itself something of an occupational skill and a factor in esteem. For example, when one of PetroHaul's less experienced and less skilled drivers blew his engine while ascending a mountain, I stopped to offer my assistance. I determined what was wrong, that an error on his part was to blame, and that this error could be inferred from reading his tachograph chart. In response to his worry and to cover his mistake, I concocted a story involving the engine's behavior and his responses. The owner, managers, and mechanics all believed the story, the driver was absolved of blame, and from that day forward the driver deferred to me as being the more skilled.

Owners also use types and frequency of truck repairs as indicators of a trucker's driving and operational skills. Problems with the mechanical items drivers most directly control, such as engines, transmissions, differentials, and suspensions, raise the suspicion that the driver is at fault. For example, almost as soon as I began my first driving job, my engine blew while I was ascending a steep hill, and the owner blamed me, attributing it to my inexperience. At first glance, his conclusion might seem reasonable. However, correlating types and frequencies of repair with skill presents several problems. For one thing, drivers rarely keep the same truck over a long period, and trucks were driven by more than one driver at all three companies, especially SandHaul and PetroHaul. While most of AgriHaul's trucks were assigned to a single driver, weekend drivers also drove these trucks, and, because of driver turnover and the addition of new equipment, drivers often moved to another truck within six to eighteen months of their most recent assignment. These switches make repair as a skill indicator invalid, because equipment malfunctions that are the result of driving abuses are most often the result of cumulative abuses over a long term rather than a single or short-term abuse. For example, long after blowing up the aforementioned engine, I was told by a company mechanic that he had suspected my engine was ready to blow up at the time I began driving that truck.

In addition to difficulties with accountability, variations in the type and original condition of equipment and the uses to which it is put render repair records suspect as indicators of driving skill. For example, the AgriHaul drivers of a new model engine were suspected of running the engines too hard because of the injector problems they were having. Later, the engine manufacturer admitted a design problem that caused premature injector failure.

A company's accounting procedures can also vitiate the worth of repair as a skill indicator. At AgriHaul, the dispatcher once told me that I was coming into disfavor because of the number of repairs my truck required. I did not think this perception accurate. My investigation revealed that mechanics reacting to a new, computerized system aimed at tracking their time regularly covered "goof-off" periods by claiming to have worked on my truck—the oldest long-haul rig and therefore the most likely to need repair—when in fact no work had been done. Because I got along well with the mechanics, they agreed to spread their goof-off time onto other trucks.

If a driver is particularly adept at or thorough about inspecting his truck, he is more likely to discover problems in need of repair. At PetroHaul, I found more cracked suspension springs than did the average driver because I inspected carefully for this defect. At first, management took this as a sign that I was doing good inspections, but after a while the general manager suggested that I was breaking more than my share of springs, a condition that is taken to indicate rough driving. In response, I began to leave all but major cracks uncited in my vehicle condition reports.

In sum, the three owners demonstrated the greatest interest in driving behaviors that had the most direct and measurable effect on profit and the smooth operation of the company. However, they also wanted to employ skilled drivers. When owners looked for finer indications of skilled driving, they were limited by their lack of knowledge of what to look for, poor measures for determining those skills, or both.

How Management's Assessments Affect Drivers' Esteem

The emphasis by owners and managers on driver behaviors associated with profit and organizational functioning in part fill the void created by drivers' own uncertainty about their driving skills. In the terms used above, "job skills" fill the gap caused by the inability of drivers to define "work skills." Like the machinists Burawoy (1979) studied, most drivers adopted as measures of their performance those standards that reflected profit and organizational demands. They thus valued behaviors that increased the quantity of completed work and the rate of productivity. Most drivers also embraced, in varying degrees, the owners' and managements' indicators of refined driving skills, such as truck cleanliness. By adopting these definitions of skill, drivers measured themselves by standards consistent with their exploitation by company owners.

When drivers at AgriHaul bragged about their accomplishments, these often had to do with their endurance. Certain drivers, especially neophytes, were chided for not being able to "stay in the saddle," that is, to drive for a long time without stopping for a break. Among the road drivers, the use of amphetamines was a part of company culture; it was a behavior that was seen as legitimate, enhanced esteem, and contributed to group bonding (though it was not necessarily done frequently by all drivers). Almost every day, I also heard AgriHaul drivers brag about how fast they could drive between points, how close to the maximum payload they hauled, overloads they managed to deliver without being detected by the police, or ruses they used to avoid complying with a variety of laws and regulations. The amount of a paycheck was another self-measure, not only in and of itself but also as an indicator of how much work was performed, how much weight carried, and the number of good-paying loads hauled. Though getting good loads was seen partly as a matter of luck, it also could be construed as signifying the owner's or dispatcher's approval of a driver's performance. It is notable, too, that in an occupation where much of the work is not readily visible, most of these behaviors are objective and measurable. Load times, miles driven, weight carried, and pay all can be stated in numbers and compared, and thereby provide a common standard.

PetroHaul's drivers included in their measures of self and other drivers the fulfillment of work quotas, trip completion times, and the speed with which they could load and unload (Chapter 3). For example, when drivers serviced their trucks at the end of a shift, they almost always recounted to their partner their successes and failures and, in doing so, used these measures.

Unlike AgriHaul drivers, PetroHaul drivers did not brag about working many consecutive hours. Since drivers were expected to work about fifteen hours per shift, that extent of endurance was taken for granted; with few opportunities to exceed this limit by notable amounts, drivers were not able to distinguish themselves by this measure. However, the bragging about the number of consecutive five-shift weeks (seventy-five to eighty hours), the complaints about being limited to a "mere" fifteen hours per shift, the recollections of a past when a driver could work as long as he wanted, and the teasing of non-PetroHaul drivers who were labeled "wimps" or "candy-asses" for working only twelve-hour shifts all appeared to indicate a positive valuation of endurance by the many PetroHaul drivers I observed expressing one or another of these attitudes.

Organizational demands at PetroHaul regularly called for late-night deliveries of gasoline at closed service stations in high-crime areas. Management recognized the very real danger of these deliveries and would not force a driver to make them, but they pressured drivers to comply by citing the customer's urgent need and complaining about schedule disruptions that would result from a refusal to deliver. While a few drivers consistently resisted this pressure and others grudgingly assented, usually after acquiring a gun, at least one-third of the drivers made these deliveries without resisting and then bragged about their fearlessness. Even the grudging assenters typically used the language of machismo to redefine their surrender to management's demands.

> *Claude:* I don't like going there at night but nobody is going to mess with me. I'll blow 'em away.

Both groups boasted of improvised shortcuts in unloading procedures, such as not hooking up the vapor recovery line, that enabled them to reduce their delivery times in these circumstances. These drivers turned satisfying an organizational demand into something akin to a work skill.

Drivers at SandHaul also displayed a certain pride in endurance that was reflected by a slang term peculiar to them, "doing the double." This term denoted working two consecutive shifts, a common practice when working a sixth or seventh consecutive day.

In addition to requiring drivers to do the double, the organization of work at SandHaul informally encouraged them to take only short, if any, on-the-road breaks (see Chapter 3). Since the hauls rarely took more than three hours of driving without an interruption for loading or unloading, working without a break was not seen by drivers as unreasonable and doing so was not particularly notable. However, the driver who couldn't stay in the saddle for these periods of time was seen as lacking skill (endurance). For example, one night in my first month of working at SandHaul, I became so tired that I pulled to the side of the road and slept for thirty minutes. Later, I was told by two drivers that the day-shift driver of the truck I drove that night had looked at my tachograph chart, seen the thirty-minute break, and passed judgment.

> *Al:* That's one lightweight truck driver. If he can't stay in the saddle any longer than that maybe he's in the wrong business.

Despite these beliefs, SandHaul drivers were less likely than those at AgriHaul and PetroHaul to measure themselves by meeting quotas or performing feats of endurance. SandHaul's shorter shifts and more routinized work made these standards less applicable, and this irrelevance was reinforced by the owner's belief, as reflected in his behavior, that the completion of work was less a problem than the manner in which it was completed. For example, when the owner monitored a driver, his concern was not with the amount of work completed so much as with driving practices that reduced fuel consumption—a very different attitude from AgriHaul's or PetroHaul's owners.

Measures used by owners and managers to assess the finer aspects of driving skills were also internalized by drivers. For example, drivers at all three companies spent two to ten unpaid hours per week maintaining their trucks' appearances. While this behavior was not totally a response to management's values, the fact that drivers repeatedly reminded owners of these efforts reveals their awareness of owners' use of this indicator. Moreover, internalization of this indicator can be seen in the reaction of conforming drivers to those few who did not keep their trucks clean; being the operator of a dirty truck overrode all other measures of a driver's standing among his peers and stigmatized him, especially if he was young and could not point to years of experience as a countervailing indicator of his standing. At SandHaul, one such driver, though he kept himself clean, was referred to as "The Pig." At PetroHaul, truck appearance was so important that a driver was informally but explicitly categorized by both management and other drivers according to his abilities as a "rag-man"—a driver who keeps his truck clean and polished. For example, when the general manager was considering hiring a certain job applicant, he asked a driver if the applicant was a good rag-man. When I was hired by PetroHaul and assigned to ride with an experienced driver for several shifts, the general manager said of the host driver, "He's a good guy and one of our best rag-men." Several PetroHaul drivers suggested that those who did not keep their trucks clean ought to be fired.

Given that drivers' work, unlike the appearance of their trucks, is unobserved, it should not be surprising that they frequently spoke to the owners, other management people, and fellow drivers about their performance. These self-promotions, depending on the company, most often centered on feats of endurance, meeting quotas in spite of adversity, outwitting police, instances where their driving skills enabled them to avoid an accident, and time spent cleaning or repairing their trucks. In other words, drivers' spoken accounts coincided with the owners' values.

Regarding the use of truck repairs as a measure of a driver's skill, that drivers adopted management's views can be seen in their reactions to drivers who experienced the failure of a major component that was under their control, such as an engine: drivers, like management, typically blamed the driver involved. This assignment of blame was clear to the SandHaul driver who told me he hoped he would not be the one driving a particular truck on the day its transmission failed (it was showing signs of early failure), because, "I'll catch hell from Will [the owner] and some of these guys will start talking shit." When I blew an engine, AgriHaul drivers teased me about having a "hot foot"—applying too much throttle. When drivers discussed such events, there was nearly always at least an undertone of blame indicting the driver who happened to be operating the equipment at the time of its failure, despite common understandings that such failures are often the result of design problems or the culmination of long-term abuse by a series of drivers. In discussing an instance where a transmission had failed, a SandHaul driver began by saying, "The other day *when Augie blew* the trans on 614 . . ." I regularly heard drivers criticize other drivers for how often their trucks were in the shop and for incurring specific types of problems. For example, injector failures are taken as a sign of running the engine too hard, although this problem also can result from design error, contaminated fuel, and normal wear and tear. After I began driving, it did not take me long to learn to feel embarrassed by mechanical failures of components that were most directly under the driver's control and to offer a defense, solicited or not, of my actions at the time of the failure.

Drivers' discussions of mishaps and driving accidents rarely exclude driver error as a causal factor. For example, when a SandHaul driver ran out of fuel, he was blamed and ridiculed by the nine drivers I spoke to that day. The blame may seem justified, but it ignores the failure of a preceding driver to fuel the truck and an organization of work that punishes drivers for thorough pretrip inspections. During an eighteen month period at SandHaul, six major accidents occurred, and only one of the drivers escaped references by other drivers that questioned his skills. The exception was so extreme that it tends to prove the rule: this driver somewhat heroically drove his truck off the road in order to avoid hitting an errant motorist. In the one accident I knew of at PetroHaul (other than my own), the driver fell asleep on a rural road, ran a stop sign, and hit a car. PetroHaul drivers who commented on the accident felt that the driver had "messed up"; none assigned major blame to the owner for overworking drivers, even though the driver was in the fourteenth hour of his shift and that week had been working approximately seventeen-hour shifts. The tendency of drivers to assign blame to those involved in accidents was particularly clear to me after my own accident; after years of listening to drivers discuss the accidents of others, I found myself greatly shamed by the knowledge that my skills were being impugned, even though the accident did nothing more than break a small light on my truck and was minor enough to go unreported to the police.

Though equipment problems contribute to accidents, drivers are not given to accepting them as the cause of another's accident.[2] For example, regulatory changes in the mid-1970s led to difficulties in matching the braking operations of tractors and the trailers they pulled, yet I never heard this problem raised as a contributing factor in accidents. Likewise, according to a University of Michigan Highway Research Institute study (*Los Angeles Times*, March 5, 1982, sec. 5, p. 1) the truck-and-trailer configuration used to haul gasoline in California as compared to a conventional semi-trailer van, requires 40 percent less force to overturn in a quick lane change. PetroHaul drivers and managers were aware of the tank truck's propensity to overturn; for example, the general manager told me, "The first time you take a corner in a loaded tanker, your asshole gets so tight [out of fear of rolling over] that light couldn't pass through it." Yet, when a driver at another tanker company overturned his truck, a Petro-Haul driver said, "It looks to me like he just wasn't careful enough. You have to watch these suckers, because it doesn't take much to flop them over." In effect, the observer notes the truck's dangerous design features but assigns blame to its driver.

The guiding assumption in assessing drivers' performances appears to be that most of a driver's work is under his control, and therefore negative outcomes are his fault. Drivers know this is not always true, but the power of the owner to define reality and the drivers' desire for visible indicators of skill lead to a certain acceptance of these judgments. However, how completely drivers have adopted such indicators must be qualified. First, the savvy driver learns to hide many of his mishaps; therefore the condemnation of a driver for a mishap is in part an indictment for the absence of this savvy. Second, drivers regularly face the very real possibility of injury or death in the performance of their duties, and they may wish to assume a greater control over these outcomes than is realistic.

In sum, drivers interpret many of the owner's values, particularly those associated with profit and organizational demands, as measures of driver skill. The power of an owner to impose his definitions of skill is enhanced by the difficulty drivers have in defining and evaluating their work skills. In several ways, accepting the owner's definitions makes the driver a more willing accomplice in his own exploitation. With self-esteem as a goal, drivers work longer, harder, and for less pay than they would if motivated only by coercion or economic need. Where drivers are ignorant, namely in the area of mechanics, their adoption of an owner's definitions makes them all the more vulnerable, because they can be put in the position of owing the owner. For example, if an engine blows and the driver is not aware that reasons other than his mistake led to this event, the owner is able to fire him without adverse consequences or to "forgive" the driver and, in so doing, make him beholden, which was my experience as a neophyte.

To see drivers, however, as empty vessels into which the owner's values and standards are poured is misleading. Aside from personal style, owners were successful in passing their values and standards on to drivers only to the degree that these were compatible with the values and myths associated with male roles, the occupation, and our culture's conceptions of work (see Chapter 5). Among the widely shared notions regarding work in general that drivers can be assumed to bring to the job are: work is an important measure of a person, especially a man (e.g., Hughes 1984, 338; Rose 1985, 89); work ought to be paid and paid fairly; there ought to be some linkage between merit and reward; employers have a general right to direct their employees; and limits exist on what an employer can fairly or rightfully ask of an employee.

The Ideal Trucker: What Drivers Want from Their Work

Male drivers carry an image of what it means to be a fully realized truck driver. While this image varies from driver to driver, its common characteristics are revealed in talking with drivers, observing what they covet, listening to talk over the CB radio, and seeing the trucking posters selected by some truck drivers to decorate a room or garage at home. The ideal driver operates over the road, that is, his hauls are not restricted to a single city or urban area; ideally he hauls for distances that take several days to cover.[3] He travels to a variety of destinations and encounters all sorts of terrain, weather, and driving conditions.

The load he carries is respectable: neither dirty (e.g., manure, asphalt), alive (e.g., chickens), or particularly unsightly; perhaps dangerous (e.g., gasoline); and, for most, carried in a van or refrigerated trailer or on a flatbed.[4]

The tractor of choice for most drivers is a long wheelbase Peterbilt or Kenworth of a conventional configuration, though some drivers prefer the roominess and superior view of the cabover design.[5] Whatever the configuration, the tractor is equipped with a large sleeper; not only does a bed increase comfort and efficiency, it also signifies over-the-road driving. Finally, the tractor is handsomely painted and ornamented, has a powerful Caterpillar or Cummins engine, and is outfitted with a full array of driver comfort options such as an air seat, stereo, and deluxe interior. This tractor is permanently and exclusively assigned to its driver, unless a two-person team operates it, and the driver is free to add personalized touches such as extra lights.

The ideal driver is given an assignment, and it is up to him to figure out the details of completing it. In the course of his work, he is able to handle his truck in the varieties of terrain, weather, and driving conditions he encounters and, in doing so, display a mix of good sense and courage. Beyond the act of driving, the ideal driver not only conforms to but exemplifies cultural notions concerning what it is to be a man. He stands on his own two feet, bargains independently with authority, and "takes no shit." Not uncommonly, the ideal driver is a bit of a rascal, a quality seen as attractive to at least some women.

Finally, the ideal driver commands fair pay. In objective terms, I estimate that for most drivers fair pay constitutes a year's gross that exceeds by at least 15 percent the national median income for a family of four; fairness in hourly and mileage pay would, at the time I worked at PetroHaul and SandHaul, be in the area of ten dollars an hour or a mileage rate whereby forty to forty-five miles an hour equaled ten dollars an hour.

The opportunity to realize elements of the ideal driver is not evenly distributed across the industry.

Contracts and How They Are Implemented

When someone enters trucking in California, it is most likely with a nonunion, competitive sector trucking company.[6] Because union companies offer a level of extrinsic rewards that insures a ready pool of experienced and skilled drivers with known records, the neophyte is usually restricted to the competitive sector, where employment is easier to obtain.

As noted, the similar environments, tasks, constraints on direct supervision, and nonunionized status of competitive sector companies contribute to similar organizations of work. In effect, the owners of the companies that employed me have, to varying degrees, motivated drivers by offering an informal contract that could be stated as follows:

> I will get as much work out of you as possible; in return you can mimic an independent contractor. You will have "your own" truck and it will be outfitted with options you would likely select if given the opportunity. You will be given a good deal of latitude in completing your assignments. Your efforts will be rewarded directly; we operate as a meritocracy in which effort and skill affect both the gross and rate of pay, perquisites can be awarded without the obstacle of seniority, and sloth is self-defeating. Finally, you will be judged primarily on the volume of your output and your ability to avoid errors.

Another way of phrasing the contract is: "You can be all the trucker you want to be in return for giving me most of your time and a high level of effort while waiving your rights under various labor laws and not demanding union-level compensation." Being all the trucker you want to be means having a good deal of control over one's work and the opportunity to act out both the mythic elements of trucking and idealized notions of traditional manhood.

This contract is compelling for several reasons. As noted, the problematic nature of driver esteem makes the highly visible indicators of output attractive as measures of the self. In addition, the contract is generally consistent with larger cultural values concerning work and with both occupational and male role values and myths embraced by drivers: the organization of work and distribution of rewards in these companies is close to the popular values extolled in this country; productivity is held as a reasonable measure of work; working long and hard is manly; accepting danger is manly, even heroic; ignoring laws and outwitting police is consistent with the masculinity implied in loosened social bonds and resonates with images of cultural icons such as the hunter, trapper, and cowboy; being on the road for long periods of time (or at least overnight) is consistent with romantic images of the truck driver and, within the occupation, has greater prestige than local hauling; good equipment is highly valued within the occupation and is consistent with romantic images of the driver; and the driver's relatively greater autonomy and opportunity to mimic truck ownership is akin to self-employment—a more noble status than employment (see Veblen 1905). Finally, by citing the company's competitive environment, owners and drivers are able, to varying extents, to explain the contract's more exploitative features. By pointing to competitors the owner can say, "This is the best I can do for you drivers," and drivers can say, "It is reasonable for me to put up with these conditions because it is the best the owner can do."

For the beginning driver who wants to be a traditional man and perhaps achieve the prestige and esteem associated with the fully realized driver, the largest problem within the competitive sector is the price he must pay.

In contrast, the monopoly sector contract says, "In return for high extrinsic rewards, security [which, for many, evaporated after deregulation], and the protections of seniority, you will forfeit your desire to be all the trucker you can be."[7] Drivers for a large, union freight carrier typically drive strictly utilitarian equipment that is not assigned permanently to them. These tractors are plain, often ugly, brands that drivers consider second-line, such as Freightliner, or third-line, such as GMC and International. The tractors are specified in ways that indicate the driver is a secondary consideration: short wheelbase, minimal interior upholstery, no radio or tape player. If a driver wishes to have a radio or CB he has to bring his own and hook it up on a temporary basis. For example, he can weld a CB antenna to vice-grip pliers that are then clamped to mirror brackets; even this violates the rules of some large companies.

Drivers at these companies work for a monolith, not an individual, and the impact of a single driver's effort is diminished by this scale. In spelling out work rules, the contract offers the driver protections but also greatly reduces the likelihood of negotiating individual deals with management—a means of linking merit and reward. The driver lacks the latitude of the AgriHaul, PetroHaul, or even SandHaul driver to decide routes and plan his time. Monotony is greater for drivers at these companies, because work is broken down into smaller components and highly routinized, and seniority rules govern assignments. For example, the driver may haul preloaded trailers between his company's terminals rather than pick up a load from a shipper and deliver it to a customer, and repeat the same route until seniority allows him to bid for another haul. Cross-country hauling by a team of two drivers virtually disappeared from these companies and was replaced by single drivers operating in hublike service areas.

In short, the monopoly sector contract emphasizes extrinsic rewards at the expense of intrinsic rewards.

When this contract is compared to the nonunion, competitive sector contract, we can see the compromises in economic rationality made by small company owners. For example, unlike large, unionized companies, they often allow drivers to put non-work mileage on their trucks (e.g., by taking it to and from home); assign trucks to drivers rather than drivers to the first available truck (which would keep equipment in operation longer); say nothing to drivers about how fast they drive (speeding typically lowers fuel economy and increases wear); restrict drivers from using another driver's truck; agree to pay for truck enhancements; and purchase expensive, accessory-filled trucks with powerful engines that get below-average fuel economy.

AgriHaul came the closest to embodying the implied competitive sector contract; the owner asked a great deal of drivers but went a long way in allowing them to be all the driver they wanted to be. AgriHaul used late-model Kenworth and Peterbilt tractors equipped with sleepers. Most were handsomely painted, had ornamentation such as chrome exhaust stacks and bumpers, and were outfitted with driver comfort options. AgriHaul originally specified engines of less than medium power but over time switched to medium- and high-powered models. Though the loads drivers hauled were often dusty, greasy, or bad smelling, they were concealed in a tarped trailer and therefore not embarrassing.

The treatment of drivers at AgriHaul was in almost complete accordance with the contract. Most drivers were the sole operators of the trucks assigned to them. Drivers were free to add lights and chrome accessories, they could take their trucks home, and some were allowed to paint their names on the door—perhaps the ultimate symbol of the driver as independent contractor. Drivers hauled over the road, though not for great distances, and were typically away from home every other night. They had great latitude in planning their work and rarely had to account for their time as long as they completed their assignments. Heavy workloads, a wide variety of hauls, and irregular scheduling meant that effort—working fast and for long periods of time—had a great impact on income and the successful completion of assignments. The assignment of nonmonetary rewards was based on a mix of seniority and merit. Finally, much individual bargaining went on between drivers and the owner.

As a consequence of the problematic nature of esteem and AgriHaul's consistency with drivers' cultural (including male role) and occupational expectations, AgriHaul's owner and drivers were quite consistent in the measures they used to evaluate driving performances. Drivers complained about the often-excessive demands made upon them yet measured one another by the ability to meet these demands.

PetroHaul exceeded AgriHaul in some areas of the contract and fell below in others. PetroHaul operated late-model conventional Peterbilts that were among the nicest-appearing tankers in the area. All of these trucks had engines of at least medium power and many driver comfort options. Further, petroleum tanker loads are more respectable than AgriHaul's or Sand-Haul's loads, and the danger in hauling gasoline made those jobs more prestigious—a valuation not lost on the drivers. For example, an oil driver at a major oil company told me, "The gas haulers from my own company won't wave to me [when we meet on the road], because they think they're such hot shit for hauling gasoline."

The use of drivers at PetroHaul deviated somewhat from the contract. Though some hauling was out of town, much was local, and all drivers returned to the yard at the end of each shift. In assigning two drivers to a truck, each driver's sense of having his own truck was diminished, though not extinguished. Drivers could and did personalize their trucks. They worked long hours, but shifts were routinized. Drivers had considerable latitude in sequencing their assignments, and effort had a major impact on job performance, as defined by both the owner and drivers.

The payment of hourly wages to PetroHaul drivers had conflicting effects. On the one hand, drivers saw hourly pay as an indication that the company was of a higher grade than nonunion companies that paid a percentage of the gross. Hourly pay thus added to the drivers' self-esteem and satisfaction with PetroHaul. On the other hand, hourly pay makes the relationship between the owner and drivers more adversarial and seemingly requires careful monitoring of drivers. PetroHaul drivers had to account for all of their time, but in reality this amounted to minor dickering over whether breaks should be paid or unpaid. Nonmonetary rewards were assigned by a combination of seniority and merit, and individual bargaining with the owner and management was common.

Thus, PetroHaul subscribed to much of the contract, and a lack in one area (no long hauls) was compensated in other areas (first-rate equipment, prestigious loads, freedom to sequence loads). As at AgriHaul, PetroHaul's consistency with driver's cultural and occupational expectations led to a general accord between management's and drivers' assessments of driving skills. This accord was furthered by management's claim that it employed first-rate drivers, because it encouraged drivers to measure themselves as the owner and managers measured them; a correspondence in values that can best be seen in the previously noted seemingly irrational efforts drivers made to meet quotas. From the point of view of hourly pay it makes little sense to complete a seventeen-hour haul in fifteen hours, but it makes considerable sense if such an achievement is considered indicative of skill, especially if that notion of skill is consistent with widely shared definitions of work and manhood.

In terms of equipment and loads, SandHaul embraced fairly closely the implied competitive sector contract. SandHaul operated attractive Peterbilt and Kenworth conventionals equipped with a full array of driver comfort options. All of the tractors had engines of at least medium power, and some had engines of great power. Like PetroHaul, SandHaul's equipment was one of its major attractions for drivers. Loads at SandHaul were somewhat dirty and did not have the prestige of PetroHaul's loads, but they were not disreputable.

In the treatment of drivers, SandHaul in some ways resembled AgriHaul and PetroHaul. Drivers worked approximately fifty-five to seventy hours a week. They were allowed to select their routes and delivery sequences (except in emergencies when one customer needed an immediate delivery), but the comparatively small number of customers qualified this freedom. Those who were assigned trucks could personalize them. SandHaul linked pay to effort and assigned nonmonetary rewards based on a combination of seniority and merit, with merit being the foremost consideration. As was the case at AgriHaul and PetroHaul, individual bargaining took place between the driver and owner.

However, substantial divergences from the contract existed at SandHaul, especially for the night-shift drivers. All drivers hauled within a 150-mile radius of the yard and returned at the end of each shift. Moreover, while each tractor was assigned to a day-shift driver, night-shift drivers took whatever was available ("slip-seat" assignments). Day-shift drivers had some control over what hour they began work, but night-shift drivers had little control over their starting times. Perhaps the greatest difference at SandHaul in terms of the implied contract was that work was highly routinized.

Routinization of work compromised the usefulness of productivity as a measure of self, because outcomes were more predictable and less dependent on effort than was the case at PetroHaul and AgriHaul. For example, AgriHaul drivers commonly were given conditional assignments:

> *Arnie:* If you can get your load off by noon and get over to Shaky Town [Los Angeles] by three o'clock, you ought to be able to load today and deliver first thing in the morning. If you can do that you'll save the day; otherwise [the customer] is going to be crying, we're going to be all screwed up, and I may have to lay you over for the night.

In successfully completing such an assignment, the AgriHaul driver probably will be thanked by the customer, praised by the dispatcher or owner, admired by other drivers (this experience will be grist for bragging in a bull session), and monetarily rewarded by the highly efficient use of his time. In comparison, SandHaul drivers could brag about load completion times, but these accomplishments did not lead to noteworthy increases in output, or to praise from the owner or customer.

The debasement of effort was underscored by SandHaul's

speed limit of fifty-five; clearly the owner did not need work to be completed as fast as possible. In addition, the speed limit breached the competitive sector contract in other ways. First, it infringed on the control drivers had over their work. Further, it was economically irrational in that it lowered drivers' rate of pay and lengthened their workday; not only did drivers have to work at a slower rate for the same gross income, but they were more likely to be passed and therefore delayed by competitors. Finally, SandHaul drivers were embarrassed by having to observe a fifty-five-mile-an-hour limit. For example, almost as soon as I departed the company yard with the driver who was charged with showing me the ropes, he commented on it.

> *Walt:* What I hate most about this company is the fifty-five speed limit. You get up on [a two-lane highway] and there you are creeping along holding up every other truck on the road. It's damn embarrassing, especially when a guy in a big road machine [i.e., an idealized truck driver] passes you and checks you out to see who the heck you are.

In this vein, SandHaul drivers complained about being mocked by competitors who were able to pass them.

The routinization of work, underscored by a company-imposed speed limit, made effort less relevant and consequently devalued the worth of drivers. When the owner, Will, violated informal deals with individual drivers, he further debased the value of effort. In addition, by breaking deals and being inconsistent in arranging them—for example, by refusing to put chrome wheels on a top driver's truck—Will devalued the worth of seniority and loyalty, both of which were proxies for skill. In short, the organization of work and the owner's actions argued against the worth of drivers; for the most part, SandHaul considered one driver as good as the next. During the exodus of drivers from SandHaul, the wife of a high-seniority driver who quit said, "Will's attitude is that drivers are a dime a dozen; now he's going to end up with dime-a-dozen drivers, and we'll see how he likes it."

As a consequence of the problematic nature of esteem and the devaluation of effort by SandHaul's owner, SandHaul drivers had particular difficulty in measuring their performances. They did not use the owner's standards to measure themselves to the same degree as did drivers at PetroHaul and AgriHaul—for example, no SandHaul driver bragged about driving at exactly fifty-five miles an hour—and they were forever searching for ways to assess themselves and one another. Tales of low completion times and strategies for maximizing speed were daily events, but without the owner's support these values took on the form of insurgency. Further, because of routinization, low completion times were more often a matter of luck than of effort or skill. The night-shift drivers, who did not have their own trucks through which they could make a visible statement about their identity, had an especially hard time. Whereas at Petro-Haul and AgriHaul owners applauded and drivers took pride in feats of endurance, low completion times, or fulfilled quotas, night-shift drivers at SandHaul, in search of indicators, seized upon steady lines on tachograph charts, backing-out times at a difficult delivery site (the one genuine indicator of work skill they found), minor mishaps such as tearing off a mudflap by backing over it, and petty infractions of informal rules such as leaving an empty pop bottle in a day-shift driver's truck, an oversight taken to indicate sloppy workmanship.

The final consequence of problematic esteem and the devaluation of the worth of drivers by SandHaul's owner was that many drivers quit, especially core-group drivers (Chapter 4). Whereas PetroHaul and AgriHaul drivers generally quit for reasons having to do with career advancement, the desire to try a different type of hauling, or the fit between the job and life at home, SandHaul drivers quit because of dissatisfaction with the way they experienced their jobs. The willingness to quit Sand-Haul is especially notable because eight of the eleven who departed were married, and for them quitting meant giving up a job that combined decent pay and benefits, excellent equipment, and the opportunity to be home for dinner every night, an uncommon combination in trucking.

Trucking offers drivers a chance to meet the requirements for the traditional man and to be a notable man. A problem arises for drivers, however, when it comes to assessing their performance: the work skills of a driver do not lend themselves to observation or measurement. On the other hand, measures of output are attractive indicators of performance because they are visible, quantitative, usually endorsed by the employer, and consistent with cultural notions regarding the worth of both work and men. But, in embracing measures of output as an indicator of performance and self-worth, drivers are at odds with certain features of idealized masculinity: employment is fundamentally ignoble, thus the effort necessary for high output may be taken as commitment to an ignoble relationship and acquiescence to exploitation—an unmanly accommodation.

Trucking company owners were able to counter the ignoble features of effort and commitment in two ways: drivers were set up as quasi-independent contractors through mimicking ownership of the means of production, granting them latitude in planning their work, and linking effort and rewards; and owners and drivers were able to cite a highly competitive environment that "explained" noticeably exploitative features of the relationship.

The treatment of drivers at PetroHaul and AgriHaul was relatively consistent with the implied competitive sector contract, and drivers at these companies worked hard, took pride in their work, and were largely satisfied with their on-the-job experiences. At SandHaul, effort was somewhat irrelevant; coupled with the problematic nature of esteem, this left drivers even more doubtful about evaluating their performances and self-worth. This uncertainty was not a major problem for drivers so long as the owner constructed deals based on the assumption that skill and effort were important and recognizable, for example, by using seniority, willingness to work weekends, and truck cleanliness as proxies. When the owner began to violate or inconsistently enter into deals, effort was devalued and commitment dishonored. Work at SandHaul moved in the direction of an activity that one does for money and nothing else. This change in relations made exploitation clear and called for drivers to redefine their self-images, especially since SandHaul was marginal in other areas of the contract due to its local hauling, compromised autonomy, and, for night-shift drivers, "slip-seat" truck assignments.

It is reasonable to ask why SandHaul drivers continued to deliver loads as fast as possible. Part of the answer already has been discussed: measures of output lend themselves to measures of self-worth, there is considerable support within the culture for using such indicators, and indicators of self-worth based on work skills were problematic.

In addition, piecework encouraged effort through a paradox: the faster drivers worked, the less they felt exploited. Because drivers were paid nothing for on-the-road delays and only five dollars per hour for loading and unloading delays, all delays reduced their *rate* of pay (see Chapter 3, notes 1 and 2). Most drivers seem to have a rough norm regarding what is an acceptable rate of pay derived from comparisons with the Teamsters' Union Master Freight Agreement, the pay of drivers at similar trucking companies, the pay of nondriver acquaintances, and general notions about what constitutes reasonable pay.

Meeting the rate norm appeared to be important to the driver's self-image and necessary for a sense of satisfaction with the job. This was best evidenced by the tendency of nearly all SandHaul drivers, like other drivers who work for a percentage of the gross, to overestimate their rate of pay (see Chapter 3, note 1). I rarely heard a SandHaul driver include in his total hours those spent within the yard on job-related tasks. When drivers made pay rate calculations, they ignored all this unpaid time and figured only the time between departure and return into the equation. Because standing time occurred during this period, it was factored into the calculation of hourly rates, and it is telling that drivers complained much more venomously about this type of "excess" work than that which occurred in the yard and was totally unpaid; standing time makes it impossible to ignore lower pay rates.

The exceptions to this implicit deceit in estimating pay rates were the few ex-union drivers at AgriHaul and SandHaul. They had a broader conception of what paid time ought to be than did drivers who had always worked in nonunion and percentage pay jobs. In addition, the ex-union drivers were the only ones to add time-and-a-half considerations into the calculation of pay rates. Not surprisingly, they expressed the most dissatisfaction with both pay and working conditions. However, with the passage of time ex-union drivers were increasingly likely to engage in the same wage rate deception as the other drivers.

Finally, while it is true that SandHaul drivers continued to deliver loads as fast as possible, they withdrew effort in other areas, particularly in truck maintenance. For example, of the SandHaul drivers who did not quit, the three top rag-men ceased to take exceptional care of their trucks, and two were looking for other jobs.

It is informative to look at the companies drivers took jobs at after quitting SandHaul. Of the eleven drivers who quit, one left the industry for a white-collar job, and four moved into unionized driving jobs. In my experience, and aside from PetroHaul where drivers had much more than average contact with unionized trucking companies, the proportion of those seeking union jobs was high—in part a consequence of the nature of the rupture in their informal contract with SandHaul's owner. Two of the four who went to unionized driving jobs went, however, to small companies that, contrary to the usual case for unionized haulers, offered relatively high intrinsic rewards such as excellent equipment assigned permanently to a single driver. I asked one of these two drivers why he sought out this company.

> *Al:* They had nice equipment, I knew they had plenty of work, and I knew the owner was decent and, after working for Will, that was important. It also was nice that it was close to home; I suppose you could say that was a secondary reason. The union? That really wasn't an issue then.

One of the two drivers who went to larger, unionized companies became dissatisfied and left within a year. I was not able to keep track of the other's career.

The remaining six drivers left for small companies that were more in sync with the competitive sector contract: trucks were first-rate and permanently assigned; loads were more prestigious and hauls were longer; a wider variety of hauls and less routinization made autonomy more meaningful; and effort was valued and rewarded. Thus, six of eleven drivers demonstrated a preference for work as constituted in the ideal competitive sector contract, and two other drivers chose unionized employers that came closest to that contract. Only three drivers ultimately rejected the rewards of working in competitive sector trucking.

What can be said in general about drivers' work values in relation to the owners' and managers' standards? Drivers valued efficiency as measured by completing the most work in the least amount of time. Sixty-hour work weeks were the norm, the point beyond which the driver might see himself as working overtime. Drivers generally wished to do the work "right," although the definition of "right," once it moved beyond efficiency varied considerably, because work skills were not clear. Almost without exception, when a driver clearly voiced a lack of concern for the quality of his work—typically, "Fuck it, I don't give a shit any-more"—it was precipitated by what he saw as an instance of management not caring about "doing the work right" (see Jura-vich 1985). In return for giving so much time and effort, drivers wanted to be paid fairly, and most wanted the opportunity to be the man and the trucker they saw themselves to be.

The self that emerges from drivers' work experiences is formed in interaction with other audiences as well as owners, managers, and driver co-workers. Three of those audiences, to which I now turn, are directly involved with the work of truck drivers: police and other government officials, company support personnel, and workers involved in the loading and unloading of trucks.

CHAPTER 7

Work Audiences

A DRIVER DOES MOST of his work in front of audiences other than owners, managers, and driver co-workers, and by interacting with these audiences he further develops a sense of himself as a trucker and as a man. Three of these groups are directly involved in drivers' work: police and other government officials, company support personnel, and workers who load and unload trucks. The first two audiences also affect a driver's self-perceptions by influencing his standing with employers and driver co-workers, a measure drivers take into account.

Police and Other Government Officials

The state, like management, can forcefully present standards that drivers embrace in their search for performance measures. Through its laws and agents, the state enacts and enforces standards for measuring drivers' work performances. The officials that truckers see most often are state and local police, including weigh station personnel and equipment inspectors, state port of entry and federal customs agents, representatives of state and federal commerce commissions, and regulators particular to certain types of loads.[1]

State departments of motor vehicles maintain the official records of drivers' performances. The central feature of these records is a listing of police-issued citations and any related judicial actions. In California, this record listed all moving violations, chargeable accidents, and weight and equipment violations for the most recent three years. In addition, it listed for five years those citations considered most serious. I have applied for driving jobs at fifteen companies, and all but one wanted to see my record. In addition, six of the eight companies employing me claimed to review these records annually. The accumulation of too many citations or the issuance of a serious citation such as reckless driving or driving while intoxicated could result in dismissal. At SandHaul, a single citation might result in the loss of an annual bonus for safe driving of from one hundred to five hundred dollars. Moreover, citations and accidents injured a driver's self-esteem.

> *Leon:* I don't know what I hate more about getting this ticket: losing my bonus and having to pay the fine or fucking up my perfect record.

Since chargeable accidents and moving violations are the aspects of drivers' formal records that are most consequential, it is the police, among government officials, who have the greatest impact on drivers' esteem.

Truck drivers believe police single them out for harassment. This belief is especially strong if the trucker works for a small company or is an owner-operator, and these feelings of persecution appear to have some basis. First, while on the road, truckers are much more visible than motorists and subject to many more regulations. In addition, trucks and truckers at times become a public issue and are subject to periodic, publicly announced "crackdowns" (*Heavy Duty Trucking*, January 1986, 12). Second, truck drivers believe that California weigh station officials, the police with whom truckers are most likely to have contact, are much more likely to single out for inspection owner-operators, out-of-state truckers, and truckers from small companies than truckers who haul for the large freight carriers.[2]

> *Lenny:* It gripes me the way [weigh station personnel] will signal through a freight hauler [a driver for a large, monopoly sector freight company] who's driving a bucket of shit and turn right around and pull us in even when we have quarterly tags [that signify a recent inspection].

Likewise, drivers believe that state police rarely cite the drivers of major firms, and my experience confirms this observation.

Drivers from smaller, nonunion companies take these occurrences as signs of unfair treatment.

Drivers also see many laws as unreasonable. While I have
heard few truckers complain about the more basic laws governing driving, such as those regulating the flow of traffic, right of
way and, to some degree, speed, they often disagree with the
way police officers interpret and enforce them. For example,
drivers of heavily loaded trucks typically exceed the speed limit
in descending a hill to gain speed for the next hill. Even drivers
who do not follow this practice may inadvertently allow their
trucks to gain speed on a downgrade. When police stationed at
the bottom of a hill cite a driver for speeding, that driver will
almost certainly feel unjustly apprehended.

In addition to motor vehicle codes, truckers are governed by
a host of other laws and regulations; drivers are more likely to
run afoul of these than of the basic driving laws. For example, I
have been cited only once for a moving violation, but in fourteen
months at PetroHaul and SandHaul, I was cited three times for
equipment violations. As with general driving laws, drivers take
issue with how these laws and regulations are enforced; they are
also less likely to accept the laws themselves as reasonable because their import is less obvious (e.g., rules governing the legal
distance between a truck's axles), some are seen as infringing
the driver's rights (e.g., limits on working hours), and some are
ludicrous or contradictory. For example, in California it is illegal
to mount on the front of the hood a plexiglass bug deflector colored amber, blue, or red. Several drivers cited for this infraction
told me that the police explained this ruling as necessary to prevent motorists from confusing the truck with an emergency vehicle. The police claimed that a motorist looking in the rearview
mirror might see the colored strip and think it the emergency
lights that identify police cars, fire engines, and ambulances.
When pressed, some police also said that the rule was intended
to prevent the truck's driver, in looking through the deflector,
from thinking that oncoming headlights were a vehicle's tail-
lights. The first reason is obviously absurd; a four-inch strip of
plastic on the hood of a truck is quite unlikely to make it look
like a police car, ambulance, or fire engine. As for the second
reason, a truck's driver could see a car's headlights through a

bug deflector only if the car were directly in front of the truck and so near that a collision would be inevitable.

Truck regulatory laws are so contradictory that truckers claim it is impossible to build a truck that would meet the standards of every state in the Union. A trade journal columnist (*Heavy Duty Trucking*, April 1986, 43) stated, "Uniformity of state laws and regulations governing motor carriers seems, like Annie's Tomorrow, to be always a day away." A driver told me he was once cited for not having on his truck a piece of equipment that was prohibited in his home state. Also, many of these laws are unenforceable or so poorly enforced that truckers find them ridiculous. For example, SandHaul's entire fleet was equipped with amber-colored bug deflectors, but only once during my employment was a truck cited for this violation; the lack of citations probably was a result of officials at the few weigh stations SandHaul regularly crossed being familiar with the drivers. On the other hand, an owner-operator told me of being ticketed for this offense the day after mounting an amber deflector on his truck.

Truckers do not feel that every citation they receive is unfairly issued or the result of an absurd law. They often feel, however, that even citations issued fairly and chargeable accidents are not totally their fault, given the demands made by management, traffic and road conditions, and equipment limitations. For example, all of the roll-over accidents at SandHaul happened to trucks that combined high center of gravity trailers with fifth-wheels designed for low center of gravity trailers. When discussing these accidents, the poor match between fifth-wheel design and trailer characteristics was always cited.

Despite drivers' frequently stated belief that citations are unfair or impossible to avoid and that accidents are often not entirely their fault, drivers paradoxically embrace these official standards to measure one another and themselves. They brag about their driving records and proudly wear safety awards in the form of belt buckles, pins, and patches. If truckers have a magic number, it is one million miles without a chargeable accident. Drivers denigrate those who receive "too many" citations and the issuance of a citation to a fellow company driver is cause for discussion. Such talk almost always mixes condemnations of police and at least mild put-downs of the cited driver, as when Ringo was cited for speeding on a city street.

> *Sid:* I've seen that chickenshit cop hiding along there just hoping to get a truck. But, if Ringo wasn't always in such a hurry he might not have gotten nailed.

If the offending driver is held in low esteem, the citation can be taken as further evidence of his poor performance. If the driver is held in high esteem, a citation may be written off to bad luck but still gives cause for doubt. Accidents stir a good deal of conversation that, again, often mixes sympathy with condemnation of the driver. For example, in my discussions with SandHaul drivers, almost all cited improperly specified fifth wheels as a factor in the roll-over accidents, yet ultimately blamed the driver; in effect, they said, "Yes, that type of fifth wheel shouldn't be on these trucks, but it's up to you to watch it."

Why do drivers at once belittle elements of their official driving records and endorse them as measures of performance? I suggest that four reasons account for this paradox. First, state standards help fill the void created by unknown and unobservable work skills, and they look objective. In the same way sociologists or psychologists can attack the validity of IQ scores yet use them to judge others and themselves, drivers question driving records yet, in the absence of sufficient alternative indicators, measure one another and themselves by these records. Second, the state is a powerful evaluator; its judgments are public and can be the determining factor in getting or keeping a job and in the distribution of work-related rewards. Given the consequences of driving records, it is difficult to dismiss the state's judgment. Third, drivers believe that these standards are not totally unreasonable. Finally, being caught is as much condemned as the violation itself. Part of the skilled driver's repertoire is the ability to avoid citations by government agents of all kinds. A favorite theme in drivers' stories is duping a government regulator.

Nonpolice government officials have less impact on drivers' esteem than do the police. For the most part, drivers view the concerns of these officials as petty or incidental to driving and therefore as having little to do with occupational skills. Further, the consequences of running afoul of these agencies are usually time delays and monetary penalties; the infractions rarely become part of a record that affects drivers' lives.

This is not to say that these agencies are inconsequential for the process of a driver's constructing an occupational self. The plethora of regulations governing trucking and of officials enforcing them means that the trucker is rarely in total compliance with all laws and will at least occasionally be found in violation of one or another. His awareness of the potential for being cited, delayed, or fined is constant. This subjection to myriad laws, regulations, and enforcement agents offers one basis for the trucker's image as an outlaw. While this image is certainly rooted in blue-collar work that is often done at night and takes the worker away from family and community (Melbin 1978), it is in more than a mythic sense that the trucker is something of an outlaw constantly pursued by government officials. Several examples based on my experiences as a driver illustrate this point. (In accumulating only one moving violation and no officially cited accidents in 800,000 miles of commercial driving, if I have a bias, it is toward the possibility of a driver working without official citations.)

Almost every day at SandHaul, I had to go through a weigh station in which the weight of each axle and the overall weight of the truck was checked, and the truck and my logbook were subject to inspection. At least once every five weeks I was signaled in for an inspection. Over the years, I have received numerous citations for equipment violations in the course of these inspections. The violations ranged from brakes out of adjustment (this could amount to one of ten brakes being one-quarter inch out of adjustment) to logbook violations; from the truck being five inches too long to a having a blue light on the side of the truck; from a cracked spring to a missing mud flap. When working a sixth day at SandHaul, approximately an every other week occurrence, night-shift drivers worked for twenty to thirty consecutive hours, a clear violation of state and federal limits that was further compounded by our need to falsify logbook entries and tachograph charts. And SandHaul was not particularly given to violating the law; compared to the other companies I have worked for, SandHaul ran a mostly legal operation. The combination of a company-enforced speed limit, two shifts (thus less driver fatigue), regular and mostly local routes, usually innocuous loads, and very good equipment reduced illegal behavior and the chance of contact with the police more at SandHaul than at any other company at which I was employed.

At PetroHaul, a combination of the type of loads hauled, competitive sector demands, and the owner's policies made illegality more common than at SandHaul. PetroHaul drivers were instructed to bypass the scale that we otherwise would have had the most contact with, because the officials stationed there were said to single out PetroHaul in particular and tankers in general. We were encouraged by management to run overweight and, at times, over the legal number of work hours. When the legal time limit was reached, management "allowed" (in effect, the situation required) us to use multiple tachograph charts and falsified logbook entries. Speeding was allowed, even at rather gross levels (seventy to eighty miles an hour), and the amount of work expected of drivers subtly encouraged speeding. When the general manager gave me a road test, I asked him if PetroHaul had a speed limit, and he said, "We like to leave that up to the drivers."

PetroHaul also encouraged the violation of laws and regulations apart from the motor vehicle code, such as air pollution standards, tax laws, and rules governing the hauling of hazardous materials. For example, when hauling jet fuel, refineries wanted us to steam clean our tanks if they had just been used to haul another product, especially gasoline. Management told us not to steam the tanks but to rid them of their telltale fumes by leaving our hatches open until we arrived at the refinery, a blatant violation of criminal law. Another sort of violation occurred when we hauled fuel for ships: the general manager told us to record this fuel as a different commodity—reportedly a tax fraud that cost the government nine hundred dollars a truckload, according to a refinery employee who explained to me why the refinery began double-checking the veracity of our bills of lading.

At gas stations the violations continued. For example, gasoline spills of as little as five gallons are, according to law, to be reported to the fire department immediately, but in practice the rule was "Don't report what you can get away with." I once told the dispatcher I had spilled five to ten gallons (quite a lot when spread on cement) during a busy period in a high-volume self-serve station, but I had handled it without calling the fire department. He asked me what station the spill had occurred in, and when I told him it was in a poor black neighborhood, he said, "Oh hell, it doesn't matter down there. You did the right thing." Also, drivers making night deliveries in neighborhoods considered dangerous rarely took the time to hook up the hose that routed gasoline fumes back into the trailer rather than letting them escape into the atmosphere, a criminal violation of air pollution laws.

Consumer laws were also violated regularly. Approximately 25 percent of my gasoline loads exceeded the gas station's available storage space for the specified grade. For example, a dealer might order six thousand gallons of regular gasoline but at delivery time have room for only five thousand in the regular gasoline storage tank. In such cases, PetroHaul's policy was to put excess gasoline into the storage tank of the most expensive grade possible. Premium gasoline was, therefore, frequently diluted with regular. The company did not mix leaded gasoline into unleaded gasoline, a decision they explained more in terms of fear of punishment than concern for the public good. Finally, for fear of being assaulted while making a delivery, about one-third to one-half of the gasoline drivers illegally carried guns.

AgriHaul drivers constantly violated laws, especially those imposing limits on hours worked in a day and week. Much of the time I would have had to use three logbooks to be able to produce one that at any given moment would be in compliance—a violation that can result in imprisonment as well as a fine (I chose to use one book that was not always up to date, a less serious violation). AgriHaul drivers were given verbal encouragement and financial rewards for running overloaded but were usually chided by management if they were caught. As noted, given the reward structure at AgriHaul, drivers often loaded in excess of the legal limits and then illegally dumped the excess before reaching a state scale.

Demanding schedules at AgriHaul encouraged speeding and brought about fatigue, both of which increased the chance of being cited or involved in an accident. Schedules and long hours pushed approximately half of the drivers to at least weekly use of amphetamines. About once a year, a driver fell asleep at the wheel and had a major accident. Equipment maintenance was fairly good, yet it was not uncommon to receive a citation as a result of an official inspection. I once had a criminal warrant issued for my arrest because AgriHaul did not properly dispose of a citation for a truck that emitted too much smoke. Problems with trailers occasionally led to encounters with the police regarding load spillage, a relatively expensive citation that the driver often had to pay. AgriHaul occasionally hauled into states for which it had no operating authority, and drivers were encouraged to use a variety of dodges to avoid complying with that state's temporary-permit laws.

At other companies I have broken laws and regulations by hauling "hot" freight (commodities my employer did not have the legal right to haul), operating without a state's required permits or with fraudulent permits, lying about loads to pass through customs or state ports of entry, using roads that were illegal for truck passage, hauling partially loaded trailers that were grossly unstable, illegally obtaining falsified weight certifications, and driving equipment that exceeded legal dimensions. As a counter to laws specifying truck lengths, I was taught how to slide a trailer forward on the tractor's frame, so as to shorten the truck's overall length to the legal limit, while approaching an inspection station and without stopping to do it the proper way. The truck itself had been altered for this purpose. Finally, I have hauled loads that left considerable debris on the roadway and have been instructed to dispose illegally of the remnants of hazardous chemicals.

In short, there is hardly a moment in the day that a driver is not in violation of some law or regulation. And for a good part of the workday, drivers are on the alert for enforcement officials who pose a threat to their driving records, time, pocketbooks, and freedom.[3]

If my reaction is typical, the result of the myriad regulations and enforcers that truck drivers face in the course of their work is a worker who feels himself to be something of an outlaw. This outlaw status appears to provoke in drivers a feeling of distance from society, no doubt heightened by work that is often done at night and that takes them away from family and community.

> *Gus* [an AgriHaul driver]: Being a driver makes you feel like you're sort of different from other people. You're gone from home a lot, you horse around with the guys on the road. . . . You're always playing cops and robbers with Smokey [the police]. You know what I mean? That ain't like other people.

> *Steve* [a PetroHaul driver]: Sometimes I feel like public enemy number one, the way these cops hassle you all the time.

Drivers' tendency to see many laws, regulations, and enforcers as capricious, arbitrary, stupid, and mean spirited erodes their respect for governmental authority.[4] Finally, some drivers thrive on the image of trucker as outlaw and actively work at projecting this image. All the drivers at these companies, as a consequence of heavy regulation, took pride in eluding and deceiving regulators, and such evasions and deceptions become an element in esteem.

A final word: drivers for nonunion companies do not have the protections afforded their unionized counterparts and therefore are less able to avoid having to operate illegally. Drivers who work for some time in competitive sector, nonunion companies are therefore more likely than union drivers to compile poor driving records. The vulnerability to citations and accidents is especially true for drivers employed by highly competitive less routinized, interstate hauling companies, because they are under much pressure, are less likely to know the habits of local police, and are more likely to be singled out for police attention. Therefore, drivers who work for such companies often compile driving records that rule them out for employment by union and desirable nonunion companies able to hire selectively. In effect, the organization of work in the competitive sector tends, over a period of time, to lock the driver into both that sector and its second-rate companies.

Trucking Company Support Personnel

Clerical staffs and mechanics at trucking companies have a direct impact on the evaluation of drivers' performances and an indirect impact on how drivers assess their occupation. Both groups are in a position to convey judgments to the owner, managers, and other drivers regarding the quality of a driver's work.

For a variety of reasons, not the least being that the owner is mostly a creature of the office, paperwork is taken as a sign of a driver's skills. The owners and managers work with the company's clerks and so derive a part of their total picture of a driver's performance from his ability to make the work of the clerks go smoothly. As a neophyte, it came as a shock to me to realize that my in-cab performance went unnoticed (and was mostly unnoticeable) as long as I avoided major errors and that I was praised rather consistently for turning in orderly and legible paperwork. At three companies, I have overheard management and clerical workers cite poorly done paperwork in order to impugn a trucker's driving skills.

While a poor reputation with the clerical staff is usually not enough to threaten a driver's job, it can color the view of other aspects of his performance. When a driver known for good paperwork commits an error in some other area of the job, the error is more likely to be viewed by management as an exception, whereas the deficiencies of the driver known for poor paperwork are more likely to be seen as consistent with lack of workmanship.

The clerical staff's central location in the company puts them in a position to affect drivers' esteem in another way. Staff can trade in information with drivers, and drivers who are not liked by the staff find it almost impossible to hide information that reflects unfavorably on their performance. Citations by police, loading or unloading errors, equipment damage, getting lost, and dumb mistakes that cannot be hidden from the owner or managers can sometimes be hidden from fellow drivers with the cooperation of company clerks, who typically know at least as much about drivers' mistakes as does the owner. Clerks also may be aware of drivers who report on their co-workers, and, as was the case at SandHaul and AgriHaul, they may share this information with favored drivers. Savvy drivers, therefore, learn to do what it takes to please office personnel and in return find their reputations throughout the company enhanced or at least not damaged.

Like the clerical staff, mechanics are in a position to affect the assessments of drivers' skills by both management and other drivers. By virtue of their specialized and superior knowledge, mechanics are thought to be able to link the condition of equipment to the operating skills of its driver. Owners usually know less than their mechanics about a truck's operating systems and defer to the superior knowledge of at least the top mechanic. Most drivers understand their equipment less well than do the mechanic and owner and so are susceptible to the opinion of mechanics. Since such transactions almost always revolve on *problems* with the equipment, mechanics are more likely to damage than to enhance a driver's reputation or self-assessment.

Because mechanics come in contact with all of the company's drivers, they, like clerks, are able to describe any other driver's equipment problems and provide a diagnosis. The shop is a prime place for a driver to develop a reputation for mishandling equipment, but it is also a place where evidence of a driver's errors and miscues can be removed, hidden, or redefined. The ability to damage or protect a driver's reputation, along with the ability to bestow favors that translate into time, money, or comfort, make the mechanic a person whom drivers are wary of crossing and, indeed, someone whom they often court.

Mechanics also have an indirect impact on drivers' self-assessment. In a small trucking company, mechanics are the only other employees who appear to the driver to be engaged in an occupation comparable to his own. At every company where I have worked, the mechanic is thought to possess rarer occupational skills than the driver. He is held by the owner to be more important than a driver and is paid more. Several times I have seen a valued mechanic secure an immediate pay raise by suggesting he may look for employment elsewhere or become a driver. I have never seen a valued driver satisfied so directly. The most valued mechanics at AgriHaul, PetroHaul, and SandHaul, though nonunion, all commanded union wages and near union-level benefits. Given the higher prestige, wage rates, benefits, and advantages of relatively regular working hours, one might expect drivers to aspire to be mechanics.

Yet, with two exceptions, I have never met a mechanic who was an ex-driver, although I have met a considerable number of drivers who worked first as mechanics. One exception was a driver who was working temporarily as a mechanic until enough time elapsed for his suspended driver's license to be restored. The second exception had sustained an injury that ended his driving career but left him able to work in a shop. Far more common is the mechanic who expresses a desire to become a driver but who never actually makes the change. The converse seems not to exist; I have never heard a driver say he wished to become a mechanic.

Three explanations for drivers' lack of desire to be mechanics seem plausible. First, and least important, not many drivers have the necessary skills to be a mechanic, so a move into this occupation would likely require training and, concurrently, a pay cut. If this explanation were sufficient, then one would expect to hear at least wishful thinking among drivers who desired to be mechanics; I have never heard such expressions. Second, gross wages of the two groups are approximately equal, though drivers attain this level by working more hours. Thus drivers are under no great financial incentive to switch occupations. Finally, and most important, drivers believe driving is more desirable work (what they *do*) and a more desirable occupation (how they are *perceived*) than repairing trucks. While the owners of AgriHaul, PetroHaul, and SandHaul treated their mechanics well and only occasionally interfered with their work—the senior mechanic in each shop had been recruited by the owner, and all the owners appeared wary of angering these men—drivers saw themselves as less subject to constraints than mechanics because driving is done away from the yard. Truck repair was also seen as dirty, repetitious, and somewhat heavy work, while driving was seen as cleaner and holding a greater potential for adventure or variety. Moreover, drivers do not feel that as mechanics they can be someone special in the eyes of the public in the way they are as drivers.

The trucker, then, looks at the mechanic and counts his blessings. In the shop, drivers see the sort of work for which those of his class or fate are typically destined, and it is not work he wants for himself. The mechanic provides for the trucker a point of occupational comparison, and from the trucker's vantage point his job compares quite favorably to that of the mechanic's.

Shippers and Customers

Other than mechanics, the nondriver blue-collar workers that truckers have the most contact with are those associated with loading or unloading the products being hauled. For the AgriHaul driver, these people worked in grain and feed processing, meat packing, rendering, and aggregate materials plants and for manufacturers of chemicals, glass, cement, plywood, fiberglass, and explosives. At PetroHaul, drivers mainly came into contact with oil refinery workers, gas station attendants, and ship and airline fueling workers. The employees of large industrial manufacturers and of producers of raw materials comprised the blue-collar workers with whom SandHaul drivers had the most contact.

Drivers do not like what they see at the places they load and deliver products. Shippers and receivers almost always have a guard posted at the entrance of their larger plants; drivers must sign in and out and are often made aware of rules regarding truckers. These guards who enforce company rules are considered by drivers to be petty tyrants and are described as "chickenshit." Inside these plants and depending on the company, drivers come into contact with posted lists of rules, bosses nosing around, and whistles or bells to denote break times. And drivers often find plant working conditions made exceptionally unpleasant by dirt, dust, noise, heat or cold, stench, and gore. Jobs appear to be repetitive, mindless, joyless, and terribly uninteresting with little hope for even the occasional exciting interlude. Many of these jobs are held by people the white male driver considers to be of lower status than himself: racial and ethnic minorities, illegal immigrants, rubes, and women (conversations with Hispanic male drivers revealed many of the same prejudices). The disreputable status of these job holders is interpreted to be an indication of the undesirability of their jobs. Finally, whereas the driver is accustomed to some leveling in the outward signs of status differences between himself and his company's managers and owner, in the large plants status differences between workers and management are pronounced and may be reinforced by separate cafeterias, considerable differences in dress, and formality in their interactions. The sense of "we-ness" drivers are likely to feel in relation to the owner and managers in small, competitive sector companies is noticeably absent in these large-scale enterprises.

I never heard a driver say he wanted the job of a blue-collar worker at any loading or unloading site. Sometimes a driver will envy the other's stable work hours, but never to the point of applying for a similar job. Conversely, I found it common for such workers to admire the driver's truck and engage in a bit of shared fantasy in which the workers picture themselves as drivers. This is not to say that most of these workers wish they could trade places with the driver. But when the subject is broached, and plant workers argue for their job over the trucker's, regular hours and a daily return home are cited as the advantages of factory work, not the work itself. In other words, almost inevitably family, not work, considerations lead plant workers to conclude they are better off than drivers. In addition, pay is not often a point of envy for the driver, because drivers usually have almost the same pay rate and a higher gross income than the workers they meet.

In the places where they load and deliver, drivers thus see undesirable jobs performed by people of their class or fate.[5] Many drivers, with parents, relatives, or friends who work in similar places, are likely to see themselves as having escaped these jobs only by their efforts, good sense, fortune, or whatever they use to explain how they came to be a driver. "Yes," a driver might say, "driving may be dirty, but it is not as dirty as these jobs; it may often be boring, but excitement is liable to be around the corner; the boss may be bothersome, but I rarely see him; my work may sometimes seem repetitive, but not nearly so when compared to the bottle inspector, grain unloader, or scale attendant; it may appear mindless, but a single misjudgment can cost in life and limb, and, besides, there is always something new to learn. And if I get to where I don't like it here, I can move on to another company." Finally, perhaps more than anything else, the driver is likely to feel that the plant worker, as a plant worker, is a "nobody," while the driver, as a driver, is a "somebody." For example, an AgriHaul driver said, "I couldn't stand to work in a factory and be a zero." At no time is this more obvious to the driver than when he leaves the dismal environment of the loading or unloading site and enters his main-stage, the road.

Drivers come away from loading and unloading sites with an enhanced appreciation for their own work. About the only blue-collar worker the driver comes into regular contact with and envies is another trucker, one who has a "better deal." At the heart of this assessment is the opportunity for the trucker to perform before large public audiences in a heroic role that enables him to see himself as a somebody.

CHAPTER 8

Highway Audiences

*O*NE NEED NOT stretch a simile to say a driver taking to the road is like an actor mounting the stage. Clothed in their trucks, drivers enter a public arena where they command attention. And in this arena drivers can evince support for the notions that what they are doing is skilled work and that they are masters of such work. Moreover, in this arena and in costume, the male truck driver can personify certain cultural icons as well as satisfactorily act out many of the requisites for traditional manhood.

Drivers are conscious of the performance quality of driving, as indicated by some of the terms in their lexicon. For example, the term "styling " is used by some drivers to denote both the work of enhancing the truck's appearance and showing off in a presumably attractive truck. As examples, when a SandHaul driver who was installing chrome lug nut covers and chrome mud flap strips on his truck was asked what he was doing, he replied, "I'm styling my ride [truck]." On another occasion, after two SandHaul drivers finished washing their trucks, which were covered with chrome and polished aluminum, one said to the other, "Now let's get up on the super slab [freeway] and do some righteous styling." Other indicators of the self-consciousness of drivers' performances include the wearing of outrageous hats while driving, obvious expenditures by the driver of time and money aimed at upgrading the appearance of his truck, and the assumption of exaggerated and often uncomfortable sitting positions that signal identification with a particular subculture.[1]

In a sense, the driver and truck can be conceptualized as one; drivers may express themselves through their trucks, for example, by enhancing the truck's appearance, and the truck shapes the reactions to its driver of those who encounter him. In the day-to-day talk at trucking companies, drivers and their trucks are continuously talked about in interchangeable terms. For example, a driver for a large, unionized company began a conversation by saying, "I saw two shiny bumpers talking to each another at the brake check [area]." "Shiny bumper" indicates that the truckers he observed drove attractive, customized trucks and therefore were probably either owner-operators or drivers for small, nonunion companies. In hailing a passing driver by CB radio, a trucker is likely to say something like, "Hey, how about that big red Petercar [Peterbilt tractor] northbound with a load of garbage [fresh produce]. Do you copy?"

This melding is not lost on drivers. After parking their trucks, it is common to see drivers glance back at them as they walk away. And I have known many drivers for whom an ideal seat in a coffee shop is one that affords a view of their trucks. The backward glance is not absentminded, and the coffee shop view is valued for more than the ability to prevent theft; both give the driver an opportunity to imagine what he looks like in costume. The desire to imagine oneself in costume was made clear by one PetroHaul and two SandHaul drivers who told me they liked driving by a particular store because its large and highly reflective windows served as a huge mirror.

Motorists as a Source of Prestige and Esteem

On the road, a truck is hard to ignore. Its size, noise, and perhaps load and appearance command attention. Drivers see motorists, including passengers, taking them into account. If nothing else, a truck poses considerable danger for motorists unlucky enough to strike or be struck by one. Many motorists are visibly fearful or annoyed by trucks close to them and take actions to avoid staying near. Beyond these actions, the truckers can see motorists consciously looking at them or their trucks. In addition, it is common for motorists to signal to truck drivers. For example, children often signal drivers to honk the truck's air horn; a fair number of adults make the same request by mimicking the motion needed to pull the horn chain that hangs from a truck cab's ceiling. Finally, motorists with CB radios appear to enjoy talking to truckers, and it is not unusual to hear them request that a trucker reply to their call for a conversation. In sum, though motorists, with some exceptions to be discussed later, have not gathered for the purpose of witnessing truckers' performances, truckers can easily see themselves as the center of attention when on the road.

From motorists, drivers gain support for the assessment that their work is skilled and notable and that they are experts in driving and thus worthy of esteem. Drivers come to these conclusions in several ways. First, the conscious attention paid by motorists to trucks and truckers is frequent enough and either sufficiently open to interpretation or clearly enough approving that a driver can conclude the public has respect for him and his work, which is not to say that truckers think the public has an unmitigated fondness for them. Many drivers feel their work is skilled, and they want to see respect for their skills; drivers are therefore predisposed to interpret responses by their audiences as indications of respect.

Second, truckers see motorists defer to them, and when the going gets tough, for example, when driving on snow or ice or in a heavy fog, motorists commonly pull in behind a truck and let it lead the way. This deference is esteem enhancing and may also heighten the sense that the trucker is engaged in skilled work; driving in extreme conditions underlines the fact that driving is not entirely rote work, and the serious consequences possible from a single error lend importance to the skills called into play.

Third, when on the road, truckers are witness to a parade of inept drivers. Truckers generally separate motorists into two skill groups: the incompetent and the barely competent. Given these two reference groups and the ample evidence, from the driver's point of view, to support this dichotomy, the trucker sees himself as a master in his domain. In addition, a simple comparison of trucks and automobiles implies the trucker has the greater skills.

Finally, in conversations with his friends and acquaintances, it is obvious to the trucker, if my experiences are typical, that many of them believe the truck driver possesses a good deal of skill, at least relative to their own skills as a motorist. For example, a frequent comment is "I can't imagine driving something so big or having to shift all those gears. It must be really hard."

Another common observation is "I can hardly back my *car* into a parking space. I can't believe the way truck drivers can back up their trucks." In addition there is the nontrucker's oft-spoken belief that drivers make "good" money. Without arguing that there is a direct and high correlation between a worker's wages and the level of skill the worker is presumed to possess, it is enough to say that good wages are more likely to command respect for an occupation than are low wages, especially in blue-collar work.

Thus, motorists' actions both on and off the road support the trucker's view that he is vastly superior in skills to the motorist, and he doesn't doubt that the motorists would agree with his estimation. The trucker also finds among motorists some belief that truck driving is skilled work.

Besides feeling superior in driving skills, the trucker, when on the road, is able to see himself as a "somebody": a masculine man in the traditional sense, and a notable man linked to cultural icons.

How does the male trucker come to know that he is manly, even perhaps a folk hero? First, as noted, many drivers are attracted to trucking by these impressions. As with skill determination, drivers who already believe that trucking is manly and heroic are predisposed to seeing these traits reflected in their audiences' responses. In addition, drivers do not have to grossly distort their audiences' responses to find support for these images and perceptions. Truckers derive evidence for their perception of themselves as macho men and cultural icons from motorists' nonverbal signing, from off-the-road conversations with friends and acquaintances, and from on-the-road interactions that have sexual overtones.

As noted, it is obvious to truck drivers that they and their trucks are noticed, and not only with a glance in passing. People frequently go out of their way to look over a truck or truck driver. Motorists crane their necks; smile; wave; blink their lights; display anger, annoyance, or disgust; make hand signs that signal approval or disapproval; move away in fear; honk their horns; display trucker-associated bumper stickers; and mimic truckers through attaching certain accessories to their cars and pick-up trucks such as dual vertical exhaust stacks. Much of this signing lends itself to a wide range of interpretations. A motorist's possibly neutral look at a truck or trucker can be interpreted as interest, awe, admiration, attraction, fear, respect, annoyance, or curiosity.

Not all signing is left to the driver's imagination; he frequently observes signing that is unmistakably positive in its assessment of the truck/trucker. For example, while I was driving a PetroHaul tanker on the freeway, a convertible filled with male blue-collar workers looked over the truck and then began exuberantly cheering the truck/me and giving vigorous thumbs-up and thrust-fist signs, much as one would applaud a rock music band or a team's successful scoring attempt. This is not at all uncommon if the truck is attractive. On another occasion, a night haul performed in a tanker that was something of a "Christmas tree," with many extra marker lights attached to it, I passed a country and western music bar in the process of closing. As I slowly rolled by, a large number of patrons were leaving the bar and many began to cheer the truck/me. Even common-appearing trucks evoke positive reactions, though not as often as an attractive truck. When I began driving, it was in a plain-looking truck hauling a low-status load, yet one of my clearest pleasures was the feeling of being onstage and commanding a certain amount of interest and respect. For example, several times a month a male motorist or pedestrian would imitate the two-handed movement used when both transmissions had to be shifted simultaneously (until the mid-1970s, trucks commonly had two transmissions) and then follow with a smile, wave, or thumbs up.

Based on my experiences it is a rare workday that a trucker does not observe at least one signing of clear approval. Such approval does not emanate solely from blue-collar workers or males. While on the road, truckers observe positive reactions from what appears to be the entire range of their audience. This experience seems to differ from that of most other blue-collar workers, who either do their work outside the public's view, or whose work does not provoke conscious interest. For example, when I was a telephone installer, the only occasions that evoked conscious public attention that could be read as something akin to interest or admiration were those times I had to use climbing hooks to scale a pole; even then I rarely noticed anyone observing me. While working in a warehouse, I had no contact with the public.

While much work occurs out of public view or, if in public

view, seemingly provokes little interest, virtually all workers have the chance to discuss their work with people who are not co-workers. Here the experience of drivers also seems to differ from that of many other occupations.

As a driver, I found considerable interest about trucking in the people I met, whether they were blue-collar or white-collar workers or academics who thought my activities novel. This interest differed from my experiences as a telephone installer or warehouse worker: warehouse work evoked little interest, and mention of telephone work most often provoked harangues against my employer. Perhaps most occupations do not excite much interest or strong feeling, positive or negative, in the non-practitioner. What is there in the occupations of machinist, forklift driver, corporate attorney, vice-president in charge of regional sales, or a host of other occupations that offers the nonpractitioner either a common ground or titillation as a basis for conversation with a practitioner?

For reasons having to do with the large number of adults who are motorists, the romance inspired by notions of travel, and the mystery associated with belonging to an identifiable but private and somewhat deviant subculture, truckers find in their friends and acquaintances considerable interest and strong feelings about trucks and truckers. People from all walks of life have asked me to take them for a ride in a truck, and not a few have openly fantasized about leaving their cares behind and heading off in a truck to parts unknown. Many outsiders suppose trucking, like New York City, to be an interesting place to visit, if not a place they would want to spend their lives.

Significantly, the questions I have been asked by blue-collar as well as white-collar and academic friends center on the very notions that compose the images of the trucker as a traditional man and cultural icon. People ask about the sights a trucker sees, the work's difficulty and danger, what goes on in a truck stop, meeting women, drug usage, prostitutes, the life of a loner, opportunities for stealing from loads, fights, driving in convoys, and problems and strategies in dealing with police. Others have expressed annoyance or fear regarding trucks/truckers. In addition, people often have their own truck stories they wish to relate: crazy driving, following a truck (ergo, professional driver) through inclement weather and driving conditions, an accident, remarkable driving skill, or assistance from a trucker. Women have complained to me about being pursued by a truck driver who was taking advantage of the truck's elevated viewing position by staring at women motorists. Even the negative images related in these questions and stories have, at their core, images of the trucker as a macho man or an adventurer who is part of a different world, one in which he is closer to society's margins than the average person.

Male truckers, simply because they are truckers, are sexual objects for some people, and this role-related attraction, as much as any other element of their working lives, supports the drivers' notion that truckers are or are perceived to be both macho and folk heroes. The most common sexual behavior involving women is exhibitionism, though more direct forms of contact do occur. In addition, a great deal of flirting takes place on the road and is interpreted within a sexual frame. Male truckers also have contact with men who are interested in a sexual liaison.

Several times when I drove for PetroHaul and SandHaul, a woman drove next to my truck, stripped off most of her clothing, and masturbated or otherwise fondled herself. In one case the woman was accompanied by a clothed male, and together they indicated they wanted me to follow them off the freeway. In another case, a woman told us by CB radio (two of us were on the same run) that she had spotted our trucks while we were taking a break, waited for us to finish, and then followed us onto the freeway where she began exposing herself to us. This woman said she was attracted to truckers, especially tanker drivers, and on her day off often hung around the area where she spotted us, an area popular with truckers taking a break. She eventually pulled over to the side of the road with a third truck driver who indicated he was interested in more direct sexual activity. In our conversation with this woman she mentioned another PetroHaul driver whom she knew and liked. When I later told him of this incident, he said that she had approached him in the same manner and that he had sex with her. Usually, however, the exhibitionism does not lead to sex. In all but two instances I have observed, the women broke contact in such a way that they could not be followed. At SandHaul, instances of female exhibitionism (not all as overt as the examples) were reported at least every other week. Only two of these incidents reportedly ended with direct sexual contact, and one of those reports was widely disbelieved because the driver who made the claim was thought to exaggerate.

As long as I have been associated with trucking, drivers have displayed enjoyment of the voyeuristic opportunities presented by their elevated seating. In the mid-1970s, in an attempt to extend these opportunities into the hours of darkness, some California truckers began attaching lights to their trucks that would illuminate the front seat of a passing auto. Eventually these "beaver" lights became common and provoked a response in some audience members. While most people remained un-aware of the function of beaver lights, some exhibitionists took advantage of the combination of darkness and the illumination of their auto interiors. Thus there was a sort of communication between drivers who had these lights and their audience; the beaver light was an open invitation to exhibitionists. (By 1993, pressure from the police had notably reduced the frequency of beaver lights.)

In addition to exhibitionists, there are women who like to ride with truck drivers and will exchange sex for the opportunity. In discussing such women, truckers typically refer to an informal contract supposedly based on custom that legitimates such a transaction. There are also women who patronize bars fre-quented by truckers for the purpose of socializing and possibly having sex with them. In addition, drivers occasionally report direct approaches offering sex without any material or social ex-change. For example, a driver told me that after he parked his truck near a café popular with truckers, a woman drove up and made a frank sexual proposition. The driver accepted, and later she explained that she was getting even with her husband and specifically had a truck driver in mind when planning her re-venge. The driver understood her to mean that she selected a trucker to wreak the greatest revenge possible, because truckers are paragons of manhood. I believe he also thought she chose him because—as the driver of a "road machine," an attractive, fully accessorized truck—he personified the macho trucker. Even if this story were a total fabrication, which would not be characteristic of this driver, it reveals his notions about the trucker as a special sort of man.

In another instance, I was told about a supposedly impotent farmer who used a rest area frequented by truckers to recruit a trucker interested in having sex with the farmer's wife. While such assignations are not common, all drivers claim to know other drivers who have had such an experience. Whether or not the bulk of these stories is true is not the important point. What matters is that drivers believe such women exist.

Besides these overt sexual behaviors, truckers report flirting with women motorists. While it is difficult precisely to define this activity, almost any positive attention paid to the trucker by a female motorist is understood as involving some sexual attraction on her part. The trucker often assumes that the anonymity of the road offers him a peek into the hearts of women, and he concludes that many would have him (at least "him" in terms of what he represents as a trucker) if they could. An example can be found in a PetroHaul driver's description of an incident of flirtation:

> *Russ:* Here she was right next to her wimp slob of a husband and she knew I was scopin' her legs. She'd look over and give me a little smile. I know she was getting off on it.

Perhaps more common than female exhibitionism are the overtures of homosexuals.[2] Three forms of contact are typical. Several times a year, a driver is likely to see a man driving next to the truck and masturbating. In most cases, the masturbator clearly has sought out a truck driver. For example, it is not uncommon for these men to have equipped their cars with an under-dashboard light that illuminates their lap or to carry a flashlight for this purpose. Almost always, the masturbator will at some point attempt to determine if the trucker is interested in engaging in sex.

The more common means whereby homosexuals make themselves known to truckers is to park next to a road at night, turn their lights off, and flash their brake lights at approaching trucks. There are areas that become known as places where such signaling is common.

Finally, homosexual men frequent certain truck stops, highway rest areas (known as, among other things, "pickle parks"), and truck brake inspection areas. The means of contact here, according to driver accounts, varies from loitering in a bathroom to an approach as direct as knocking on the door of a sleeping driver's truck and asking him if he is interested in having sex.

All of this sexual activity, by both women and men, is easily read by drivers as evidence that they as drivers are notably macho and, moreover, someone special. It could be argued that many making these approaches are simply taking advantage of the opportunity provided by the circumstances of trucking and are not particularly attracted to truckers, but I have never heard a trucker offer this explanation. The stories about meetings and about occasional experiences with women who specifically want to have sex with truck drivers, buttressed by encounters with exhibitionists and frequent flirting, lead the driver to believe that a category of women exists akin to those attracted to particularly notable occupations or groups such as musicians or athletes; the trucker believes he has "groupies." And the presence of groupies signals an occupation that is in some way special. "After all," the trucker might ask himself, "how many of my friends or acquaintances have groupies?"

What is it about truckers that certain women find attractive? Other occupations or groups reputed to have groupies—artists, musicians, athletes, police, firefighters, and motorcycle gangs— seem to share qualities that could be generally categorized under dramatic performance and social license. First, in the course of its performance, each engages in activities that have a dramatic quality of considerable interest to their audience. Musicians and artists offer varying mixes of intellectual provocation and entertainment. Athletes entertain us. Police, firefighters, and motorcycle gang members have captured the popular imagination to the extent of (and because of) being commonly featured in such mass entertainments as television dramas and newscasts, movies, newspapers, magazines, and novels. The performances of these groups involve celebrity or heroism—antiheroism in the case of motorcycle gang members. With the general exception of artists and musicians—but varying considerably according to their music and its presentation—this heroic quality is associated with traditional machismo. These occupations and groups, excepting some artists, are alike also in that they perform publicly and are readily identifiable while performing.

The second special quality about occupations and groups

having groupies is that they seem to have power or privileges beyond those of the average citizen. Successful musicians and athletes are accorded social privileges by virtue of their celebrity or association with celebrity. If the classically defined hero is still accorded privileges, then athletes, police, and firefighters are such beneficiaries. In a more active sense, police are obviously powerful, at least at the street level, as law enforcers with the right to use deadly force and detention in the discharge of their duties. Motorcycle gang members have no power of office, but they are people to be reckoned with; nonmembers cannot count on shared norms and mores to predict the gang member's behavior. The motorcycle gang claims social license.

Trucking also has a dramatic quality and has served as an image for popular entertainment. It is traditionally manly work, and the combination of travel, danger, mystery, the potential for adventure, and the public handling of huge machinery suggests the existence of heroic qualities.

Further, trucking is similar to the occupations and groups that have groupies in that it is public, the trucker is readily identifiable, and the basis for attraction on the part of the audience has to be the occupation, given that the work is usually performed without verbal interaction with the audience.

Finally, like the motorcycle gang member and some musicians (Becker 1963), the trucker as part of a somewhat deviant subculture possesses the power implicit in loosened social ties, the power of someone who in effect publicly declares, "I'll do things my way."

That truckers believe trucking calls up in the public the sort of attraction associated with folk heroes was nicely summed up in separate discussions with two SandHaul drivers. One driver, after an encounter with a female exhibitionist, said, "Well, you know, like the song says, 'ladies love outlaws.'" The second SandHaul driver and I were talking by the side of a road next to our trucks when a man and woman, both in their twenties, drove by and signaled exuberant approval of our trucks/us. The SandHaul driver turned to me and said, "We'll let the dork play with our trucks while we fuck the shit out of his old lady." Implicit in his comment was the notion of the truck's/trucking's/ trucker's special attraction. There are many manly jobs, but few where "let[ting] the dork" take your place would, even jokingly, be thought sufficient to mollify him while his lover fulfills her assumed wish to have sex with the job holder.

The homosexual overtures truckers encounter, like the overtures they receive from women, are mostly read as evidence of truckers' machismo. When drivers tell of homosexual overtures they, like many men, usually express annoyance and cast the story in terms that emphasize the storyteller's superior masculinity. But homosexual overtures are common, and I have rarely seen drivers react angrily (unless they are disturbed while sleeping) or report responding with an attack. A common response by AgriHaul drivers, who in the course of certain hauls passed a desert area used by homosexuals to signal to truckers, was to signal back to lure the homosexual into following them. Drivers competed in seeing how far they could get one of these men to follow them, and they reported the results with great glee. However, I have heard two drivers report having roadside sex with a homosexual (in both instances the driver was fellated), and both claimed to have treated the homosexual roughly.

Other than flirting, most of the sexual activity drivers experience in the course of their work is viewed by the public as deviant. In addition to the behaviors already described, I have observed or been told of on-the-road transvestite strippers, couples engaged in exhibitionistic sex, flirtation with motorists that led to group sex, and bestiality. The fact that the trucker usually is the one who is approached in these sexual encounters, plus the often deviant nature of the sexual activity, attest to the special and somewhat deviant nature of his occupation. This image of the occupation reinforces the male trucker's notions of himself as a man apart; a rascal, adventurer, or outlaw; someone special; perhaps a cultural icon.

This apparent contradiction reflects a more general paradox. On one hand, truckers see themselves as special in that they personify traditional conceptions of manliness and, more important, they are living embodiments of cultural icons. On the other hand, when the public is asked to rate the prestige of various occupations, truck driving is ranked relatively low (Reiss 1961). In a general sense, drivers are well aware of the low prestige accorded trucking. They know that their work is thought to require little intelligence and is considered more or less dirty work. Who has not heard someone say, in an attempt to emphasize the undesirability of a job feature, "I'd drive a truck before I'd [submit to that feature of my job]." So, which is it? Do drivers sees themselves as a blue-collar elite or as ill-regarded workers doing unintelligent work? The answer is, both.

The low ranking of truckers on prestige scales indicates, among other things, that trucking is seen as relatively unskilled work. The question arises: Even when truckers are rated the most skilled drivers, is trucking skilled work? Drivers have mixed feelings on this subject. Like the public, they sometimes see driving as mindless work. For example, when I said that stress was associated with boring work, a SandHaul driver said, "Then driving must be damn stressful. A trained monkey could do this job." On the other hand, there is much to learn in the way of driving skills, and lack of skill or an error can result in horrific outcomes. In addition, in their daily observation of motorists, truckers feel justified in thinking that if driving is easy to do, why are so many motorists inept? Finally, drivers use their relatively good incomes as a trump card in imagined arguments about skill with the public.

This ambiguity about whether or not truck driving is skilled work turns on the notion of prestige. While drivers know that, if the public is asked to rank occupations, trucking will be placed close to the low end of the scale, this is not how they *experience* the public in their daily contacts. Despite some hostility and a certain amount of indifference toward trucking, the public on the road displays deference, respect, admiration, awe, and a host of other positive reactions. Negative reactions are also displayed, such as a raised middle finger or a look of disgust, but are easily explained by the trucker and present scant threat to his ego. Like the jazz musicians among whom Becker (1963) found little respect for even informed audience members, truckers see even the best motorists as unqualified to criticize their work.

It would seem that in occupations with an audience composed of the general public, prestige is likely to be understood by practitioners in terms of their daily work experiences rather than of a more abstract social ranking. Truckers occupy a public subworld where they are the elite. In this world, since the public is also a work-related other and is engaged in a similar activity (driving a vehicle), prestige and esteem tend to merge in the minds of drivers. That is, the esteem granted to truckers for their driving skill can take on the appearance of respect for their work, or prestige; whatever deference truckers detect in motorists supports this inflation of prestige. And while motorists can enhance trucker esteem, they rarely have the power to deflate it. The trucker, although detesting motorists, finds them an audience before which failure is almost impossible.

Truck Drivers As an Audience

To the driver on the the road, truckers who are not co-workers at once become fellow performers and informed audience members. In encounters between unrelated drivers, the two size up one another; the primary indicators for these judgments are trucks (costumes), personal appearance, and performances (in practice, not wholly separable from costume). In these encounters, the trucker also sees who or what he could be and receives some feedback regarding who or what he thinks he is. Such interaction takes place against a background of understandings about prestige among truckers.

If an outsider asks drivers whether a truck drivers' hierarchy exists, the reply almost certainly will be that all drivers are equal and some are not better or higher than others as a consequence of their jobs. For example, Runcie (1971) states: "Rather than being composed of many subgroups, the occupation of truck driver constitutes a single social group. Some subgroupings are mentioned but they are of little importance to the respondents" (iii). While Runcie was not necessarily wrong—the key is his definition of group—I think he overstated the occupation's homogeneity. On one hand, possession of a license and having experience with more than one type of hauling leads drivers to see one another as equal. (At SandHaul, twenty-one drivers have worked in more than one speciality area of trucking.) On the other hand, drivers make distinctions among their own ranks in terms of the rewards they are able or unable to command and skills they are thought to possess. These valuations are perhaps most clear when a driver hires on at a company and goes about establishing who he is. For example, the young and relatively inexperienced driver I first rode with at SandHaul began by talking down to me, but after seeing a truck belonging to my last employer (PetroHaul), a prestigious piece of equipment hauling a prestigious load, he became unmistakably deferential. These interactions sometimes take the form of battles as a new driver fights for position in the company pecking order. A newly hired SandHaul driver assigned to ride with me wasted no time in asserting his superiority, based on his prior job, a coast-to-coast haul performed in a prestigious truck. In return, I related past experiences in jobs more prestigious than working at SandHaul such as cross-country driving and gasoline hauling. Our one-upmanship went on for at least thirty minutes.

While drivers apply notions of an occupational hierarchy, rankings are not clearly specified or unanimous for two reasons. As noted, skill is difficult to determine, so drivers have an impaired sense of what skills exist and must use indirect indicators to identify skill levels. This doubt about skills leads to differing interpretations of indicators. For example, some drivers believe hauling hazardous loads indicates superior driving skills; others see it as a mark of foolishness. Moreover, as members of a low-status occupation, truckers are in an ignoble position: they are subservient, and their work does not have the nobility of, for example, the professions that makes effort honorable. These conditions color the indicators used to assess occupational rankings. For example, does driving a first-rate truck signal skill or a driver who is willing to work for low wages? To understand the interactions of truck drivers who are not co-workers, one needs to understand the meanings attached to the cues they interpret.

People who work decide how much to identify their selves with their jobs. Two considerations loom large in this decision: Is identification with work honorable, and is the honor sufficient to warrant a commitment at the expense of nonwork life? Conflicting demands and variations in the respective costs and rewards of occupational and nonwork selves may force a choice. For example, academics who wish to publish may have to decide between spending evenings with their families and working in solitude. As noted, professions successfully claim honor for their work. Because of this honor, many professionals can suppress problems and reap rewards from identities based on their work activities; the choice to emphasize the occupational self is not only easy, it is expected.

Other employments, for example, assembly-line work, are so devoid of ego rewards and so clearly emphasize the employment contract as the rationale for the workers' efforts that the worker, like the professional, has relatively little difficulty in deciding which self to emphasize; given an absence of intrinsic rewards, a job makes sense only in terms of how much it contributes to one's nonwork life (Chinoy 1965).

If the problem of identity and commitment is resolved—in these examples identity and commitment are proper for a professional but irrelevant or shameful for the assembly-line worker—it is much less difficult for members of an occupation to rate the various aspects of their work. If commitment to work is not embarrassing, then a worker can award high value to specific work tasks, the mastery of those tasks, and work activities as factors in career decisions such as changing jobs to improve skills. The more embarrassing it is to be committed to one's job, the more difficult it is to place value on its intrinsic aspects and the more likely a job will be evaluated by its payoffs in one's nonwork life. Thus, for example, academics trying to demonstrate their worth before peers cite indicators that show them identified with and committed to their occupation: employers and publishers, number of publications, affiliations with scholarly journals and professional societies, and research plans. If these academics satisfy their employers' qualifications for continued employment and advancement, they are likely to feel proud; if they fail to win tenure and promotions they are likely to be embarrassed and ashamed.

On the other hand, automobile assembly-line workers (Turkel 1974) brag about establishing a routine or learning shortcuts that conserve their energy and make time pass faster (235), show respect for those who have "enough willpower to stick it out for thirty years" (226), see promotion as shameful (224), or say: "I'm proud of what my job gives me. Not the job. I can't say, I'm proud of working for Ford Motor Car Company" (238). Likewise, machinists defining their worth cite jobs likely to earn a piece-rate bonus rather than their ability to do precision work (Burawoy 1979). To earn a piece-rate bonus and make as much money as possible is seen as beating the employer. Where academics cast themselves in terms of the work they do, these machinists and assemblers emphasize the roles of provider and consumer and find dignity in countering the ignobility of their employment.

Trucking, in offering freedom, variety, tasks that are relatively whole and therefore make sense, work appropriate for the traditional male, and the opportunity to be a notable man, encourages commitment to the occupation; male truckers are able to find considerable rewards in being all the trucker they can be.

On the other hand, it is not entirely respectable for the trucker to pursue these rewards, because pursuit typically comes at the expense of high extrinsic rewards and implies he has allowed his employer to exploit him. For example, in my experience, driving jobs high in autonomy are also high in the unpaid work they demand. Failure to earn the highest possible extrinsic rewards signals at least a partial rejection of the roles of provider and consumer and a failure to fully counter the ignobility of employment by making the employer pay as much as possible.

Even if the pursuit of intrinsic rewards is not at the cost of extrinsic rewards, it implies a commitment that may be embarrassing if an occupation's activities have not been defined as noble. Most blue-collar work is not seen as having enough innate worth for workers to immerse themselves in their jobs. For example, the term "dedicated doctor" is likely to conjure a positive and believable image, whereas "dedicated auto worker" either strikes us as an oxymoron or conjures an image of a fool, a "company man" not to be trusted, or perhaps a Japanese who labors under an employment contract in which communalism makes commitment honorable.

Though the work of trucking lacks the nobility of the work of the professions, its intrinsic rewards make their pursuit understandable. The differences between developing an occupational self (to be all the trucker possible) or a nonwork self (to be all the provider, consumer, family man possible) are relatively clear: the former involves the pursuit of intrinsic rewards, the latter, of extrinsic. Extrinsic rewards include gross income and rate of pay; fringe benefits such as insurance, paid holidays and sick leave, additional pay for overtime, and retirement pensions; and protections such as institutionalized seniority rights, hearings before dismissal, and work rules designed to protect drivers' time and safety. Extrinsic rewards are considered by drivers to be high when they match the provisions of the Teamsters' Master Freight Agreement.

Intrinsic rewards are satisfactions that emanate from the work itself and include equipment, autonomy, variety, the opportunity to develop skills in greater depth and breadth, work that makes sense by its task wholeness, the fulfillment of traditional male expectations, and the opportunity to be a notable man.[3] Jobs in which drivers plan their work, personally negotiate with the owner, use their trucks as if they were their own, haul over the road in a variety of weather conditions and over challenging terrain, travel to a variety of destinations, haul respectable loads, and drive nice equipment are considered high in intrinsic rewards. This is the work of the ideal trucker noted earlier.

It is clear that truckers value extrinsic rewards; in a culture where it is said that "money may not buy happiness, but it will buy everything else" and where money is to a large degree the measure of the man, how could truck drivers feel otherwise? As a reflection of social values and the fulfillment of the role expectations of husband, father, and man, extrinsic rewards become something of a moral metric. Husbands and fathers are judged at least in part by how well they provide for their dependents. And, as noted, respectable wages counter the ignobility of employment. By being well paid, the driver does not allow the owner to "make a chump" of him. In these ways, high extrinsic rewards satisfactorily explain, both to himself and others, the driver's occupational choices and behavior. It is respectable for the driver to say, "I am doing this because it will bring me the most money." Thus, as a reflection of general cultural and particular class values, drivers accord high prestige to driving jobs that collect high extrinsic rewards.

Drivers also value intrinsic rewards. As noted, over half the SandHaul drivers did not speak of pay, insurance, pensions, and the like as their primary motivations for entering trucking but cited intrinsic rewards as trucking's most attractive feature. Further, intrinsic rewards later became attractive to many of those who entered trucking primarily for money. Most SandHaul drivers not only talked about wanting intrinsic rewards but demonstrated their interest by customizing trucks, negotiating for enjoyable hauls at the expense of higher-paying hauls, and seeking employment at firms that emphasized these rewards.

> *Jack* [a SandHaul driver]: My idea of trucking is pulling a reefer [refrigerated trailer] coast to coast in a Peterbilt conventional with a big walk-in [sleeper] and dual thirteen-foot chrome stacks.

The avenues for earning the greatest extrinsic and intrinsic rewards are clear. In general, extrinsic rewards are highest in large, unionized, monopoly sector companies, while intrinsic rewards are highest in small, nonunion, competitive sector companies.

The problem with assessing prestige among truckers is that they do not agree on the relative merits of being all the trucker one can be and enjoying nonwork life. The problem of commitment has not been resolved in trucking, because truck driving is neither so devoid of ego rewards that identifying oneself by one's nonwork life is the only option nor honorable enough to legitimize a self centered on the occupation. In relation to motorists and the public, being all the trucker one can be is not a cause for embarrassment, because it is manly and conjures the image of a cultural icon. Further, motorists lack the credibility to impugn the trucker's skills. On the other hand, fellow truck drivers know the costs of the decision to go for intrinsic rewards: lower wages, fewer benefits, unpaid labor, and time away from family and friends. In addition, the driver's family is likely to emphasize nonwork life over the driver's wish to be all the trucker possible.

Prestige from the standpoint of the driver is, therefore, determined from two often antithetical perspectives. From the perspective of the nonwork self, the man apart from the driver, he stands as a member of a culture engaged in relationships with nondrivers and held accountable in terms of the responsibilities and expectations associated with his nonwork roles in that culture. The nonwork self is a somewhat abstract and broadly based notion regarding what it means to be an adult man.

From the other perspective, the occupational self, the driver stands as a member of an occupation and a subculture and in this milieu is beholden first to himself. Here the driver is grounded in daily work experience, a set of activities that typically occupies most of his waking hours. Compared to the non-work self, the occupational self is a more concrete and specific definition of identity and likely to be more compelling.

Truckers, then, are of two minds when they evaluate driving jobs. On the one hand they size up a job from the point of view of the husband, father, provider, consumer, occupant of a class, and member of the general public. On the other hand, they size up a job from the point of view of the driver they wish they could be if unencumbered by other considerations. For example, in a study of English lorry drivers (Ouellet 1981), twenty-seven of twenty-nine (93 percent) claimed the type of driving they were engaged in was what they preferred. When asked, however, "If you had no family obligations, or had a wife who did not care what you did, what type of driving would you prefer?" eighteen of the twenty-one drivers not engaged in intercontinental hauling (the longest hauling possible) said they would like to do longer hauls. While this point of view is somewhat contradictory, it reflects the way drivers talk about a trucking hierarchy. Furthermore, drivers' conversation and behavior introduces some order into this hierarchy. The major variations in ranking center on the relative importance to a driver of intrinsic and extrinsic rewards, which affects the perspective from which the job is being assessed. In other words, it is not difficult to say which jobs are the best in terms of one or the other set of rewards. The difficulty lies in comparing the relative worth of intrinsic and extrinsic rewards.

I am not aware of any driving job that combines union-level extrinsic rewards with a full measure of intrinsic satisfactions; there seem to be no widely known and agreed-upon ideal jobs in trucking. However, a certain calculus exists among drivers by which jobs are assessed. As noted, jobs known to be high in extrinsic rewards, union jobs for the most part, generally command high prestige. However, extrinsic rewards do not explain entirely the high prestige accorded union jobs, because these jobs also imply high skill levels. Since union jobs attract many applicants, union companies are able to hire only those with a considerable amount of experience and a good driving record. Thus, in general, the union driver is thought to be experienced and skilled, and acquiring such a job is seen by some drivers as acknowledgment of advanced driving skills.

On the other hand, the prestige of jobs with high extrinsic rewards may be reduced by factors involving intrinsic rewards. For example, unionized automobile haulers have one of the more lucrative pay scales in the industry, but their low-status, aesthetically offensive trucks make them more often the butt of jokes than objects of envy. When a SandHaul driver took a job hauling automobiles, several SandHaul drivers teased him about needing to drive at night so nobody would recognize him in his new employer's truck. In the same vein, a SandHaul driver expressed the belief that unionized freight haulers, given the equipment they had to drive, had lost the opportunity to be notable men.

> *Jack:* Sometimes I feel sorry for those chicken haulers [perhaps the most embarrassing load] and freight haulers [drivers for the large, monopoly sector companies]; no woman is going to show her stuff to guys who'll drive shit like that.

And at AgriHaul, where hauls were the most varied and drivers had the greatest freedom in performing their work, it was not uncommon to hear drivers wonder how union drivers for the large freight haulers could stand the boredom of their permanently assigned hauls. The few permanently assigned hauls at AgriHaul were the province of men in their late fifties and sixties, who were seen by most of the younger drivers as over-the-hill.

On a prestige scale of low, medium, and high, however, a job with high extrinsic rewards rarely will be accorded low prestige. High extrinsic rewards satisfactorily explain why a driver would work in a job low on intrinsic rewards. Automobile hauling is probably the major exception, in part because drivers often are unaware of its high pay scales.

Jobs high in intrinsic rewards vary more widely in prestige than do jobs high in extrinsic rewards. Something of a rule informs this calculus: the more a driver is seen as "buying" his intrinsic rewards, the less prestige his job will command. That is, a job loses prestige if the satisfactions inherent in good equipment, autonomy, and variety are thought to be financed to an unreasonable degree by low pay and few perquisites. For example, after we were passed by a first-rate truck engaged in cross-country hauling, a SandHaul driver offered his view of the driver.

> *Warren:* That guy thinks he's a real big strap [big jockstrap, i.e., stud], but the way his chickenshit company pays for those rigs is to hire dummies who'll work for free.

A driver in such a job violates cultural expectations regarding his responsibility to garner extrinsic rewards and violates a class norm by "allowing" himself to be "made a chump" by the owner.

On the other hand, jobs high in intrinsic satisfactions and at least moderate in extrinsic rewards command considerable prestige. For example, such jobs at one company, PetroHaul, were well regarded by many of its drivers. Drivers at AgriHaul and SandHaul who knew of PetroHaul also thought well of the company and assumed one had to be a good driver to get a job there.

As in the case of union jobs, the correlation between extrinsic rewards and prestige is confounded by the implications concerning skill that are read into such jobs. Drivers who "work for nothing" are typically thought to be either neophytes, of devalued status, or so unskilled that they have no choice. One SandHaul driver described drivers willing to work for a low-paying competitor as "a bunch of losers who can't do any better."

In sum, a driver thinking from the perspective of his nonwork self will likely value jobs high in extrinsic rewards. This perspective encompasses powerful social values and demands and is nearly impossible to ignore; consequently, drivers find it difficult under any circumstances to dismiss jobs high in extrinsic rewards. But a driver on the road and absorbed in his work or indulging in a work-associated reverie, which is to say viewing the world from the perspective of the occupational self, is most likely to value intrinsic rewards, such as those described to me, while I was loading at a major, unionized oil company, by one of their drivers.

> *Driver:* You know, I've been loading off this rack for fifteen years. I have a good deal here, but it's boring. I work four days a week and make $35,000 a year, and I wouldn't want to give that up. But, damn, I wish I could haul to some different places, get out of town like you guys. I'd love to take off in a Peterbilt with a big walk-in [sleeper] and all the goodies and head over the hill passing everybody up with a four'n-a-quarter [425 hp] Cat. . . . I have a good deal, but this is *it?*

Equipment is the main indicator by which unrelated drivers judge one another. Therefore, beyond its practical usefulness, equipment has symbolic value. To the knowing observer, a truck is a proxy for work skill and indicates the type, amounts, and proportions of rewards provided by it operator's job. And through their trucks, drivers are able to say, "Here is the sort of man I am."

That drivers rank equipment and judge operators by this is evident in the following graffiti found in truck-stop bathrooms: "Peterbilt—God's way of blessing the truck driver." "A Mack truck is like a short dick—it'll do the job at home but it ain't worth a shit on the road." "Driving an Astro [GMC] is like fucking a nigger—it's ok as long as no one sees you doing it."

If unencumbered by nonwork considerations, drivers typically would choose to drive equipment high in prestige (see table). For example, a driver who wants to have a job that allows him to return home each night will rarely be able to drive the sort of truck described in the right-hand column of the table. Note that most of the items listed can be determined by an observer on the road, an important consideration in an occupation where work skills are mostly hidden.[4]

Equipment varies enormously. Some trucks are as close to being torture chambers as they are vehicles designed to haul large loads. In such a truck a driver might be subjected to an inordinate beating from a cushionless ride, work in extreme heat or cold, be surrounded by dirt and grime, breathe noxious fumes, be deafened by noise, and otherwise be at peril from inferior equipment specifications and poor maintenance. Conversely, a driver could have a truck that rides almost as smoothly as an automobile, sit in an oscillating and air-cushioned seat, listen to a stereo in a relatively quiet environment, set a thermostat to govern the temperature in which he wishes to work, and have at hand a CB radio, large bed, television, telephone, refrigerator, and microwave oven.

In general, but with many qualifications, the make, model, and condition of a truck can be read as the sort of equipment the driver is able to command. Drivers of good equipment are usually more highly thought of than drivers of poor equipment. I have heard the drivers for nonunion companies that operate poor fleets referred to as "that bunch of clowns" and similar de-

Prestige Ranking of Equipment

	Low	Medium	High
Make	International, Ford, Mack, GMC	Freightliner	Peterbilt, Kenworth
Model	Radical aerodynamic designs, integrated conventional sleepers, short-nose conventional	Standard conventional, cabover with small sleeper	Long-nose and wide-nose conventional with large sleeper, cabover with large sleeper
Horsepower	Less than 350 hp	350–400 hp	400^+ hp
Engine make	Detroit, Mack	Cummins	Caterpillar
Configuration	Short wheelbase, or 2-axle tractor	Medium wheelbase 3-axle tractor	Long wheelbase 3-axle tractor, truck-and-trailer
Type	Automobile transporter, poultry trailer, furniture van, dirt trailers	Bulk hoppers, liquid gas tank, pneumatic tank, vacuum tank	Refrigerated and dry vans, flatbed, tanker
Accessories	No accessories, lighted rods on front bumper, bull horns	Aluminum wheels, chrome exhaust stack, engine brake	Polished aluminum wheels, dual chrome exhaust stacks, TV

rogatory terms. As noted, however, if the driver is known to be highly paid, then poor equipment is much less likely to impugn his skills. Likewise, low pay compromises the prestige of first-rate equipment.

Besides equipment make and quality, the truck and load tell drivers much about each other's jobs. The presence of a sleeper indicates that a driver is probably engaged in over-the-road hauling, which in turn suggests variety and considerable latitude in completing the work. For each such indicator, other clues help flesh out the story. For example, if a truck has a sleeper and is hauling dirt, chances are the truck was originally intended for another type of work in which the owner failed before turning to this local and low-prestige hauling. If the truck has a very large sleeper and is pulling a refrigerated trailer, it is likely the driver hauls long distances. Trucks with certain types of fenders are not likely to be operated in areas that have snow (driving in snow indicates greater skill), because such fenders make using tire chains impossible. A load of produce is likely to be hauled a much greater distance than a load of hay. Dry bulk loads in California are likely to be hauled by nonunion companies, while freight, at least before industry deregulation, was typically hauled by unionized companies.

Even driver biographies are suggested by a driver's truck and load. For example, a dilapidated truck with a low-status load that is not operated by a known unionized company indicates to other truckers that the driver may be a poorly capitalized owner-operator, a neophyte, of a perceived disreputable status such as "recent immigrant," or in possession of a record so poor as to limit his options only to the worst companies. A truck obviously used for long hauling indicates that the driver is likely to know how to drive in a wide range of adverse weather conditions. Much bulk tomato hauling in California is thought to be done by young rural men who do not drive trucks year around, and many jokes circulate about these "kamikaze" and their unorthodox driving habits. In Los Angeles, dirt and demolition hauling in semi-end dumps was, by 1981, dominated by African Americans to the extent that a driver seeing such a vehicle would presume the driver to be African American.

Equipment and loads, then, can tell much about distances covered, length of time on the road, what areas are hauled to, hazards encountered, variety, freedom, pay, skill levels, and even driver biographies.

Equipment also gives an indication of the driver's commitment to trucking. A truck that is a prestigious make and model, accessory laden, or has obviously had money and effort expended for aesthetic enhancements indicates a driver who is likely to identify himself strongly with the occupation. Such a driver, in my experience, makes broad judgments about others based on their trucks and wants to be judged accordingly. A somewhat weaker implication in the same vein can be drawn from the type of haul: over-the-road hauling is generally preferred to local hauling but is done at the expense of family life. The local driver, as compared to the long-distance driver, is more likely to have put his family and nonwork life ahead of his occupational life.

Truckers, as noted, also take note of one another's driving performances and make judgments about both the other driver and his job. For example, drivers who speed excessively are, contrary to popular opinion, often thought of in derisive terms. Such a driver may be called "cowboy," "hot shoe," or "hot dog." Drivers often explain another's poor driving performance in terms that reveal occupational differentiations. For example, if a speeding driver works for a unionized company, his behavior may be explained by a nonunion driver as an attempt to garner extra time for a coffee break. In turn, this attempt may be read as evidence of both the laziness of union drivers and the constraints—here in the form of regulated breaks—of unionized work. Likewise, I have heard union drivers explain a nonunion driver's speeding in derogatory terms: a mark of the inferior drivers such companies hire, a reaction to a low pay rate that can be made reasonable only by speeding, or a necessity because of the demands made upon drivers who are without the protections of a union. In the same manner, drivers castigate one another for unsafe, impolite, or stupid driving. For example, a driver using an illegal lane (the "$100 lane") is thought to be a neophyte, an out-of-state driver, a rube, or a cowboy.

Even behaviors that a motorist is not likely to notice can have meaning for truckers. For example, it is fairly well known that truckers signal one another with their lights. A trucker that has been passed will blink his headlights when the passing truck has cleared and has room to pull back into the passed truck's lane; in turn, the passing trucker will blink his marker lights to say thank you. Less commonly known is that blinking patterns are read for data about the driver. The standard thank you is two blinks. A failure to blink is seen as indicating a rude or forgetful driver or is used as the equivalent of a raised middle finger, not uncommon if the passed truck has needlessly held up the passing driver. One quick blink is generally perceived as curt and may be taken to indicate a driver who is either mad or cares little for the occupational subculture.

Two blinks can be done with different rhythms and can signify good humor. For example, drivers sometimes blink the visual equivalent of the shave-and-a-haircut sequence; a much-delayed final "dot" leaves one hanging, then relieved. Other patterns can indicate friendliness or an emphatic thank you. Three blinks, especially in off-beat rhythms, may be taken to indicate, depending on the equipment, that the driver is really enjoying himself, may be using amphetamines, or is a hot dog. For example, when a long-haul driver of a fancy Peterbilt passed us and responded to our headlight blinks with an off-beat, three-blink "thank you," an AgriHaul driver said, "Man, that guy is pilled-up and having a good time." Four blinks are rare, and five or more blinks always led me to believe that the truck had a short in its electrical wiring.

Older drivers may see any signal discrepancies by younger drivers as indicative of the general inferiority of trucking's newer members, as did one twenty-six year veteran of trucking.

> *Big George:* These new assholes driving are something else. You pass them and instead of giving you the lights they'll tell you over the CB to pull in. Hell, how do you know who's talking to who? It could be another driver telling someone else to pull in. These young guys just aren't worth a shit.

Others object to the increasing tendency of drivers to signal with their headlights by turning on their high beams rather than flashing the lights on and off.

While on the road, drivers are also able to connect trucks (costumes) and performances with their respective actors. For example, before affirmative-action laws went into effect, one rarely saw anyone other than white, more or less middle-aged and older men driving for union companies. Now that African Americans, Hispanics, and women hold union jobs, the old association of union jobs with white males is limited. African Americans in 1981, however, continued to be found in the low-paying and inferior-equipment jobs they have traditionally held, and few women or African Americans drove for the better small, competitive sector companies—generally jobs that are medium to high in intrinsic rewards and medium to medium-high in extrinsic rewards.

Other general social categories besides race, ethnicity, and sex are used to classify drivers simply on sight. These include: farmer, biker, cowboy, straight, low rider, hippie, bum, and regular guy. All of these categories imply value judgments by the user and, when associated with specific jobs, indicate value judgments about those jobs. For example, a co-driver suggested that we observe drivers as they entered the truck stop café we were eating in and guess what sort of hauling they did. This white, Midwestern, ex-farmer was quite sure he could correctly match drivers with their hauls more often than not, and in trying to do so he clearly matched social categories he looked down on with lower-status types of trucking. As an example, this driver guessed African Americans to be "bedbuggers," that is, furniture haulers. Another driving partner regularly associated "biker types" with drivers who operate impressive equipment for little pay.

Finally, drivers get feedback about the impressions they present while performing. By looking at a truck like their own, drivers can imagine how they appear to others. And drivers often take the looks and signals of other drivers for appraisals. Drivers of top-quality trucks appear particularly to enjoy the looks and hand waving of drivers of similar trucks, because they see in such signs an acknowledgment of their truck's attraction. In turn, this acknowledgment is read as approval of the truck driver they present themselves to be and therefore as recognition of themselves as notable men.

> *Dallas* [a PetroHaul driver]: I had [my truck] cleaned, waxed, and looking good, and as soon as I got up on the boulevard [freeway] a super-fine Petercar [Peterbilt] checked me out, smiled, and gave me a thumbs up and that really got me off.

> *Al* [a SandHaul driver]: I was checking out his [beautiful] rig, and he was looking me over; then we both nodded and waved at the same time—it was cool.

Adding to the positive responses of these two drivers is the belief that some drivers of first-rate trucks will acknowledge only the drivers of similar equipment. In this vein, a driver of low-status equipment or loads is likely to take absences of acknowledgment as signs of his job's low-status.

When on the road and among other truckers, drivers see the full spectrum of possibilities in their occupation. They see the well paid and the price they pay, the outlaws, cowboys, easy-money drivers, road kings, and the winners and losers; they see the spartan equipment, unsafe equipment, and rolling palaces; they see jobs that suggest adventure and freedom and jobs that represent monotony and bondage; and they observe the continual tension between having work that is enjoyable and being a somebody, and the dishonor of acquiring these intrinsic rewards through acquiescence to exploitation. In this spectrum, drivers locate themselves, see who they could be, decide if what they are doing and who they want to be are consistent, and monitor feedback about the self they project.

CHAPTER 9

Careers, Magic, and Masculinity

SOONER OR LATER, and perhaps several times in his career, the male truck driver confronts a two-sided question: What kind of trucker do I want to be? What kind of man do I want to be? The choices drivers make about their careers are similar to the choices faced by the dance musicians Becker (1963) studied.

The musicians placed great value on playing authentic jazz. This was the essence of their occupation, it was what challenged them, and the ability to excel at it appeared to be the most positive basis for constructing their occupational self. But musicians who played real jazz found it difficult to make a living. Sooner or later the jazzman, particularly one with a family to support, had to choose between playing commercially viable music and music that better suited his artistic standards and self-concept. Although commercial jobs had more prestige within the occupation, they were seen as compromising one's artistic integrity. A jazzman who pursues a commercial career "finds it necessary to make a radical change in his self-conception; he must learn to think of himself in a new way, to regard himself as a different kind of person" (111).

The truck driver's equivalent of playing jazz is to use first-rate equipment to perform work over which he has considerable control, that varies and challenges him, suggests heroic qualities, and provides the opportunity to experience the magical times I describe, all intrinsic rewards most often found in small nonunion companies. As in the world of dance musicians, drivers who want to "play jazz" usually have to accept fewer extrinsic rewards.[1] And such drivers are likely to run afoul of their families, because work hours in the companies where the most intrinsic rewards are found typically are long and erratic.

In deciding what kind of truck driver and man they are, drivers make career decisions and organize their identities around one of three general roles: super trucker, trucker, or worker.[2] Implicit in each role is a particular view of labor unions.

The super trucker is immersed in his occupation. Rather than attempting to even the balance between work and nonwork life, the super trucker invests almost all his nonsleeping hours in his work. If he is not actually on duty, he is likely to be either enhancing his truck's appearance or socializing with other drivers. What most marks the super trucker is how much he derives his self-identity from his occupation and the fervor of that identification. The most common manifestations of a super-trucker orientation are conversations that rarely stray from trucking and a large investment of time, effort, and money to improve a truck's appearance. Some of these men go so far as to have themselves tattooed with pictures of trucks or a favorite truck manufacturer's logo.

The super trucker is as likely as other drivers to be married or living with a female partner and to have children at home; between AgriHaul, PetroHaul, and SandHaul, only one super trucker lived alone. However, the super trucker clearly strikes or forces a bargain with his family in which it is understood that the vast majority of his time will be devoted to his job.

> *Brian:* [My wife] understands that my job is important to me, so she doesn't complain if I get home late 'cause I was waxing my truck or having a few beers with the guys.

If a super trucker makes a concession to his family, it is likely to be in taking a job that allows him to sleep at home more. Since the typical super trucker is willing to work many hours, he is among the top money earners at his company; he brings home more money than his less-eager co-workers and perhaps many of his family's acquaintances bring home. From this point of view, the super trucker can think well of himself as a provider.

Extrinsic rewards are not, however, what propel the super trucker. On the contrary, pay seems to hold little value for him other than providing a satisfactory rationale for his work commitment, for the long work hours inherent in his devotion to his job make it nearly impossible for him to enjoy the material goods that his income provides.

What motivates the super trucker is the positive feedback of audiences to those who embody trucking's mythic elements. In a theatrical sense, he wants to be a star in the ongoing productions acted out on the highway. The super trucker is therefore most keenly interested in intrinsic rewards, especially in terms of equipment and hauling, for these are the visible signs of his worth as a driver. While he may be among the top money earners at his company, his orientation is antithetical to extrinsic rewards in that it forecloses working for most large, unionized enterprises, the very jobs that bear the highest extrinsic rewards.

Super truckers constituted about 15–25 percent of the drivers at the three companies, which is not to say that these distributions are typical. Because the three companies provide the equipment and organization of work, such as permanent truck assignments, in which drivers can give vent to super-trucker inclinations, they attract and nurture super truckers. In contrast, I worked for one company that offered high pay but little autonomy and only low-status, local loads hauled in poor equipment, and here there were no super truckers. I also know of companies in which super truckers are the majority.

Super truckers are found at all ages and levels of driving experience, but they are underrepresented among older truckers who have driven for many years. The three companies had a total of nineteen drivers over forty years old (22 percent), but only two super truckers (11 percent) were in this age group.

Given his desire to assume the role of the mythic truck driver, the super trucker is not necessarily a company man. Although he expects the owner to share his own commitment to work and trucking, this commitment, in its fervor and in not being centered solely on profit, can be an aggravation for the owner. For example, the extensive washings SandHaul super truckers gave their trucks often delayed the departure of night-shift drivers. Some super truckers are close to owners, while others are indifferent or opposed—some cultivate an outlaw persona antagonistic to all authority—but all super truckers, in their desire to reap high intrinsic rewards, engage in conflict with owners. For example, super truckers typically badger owners for more autonomy, truck accessories, and truck maintenance than they are inclined to provide.

The super trucker typically does not support unionization. No super trucker at SandHaul was interested in seeing Sand-Haul unionized. Of the drivers who left SandHaul for union work, only one was a super trucker, and his new job was at one of the rare small unionized companies that have first-rate equipment and allow their drivers considerable autonomy. Further, this driver told me that the union was not a consideration in his decision to seek or accept work at that company (Chapter 6). For the super trucker to become interested in unionization would demand a reordering of what he wants out of work, because he believes unionization would wipe out most of the intrinsic rewards that are central to his life, that in fact define it. When on the road, super truckers see union drivers in their typically unattractive trucks; they see that union drivers cannot distinguish themselves by, for example, attaching extra lighting to their trucks (SandHaul, PetroHaul, and AgriHaul drivers can almost always recognize co-workers at night by the individualized lighting patterns on their trucks); they see some union drivers driving in a fashion that indicates direct and overbearing company monitoring; and they sometimes see and hear union drivers who are envious of the super trucker's intrinsic rewards. For example, as I pulled out of a weigh station I heard the union driver in front of me tell his partner over the CB radio, "Look at me, I'm driving a big CAT [Caterpillar engine]" while purposely lugging his own low-power engine after each shift to make it emulate the CAT's characteristic burst of exhaust smoke. I was driving a fully accessorized, CAT-powered Kenworth, and here on the road I felt that my job, not his, was the one to be envied. I once asked an AgriHaul super trucker if it was true that he had applied for a job at a particular union company.

> *Dale:* Hell no! You see those guys poking along at fifty-five miles an hour in those shit wagons they drive; the day I drive junk like that and have some asshole telling me how fast I can drive is the day I get out of trucking.

Everything about a large unionized operation appears utilitarian and without regard for intrinsic satisfactions, and these jobs do not spur the super trucker into thinking, "That looks like fun."[3] The super trucker viewing the union driver at work sees neither the work he wishes to do nor the man he wants to be.

Nonunion truck drivers also have ideas about union work that are not born of direct observation but originate in conversations with other drivers, in general impressions regarding work at large enterprises, and in the experiences of their families or friends. They know that high extrinsic rewards are available in such jobs, but they also associate unionization with a plethora of rules covering nearly all aspects of the work, the absence of individualization, the loss of personal relationships and deals with management, and possibly a greater division of labor that will result in boredom. Unionization is associated with bureaucracy, a word that comes like a curse from the lips of a super trucker.

Finally, to support unionization of the company that employs him would require the super trucker to radically redefine his relationship with the owner. Whether he is a company man, an outlaw, or someone in between, the super trucker is likely to have a personal relationship with the owner in which he, through the exercise of his wiles and "rights" as an exceptionally dedicated employee, tries to convince the owner to act in his favor. The super trucker understands this relationship to be man-to-man and values it as such. Unionization would mean giving up the right to bargain individually and man-to-man, something the super trucker is successful at. Moreover, a super trucker who saw his employer as basically exploitative, as he would have to if embracing unionization, would be forced to draw the unhappy conclusion that his very fervor had been a measure of his foolishness, that he had been "made a chump."

The few super truckers I have known to seek union trucking jobs either were greatly pressured by their families or underwent a dramatic change in their ideas about what is possible in work.[4] Among those not pressured by their families, the decision was precipitated by the owner's lack of commitment to the super trucker's values. If the owner rejects the super trucker's orientation to work, a super trucker may find it impossible or unreasonable to sustain belief in the worth of his commitment. In either case, the decision to seek union employment marks a defeat of sorts for the super trucker. If his family has pressured him, he goes unwillingly and not wholly divested of his notion that work can provide more than extrinsic satisfactions. In the face of a clash with the owner's values, though he goes of his own accord it is only after work has lost meaning even beyond extrinsic rewards; this bitter conclusion marks the destruction of his once-fulfilling self-image and leaves in its place a notion of work as little more than bondage and of himself as little more than a bonded toiler.

> *Pat:* It was clear to me that [the owner] didn't appreciate what I was doing. All they want to do is make the most money they can. So I finally decided that if I was going to get fucked around, I may as well get a union job and make them pay the max for fucking me.

At the other end of the continuum from the super trucker is the worker, who views trucking as little more than a means of earning money. The worker's self-image is that of a blue-collar employee and could be rooted in a host of other jobs. Like the super trucker, the worker does not attempt to strike an even balance between his work and nonwork life. He wants to spend as much time as possible with his family or at his favorite pursuits while still maintaining a satisfactory income.

The worker assesses the equipment he operates only in utilitarian terms: Does it keep his earning potential high (e.g., low weight when empty)? Is it comfortable? The prestige bestowed by equipment is lost on the worker. He is unlikely to customize the truck he drives, and he ridicules others for spending their time and money doing so. Likewise, he spends little time at the wash rack, and in return owners often assign him some of the least attractive trucks. While workers in the three companies in this book typically want to do work "the right way," they were more inclined than other drivers to say, "As long as the man [owner] pays me, I'll do it any stupid way he wants it done." Thus, the worker is more likely than other truck drivers to accept the loss of intrinsic satisfactions, as long as the level of extrinsic rewards is satisfactory.

Workers constituted about 15 percent of the drivers at the three companies and usually had more than ten years of experience as drivers. I have also encountered neophytes who exhibit a worker orientation, but they tend to leave trucking, or at least its competitive sector. Most workers, therefore, are drivers who once had another orientation to their work. Over a period of time, these men have found that they are no longer able to enjoy the ego satisfactions they once found in trucking, or that these satisfactions are outweighed by the personal costs of trucking or by their resentment of exploitation by the owner.

> *Milt:* I used to really be into trucking. I loved it. I cared a lot about what sort of truck I drove, I fixed it all up, you know, ten thousand lights and plenty of chrome. I got off as much as anyone when I was cruising down the boulevard in a nice truck. Then [my ex-employer] screwed me, and that changed things. I just stopped caring; the thrill was gone. When it comes down to it, you don't own the truck, and all the owners really care about is money. They don't really give a damn about you. I got into other things. I've been driving twelve years, I'm thirty-six years old, and I want to do other things. I'm getting tired of this business; it's too much work. I'd like to get into something where I could lead a more normal life or work for myself.

Workers generally are supportive of unions. The one exception at SandHaul was unhappy with the Teamsters' Union and thought that deregulation eliminated much of the security once found in union jobs. When the worker sees union drivers on the road, he may well agree with the super trucker's assessment of them, but since he experiences few of the joys of the super trucker, he is likely to view himself as worse off than the union driver. "Sure," the worker may say, "union jobs don't look like they're any fun, but neither is this job, and at least those guys get screwed less." The worker, then, usually defines the relationship between the owner and drivers as exploitive on the part of the owner and sees unionization as a reasonable alternative. This advocacy is all the stronger if the worker has previously held a union job.

The third role, that of trucker, applied to the remaining 60–70 percent of those working at the three companies. The role is more broadly drawn than that of super trucker or worker, and truckers range in their orientations from those who are more like workers to those who are more like super truckers. The trucker is attracted to the mythic images of trucking and the nature of the work but also wants to be with his family or to enjoy other personal off-duty relations and activities. As a consequence of his split allegiances, the trucker tries to strike a relatively even balance between work and nonwork life. Much like the super trucker, he derives ego satisfaction from trucking, but, like the worker, he has nonwork interests and obligations that impinge significantly on his work commitment. To be the trucker he wants to be requires a commitment that he is unwilling or unable to make.

Equipment is important to the trucker in both utilitarian and ego-enhancing terms. The ego satisfactions of equipment are much more important to the trucker than to the worker, and somewhat less important than for the super trucker. He keeps his truck clean and is given to customizing it, but he berates the super trucker's fanaticism while condemning the worker's lack of concern.

The trucker is engaged in a sort of war with his family; unlike the cases of super truckers and workers, he and his family seem to have no clear deal regarding the apportionment of work and nonwork time. The super trucker's family has reconciled itself to his obvious work commitment, and the worker's family sees that he is doing all he can to be with them. The trucker's family, however, sees someone who wants or acknowledges a duty to spend as much time as possible with them, but whose notion differs from theirs over what is possible. Given trucking's heavy demands on its employees' time, what the trucker sees as a minimum work commitment his family is likely to see as an over-commitment.

> *Floyd:* She wants me to put in as little time as possible, but I want my truck to look nice and that takes time. I like to stop on the road with the guys, but she thinks that is screwing around. I dig my family, but I don't want to have a job where I just put in my time and that's that.

Compounding the conflict between truckers and their families is the fact that often the worktime argued about is time spent in non-income-producing activities such as enhancing a truck or socializing with other drivers. For example, to enjoy full acceptance by co-workers, AgriHaul drivers with a common destination had to wait for one another to load so that they could convoy. This strategy was arranged at the expense of time that ultimately could be spent at home. It was common to hear these

AgriHaul drivers say, "If my wife knew why I'm going to be late getting home, she'd give me hell."

A common lament among truckers is that they cannot explain to their spouses what it is about their work that makes them willing to sacrifice family time for work time. Where fun is a feeble explanation for "excess" time spent at work, the desire to live out a mythic character that is the opposite of a family man is no explanation at all. The trucker, therefore, is likely to cast the deals he negotiates with his family in terms of self-sacrifice and to hold his family at least partly responsible for preventing him from being the trucker he would like to be. To the degree he is inclined in the direction of super trucker, his family stands in the way. Given this opposition of interests, it seems likely that the more the trucker is motivated by allegiance to his family rather than attraction to it, the more he is likely to blame his family, as opposed to the owner or industry, for dissatisfactions he experiences.

Aside from the roles of husband, father, and provider, it is worth considering the trucker as a member both of the wider culture and of a class. To the degree he is less committed to the occupation than is the super trucker, the more he is in conformity with our culture's notions about the worth of blue-collar work. Generally, blue-collar work lacks the honor sufficient to explain ardent devotion. Except for those truckers who would be super truckers were it not for their family's resistance, truckers are slightly embarrassed by the super trucker's rabid commitment. Even though most of them share the super trucker's basic orientation toward the occupation, they have some difficulty in justifying his monomania because they also have bought into norms that denigrate their work. This is quite different from the experience of elite professionals; for example, university professors who make an obvious commitment to their families or nonwork activities at the expense of academic pursuits are the ones likely to be denigrated by colleagues, and to worry about acting in an inappropriate manner.

Finally, the trucker, in an expression of class awareness, does not want to be "made a chump" by the owner. What constitutes being made a chump varies according to the perspectives of driver roles: such terms are rare in the mouths of super truckers but something of a leitmotif for the worker. For the trucker, determining when one has been made a chump is not so simple. On one hand, the trucker derives considerable enjoyment from intrinsic satisfactions, and he dreams the mythic occupational dreams. On the other hand, he sees employers as at least somewhat exploitive. With no clear calculus for measuring exploitation, it is usually determined by a fluid norm worked out in conjunction with fellow drivers in general and co-truckers, in particular. For example, truckers and workers commonly admonish one another to "remember who owns this truck." The use of this admonition is one means of working out a definition of exploitation; a driver so admonished is being told that he is overdoing his unpaid efforts at enhancing his truck. From the trucker's point of view, the super trucker, in putting too much of his own time and money into his truck, at some point begins to look like a chump.

Truckers fall between super truckers and workers in their assessments of unions and unionization. They express neither the super trucker's rejection nor the worker's easy endorsement of the idea of unionizing or taking a union job. Truckers themselves vary in this orientation, as some are workerlike while others are super-trucker-like. In the main, truckers have some recognition and resentment of exploitation by the owner but are reluctant to forgo the work and ego pleasures that attracted them to trucking and that continue to occupy a central and satisfying place in their self-conceptions. This orientation is obvious in the decision by almost all truckers who quit SandHaul to seek jobs at companies that offered intrinsic rewards at least equal to what SandHaul offered before it changed in the ways that led to their departures. For example, three SandHaul truckers went to companies that operated beautifully outfitted Peterbilt tankers that drivers could customize.

To take a union job is a mixed blessing for a trucker. He can feel satisfied in knowing that he is not being overly exploited and is doing right by his family. A union job also may increase his nonwork time and allow him to further indulge in pleasurable nonwork activities. And a union job signifies that he has the credentials necessary to obtain such employment. But, a union job takes on the tones of self-sacrifice because it means forgoing some of the pleasures of the work and the satisfaction of being a somebody. While defining employer-employee relations in the conflictual terms implied by unionization is easier for the trucker than the super-trucker, abandoning his occupational dreams is almost as difficult.

For the trucker, an attempt to unionize the company where he works holds the potential for the same mixed blessings as taking a union job, plus worries about being fired, blacklisted, or ill-treated, having the company go out of business, or making an enemy of an owner who is something of a friend. The trucker is likely to see the risks of successful unionization as outweighing the rewards.

The example of an ex-SandHaul trucker, Joe, is informative: Joe is twenty-seven years old, claims to be happily married, has two children, and is a home owner. When he became dissatisfied with SandHaul and began to search for another job, he refused to apply for one of the jobs advertised by a large union trucking company, even though it was near his home and continued to prosper after deregulation. Joe has an excellent driving record, is in good health, and could be expected to qualify for a job with this company. He told me he did not want to work there because of the equipment they use—typically a fairly new truck, but of low-status make and model and totally utilitarian in specification—the boredom he suspects in their routinized runs, and the fetters he associates with a large bureaucratized company. He has sympathy for the union and would enjoy the union-level extrinsic rewards, but he saw working for this company as the end of much that he enjoys about trucking and of any hope for being the trucker he would like to be.

> *Joe:* I'm too young to pack it in for a job like that. To me, working at [the union company] is like giving up being a trucker.

Joe's orientation is clear in the choices to which he gave serious consideration. He applied for work at two companies that offer somewhat lower extrinsic but greater intrinsic rewards than his job at SandHaul. The offer he accepted from one of them resulted in the equivalent of an hourly pay cut of approximately seventy-five cents (a gross of about two thousand dollars less a year) and the loss of about fifteen hundred dollars a year in profit sharing for the first five years. In addition, he had to commute thirty miles each way (in comparison, the union company was about seven miles from his home). On the other hand, Joe was delighted to be driving superior and excellently maintained equipment that he could customize at the owner's expense; to be hauling high-status loads on a greater variety of runs; and to work for an owner who was nearly invisible, which gave drivers high autonomy. In effect, Joe moved to a company that offered the competitive sector contract in near ideal form.

Joe convinced his wife that his job change was in order because of his unhappiness with SandHaul's owner. He convinced her that it was reasonable by asserting his income would be close to what it was at SandHaul, pointing to a shift rotation that would regularly give him three consecutive days off, and claiming that the new job would be less physically wearing. Several times Joe attempted to convey to his wife his desire for greater intrinsic satisfactions and ego rewards, but he felt that she did not understand what he was saying or did not think it compelling, so he dropped this line of reasoning.

In choosing to be super truckers, workers, or truckers, drivers, like dance musicians, deal with significant questions regarding their sense of self. The decision to forgo valued intrinsic rewards and seek work at a large union company usually required the super trucker and trucker to redefine themselves as drivers and as men. No longer could they be somebody special, kings of the road (at least not in the eyes of peers and other informed audience members who know the signs that indicate the super trucker or trucker). Hauling probably would be more mundane, and they would just be another face.

> *Harley:* If a guy just wants to drive and collect his check, and he doesn't give a fuck about what he drives or what his truck looks like or doing the same thing over and over, then a union job makes a lot of sense. For a guy that doesn't give a shit, that's what he should be doing.

Where effort once had been something they willingly gave, something that attested to their skill and was honored by the employer, it would now be something specified in a formal contract and extracted by the employer. Nor was the promise of easier work necessarily appealing.

> *Burt:* Guys see the the bullshit those union guys pull [loafing and enforcing work rules he thought absurd] and they don't respect it.

It makes a mockery of work, it's an insult to guys who give a damn.

And working for a large company and under a formal contract threatened to end the chance to have a personal relationship with an owner wherein the driver could negotiate for individual advantage, man-to-man, by trading on his high effort, commitment, and skills (most likely what I call "job skills").

In short, the super trucker and trucker felt that a union job was more for a worker than for the last American cowboy. As with dance musicians, union jobs were accorded relatively high prestige because they paid more, had better hours and more job protections, were more difficult to obtain, and consequently were seen as something of an indicator of skill. But, while those at union companies were thought to be skilled drivers with easy jobs, their lesser efforts were not respected and they were thought to have given up what makes trucking special. To hold a union job is, for most of these truck drivers, both a victory and a defeat: as providers, consumers, and family men, they would be happy at the increase in extrinsic rewards and job protections; as truck drivers, they believe they would lose many of the work's pleasures, not least the sense of being someone special. Most of these truck drivers respect union jobs, some desire a union job, but none dreams of a union job. Their dreams are of high intrinsic rewards, and the successful pursuit of a union job is more often seen not as a dream realized so much as a dream surrendered—a surrender to bureaucracy, to sameness, to work without meaning.

To this day, whenever I spend time with truck drivers—always employees of small firms, or owner-operators who once worked for such companies—I am inevitably asked, "Do you miss it?" We both understand that this simple question is full of unspoken meaning.

What is there to miss about trucking? Not the long weeks, the shifts that are an insult to human biological cycles, the pain of trying to maintain domestic relationships despite spending so much time away from home. Not the boredom of interstate highways that sometimes seem to vary only in the shrubbery framing the ubiquitous Burger King, McDonald's, Day's Inn, and

Union 76 truck stop. Not choking on a cloud of greasy, stinking meat-meal I have knocked loose from the inside of my trailer so that it will unload. Not slaughterhouses, smelling of fish, or being green-colored after handling alfalfa. Not fighting with fellow night-shift drivers at SandHaul, constantly trying to stay a step ahead of other AgriHaul drivers, and conning or ingratiating myself with the people who load and unload my truck so that I can get on the road sooner. Even when I was paid by the hour I hated the stop-and-go crawl of traffic jams and the constant clutching and shifting they require; to be in a traffic jam while working for a percentage of the gross compounds the aggravation. Certainly, I do not miss the hundreds of other irritations caused by incompetent dispatchers; cutthroat competitors; machinery that malfunctions during loading and unloading; clients who place orders they have no space for; underpowered, hard-riding trucks devoid of creature comforts; unsafe equipment; crossing Los Angeles in the glare, heat, and smog of a typical August day; breakdowns when I am being paid other than hourly wages; getting lost; being the most convenient target for blame whenever deliveries go wrong; inspectors at border stations who act like I am smuggling contraband rather than hauling food for their fellow citizens; motorists like the two who forced me off freeways to reach desired off-ramps (one drove a station wagon filled with children and swerved so abruptly that I almost overturned my trailer to avoid a collision); loading and delivery sites where maneuvering a truck is almost impossible, where the air is filled with dust and noise, where poor scheduling causes long delays; police who, as embodiments of Merton's (1938) ritualists, issue citations for infractions that threaten no one. At times, most drivers would argue that this list is infinite.

When a driver asks if I miss trucking he is in part asking me about these sorts of frustrations and ennui. But this is superficial, the part of the question that we chuckle over. There is little interest here in a balanced weighing of trucking's pluses and minuses. More to the point are valuations of autonomy, travel, working outdoors, and work that, in being relatively whole, makes sense. Do I miss these features of the work? The question runs deeper still. I am being asked about pleasures: of operating huge machinery, of danger, of public performances that are admired or at least feared, of the outlawlike perspective rooted in both the constant encounters with government authorities and a life-style considered somewhat deviant, of being able to fulfill notions of traditional masculinity and perform iconic roles, of being a somebody. And at its very heart, the question asks about those times when all these features of the work coalesce to produce a state of utter satisfaction, sometimes even magic, that I will try to convey by describing an ideal haul.

Slowly, I roll off the scale with a weight slip that says everything is okay—the truck is just under eighty thousand pounds and I correctly distributed the load so that all my axles are within legal limits. With loading done, I give final consideration to traffic conditions, distance, weather, and the time of day before choosing a route I enjoy. Today I'm not in an aggravating race against a snake intent on beating me to the unloading site—which is not to say that no one else is headed there.

I like my rig; when I'm stuck driving a bucket of bolts my work is boring, just something I do for money. The truck is clean and running well, I'm not filthy or drop-dead tired, and I know sooner or later I'll be on open road. I adjust my air-seat so that it has a lot of bounce without easily bottoming out.

With a load on, the truck settles down. I can feel the weight behind me, and it is both friend and foe; it improves the truck's grip on the road but looms over my shoulder waiting for a chance to seize control. First gear, second gear, third and fourth, shift into high range and start the pattern over again, this time splitting each gear. One measure of the old days is that we used to do this with two transmissions. As a neophyte, I often could not remember what gear I was in. When I scaled my first hill, I was unable to downshift the lower gears accurately and quickly enough to keep the truck moving. A team of over-the-road drivers laughed as they passed, and I wanted to disappear. Now, my shifts are smooth as butter, the truck doesn't lurch, the gears don't grind.

I head into a curve and begin gently turning an instant sooner than would the driver of a car to get control of the truck's weight. I feel the lean of my tanker, of my thirteen-foot, six-inch high reefer, of my narrow-at-the-bottom and fat-at-the-top set of hoppers. With doubles, the pull trailer sometimes acts like a tail wagging the dog, especially if oversteered.

I look out over the hood, over the shining, hard-as-glass

paint, glad that I washed it to its present shine. The Peterbilt conventional is a work of art. Somehow its boxy hood and precise lines make it even more masculine than its handsome corporate sibling, the Kenworth.

Today, I go over the Ridge Route—truckers call it "the hill"— the mountainous section of Interstate 5 between Los Angeles and Bakersfield. Both the north and south sides have long, steep grades that test a truck's brakes; the north side's continuous five-mile grade is particularly dangerous. The first time I crossed it I drove a 1957 Kenworth, pulling a set of homemade trailers, and weighing over 76,000 pounds. Going up the south side, I was afraid of embarrassing myself by missing low-gear shifts and stopping the truck in its tracks. At the top I felt not relief, but terror. A veteran driver had coached me on how to get to the bottom without igniting my brakes, but I knew if I got it wrong I could die a scary death. Old-timers claimed that if a truck lost its brakes early and didn't flip on a turn, it would reach such high speeds that the front end would begin bouncing off the pavement. I had no reason to doubt their stories. My descent, though uneventful, is forever etched in memory, and I have come down that grade many times since. Today, between my "jake brake"—an engine retarder that helps slow the truck— and plenty of experience, I enjoy coming off the hill. As I descend to the crackling, assuring rumble of my jake, I do not forget how quickly a loaded rig on a grade this steep can get away from its driver; instead I take pleasure in facing and defeating that possibility.

My fear as a beginning driver did not end with crossing "the hill." Driving in ice and snow was frightening at first; under certain conditions it still provokes fear. I know an old-timer paralyzed from the waist down after losing control and crashing while coming off an icy mountain in a truck I once drove and on a road I used. On US 99 I go through an underpass and recall the wreckage of a cabover that slammed into it after the driver fell asleep. Fog, too, can induce fear. In the San Joaquin Valley it gets so thick that just seeing the painted lines that divide lanes becomes difficult. Before northbound drivers descend from the mountains into this fog, many more than normal stop and linger at the brake check area, where the tension is palpable.

I doubt there is a driver who has not come close to disaster at least once, and driving is likely to stir memories of these occasions. I recall when my double-trailered truck was fitted for the first time with radial tires and I assumed they provided good traction in the rain until I began sliding at the bottom of a steep, curving hill. I congratulated myself for not panicking and for having the skills to keep the trailers in line, but the more profound feeling was that I had made a serious mistake and that luck, not just skill, kept me from crashing. I think about the rookie blunder I made at PetroHaul that put me into a skid and almost upended my tanker, which was nearly full of gasoline. Time stood still. I imagined the gasoline exploding. Again, I took comfort in possessing enough skill to get myself out of harm's way, but I was frightened by my error and aware that luck had intervened. Once when I was loading next to a huge mound of sand, a bulldozer set off an avalanche that almost buried me under my truck. One of my worst memories is of turning a truck around in front of my house so that I could wash it and having the steering column snap; the steering wheel spun freely in my hands, unattached to the front wheels of the Peterbilt I regularly drove over the mountains between Santa Cruz and San Jose.

The point here is not to dramatize the act of truck driving but to show the constant threat of injury or death from driving accidents, and even from mishaps while loading or unloading. And drivers remain constant in their awareness of these dangers. For example, I became annoyed when my wife warned me to be careful each time I left for work. I worried that by speaking out loud about my work's dangers she might jinx me. One day she forgot or chose not to offer her warning. As I went out the door, I became uneasy thinking that her breaking a routine that so far had been successful might be a worse jinx than the one I originally feared. When I got to work, I told other drivers about this incident and was surprised to hear a number of them more or less repeat my story. All agreed I did the right thing by asking my wife to resume her warnings. In retrospect, such suspicions seem to reflect the understanding drivers have that, while on any given day they are not likely to be hurt, serious harm and even death are possibilities and not always under their control.

I check out other rigs and see many of their drivers doing the same. The nicer my truck, the more likely I will tap into a camaraderie with drivers of other superior trucks. We might only exchange nods or slight hand waves, the most likely scenarios, or we might openly acknowledge each other on our CB radios; either way, the mutual appreciation is clear. It is as if a stage actor could deliver a winning performance while sitting in the audience and watching himself perform.

Maybe I enter into the omnipresent banter on my CB, maybe I listen, maybe I turn it off. Some of my favorite times occur while running with a friend in another truck. Often we find a CB station not in use, make it ours, and engage in gossip about work, in talk of home life, in one-upmanship at put-downs, and perhaps we even act out satirical roles in improvised bits of melodrama. Or I might ignore the CB and instead put a tape of favored music into the "jukebox."

Kids always check out my truck, often begging to hear the horn. Plenty of adults do the same. I always enjoy the kids. At times the adults are annoying, at times fun, and sometimes flirtatious.

Early and late in the day, armies of motorists pass by on their way to and from work, some dressed in business suits and some dressed like me, and they appear locked into boring and overly domesticated routines with few prospects for adventure, for even the chance of something different. I feel a tad smug. In more than a few of their faces and gestures I detect the fantasy that friends and acquaintances have so often confessed: to do my job, to be king of the road, to head down a highway toward the unknown and away from their lives.

I grin to myself, recalling the time George and I, while passing through Los Angeles in his beautiful Kenworth with its gleaming Great Dane trailer, encountered that fool in a convertible Porsche. Apparently the fool imagined himself a man of the road, what with his manner, his cowboy hat and driving gloves—the latter we derisively refer to as "hand shoes." As a man of the road, he seemed to think he had something in common with us. He drove beside us overdoing his thumbs-up signing and then gunned his car ahead of us, charged into our lane, and continued his waving and fist-pumping. At that point his cowboy hat blew off and landed on the shoulder of the road. George carefully aimed the truck and went out of his way to flatten the hat, which sent us both into gut-wrenching laughter.

That this urban cowboy was accompanied by a female companion made the moment that much more delicious.

It's a sea of assholes and incompetents out here. How many times in a day, week, year do I save their damn lives, save them from themselves? It's even worse when it rains. I swear rain brings out people who have not driven in ten years, people who have never driven, people with a death wish. In California, I exercise particular caution for at least an hour after 1:30 A.M., the time bars start kicking out their customers. Twice I've seen drunks going the wrong direction on a freeway. Almost every trucker I know who hauls the mostly two-lane route from California to Alberta has been hit by a drunk.

Usually it is my defensive driving that keeps motorists from killing themselves, and I almost always know they are going to screw up before they actually do it. Sometimes things just happen, and occasionally I've been downright inspired. Today I think about the motorcyclist who accelerated to get in front of me and then drove slower than my fifty-nine miles an hour, a common experience. Do they do it out of spite or ignorance? I felt like tailgating him to retaliate, but then I considered the time I blew a tire while riding a motorcycle and how badly that would have turned out if someone had been right behind me. I backed off, and an instant later the motorcycle's engine or transmission seized up and the bike went into a wild skid. I braked, though not fully, checked my mirrors, turned on my four-way blinkers, and started weaving so that no one could pass me and run into him. Eventually, he made it safely off the road with me shielding him, but I doubt he has any idea of my role in that outcome. More often I quietly avoid trouble. Those errant motorists, if aware of my truck, probably think pure luck kept them from colliding with it. I have been a fool behind the wheel, too, but amid the ineptness of these people those occasions are easy to forget.

A recent head-on collision between a car and truck in the desert was said to be the work of a motorist bent on suicide. The trucker was okay and that was all we cared about.

I pull into a state weigh station, my logbook on my lap. I'm good at this now. If they signal me in for an inspection, I'll have it updated by the time I stop. If they don't pull me in, I'll have more latitude in filling it out to make my work hours appear legal. I don't feel guilty. When they determined these limitations on hours, were drivers driving the comfortable rigs and good roads we have now? And don't human biorhythms matter? PetroHaul's fifteen-hour shifts are perfectly legal and totally insane for the safe hauling of gasoline. Many times over the years, I have been dangerously tired despite being within legal limits on my work hours, or absolutely alert though in violation of the law. If they were really serious about limiting driving time, it could be done. The current system keeps shipping prices down and profit and drivers' incomes up, and they can blame drivers for infractions and wrecks. No, I don't feel guilty; I feel sharp.

Take a break every four hours? Ha! That's for men who can't stay in the saddle, the truck stop cowboys, the neophytes.

Driving begins to get especially pleasurable in the evening. Assuming sunshine, the world takes on a golden glow that is both relaxing and inspiring. And the evening promises night, a time of possibilities, a frontier. At night in my world, prostitutes and drug dealers begin working in earnest at favored truck stops, homosexuals at the "pickle parks," exhibitionists on the highways. Young people looking for a good time are out and about, and so are thieves and muggers, the bane of gasoline haulers. Talk on the CB becomes more sexual, players emerge as the domesticated public recedes, neon replaces sun. Out here, anything could happen.

Devil's wind blowing across the Mojave, stars like swarms of fireflies, Hendrix or Hank Williams on my jukebox; the muscular pull of a Caterpillar or big Cummins engine; blood-red moon the size of Jupiter; spooky old woman who hitchhikes across the desert at night; humid Valley air dark and heavy with the scents of cattle, sheep, and agriculture; the couple that slowly passes by, her dress up, his hand between her legs (Did she look at me and smile?); the glow of distant towns; truck stops with rigs everywhere, heat radiating off deep-throated engines, the smell of diesel, reefers cycling, and a thousand amber lights punctuated with reds and blues.

Rolling down the highway, the truck's bouncing and lurching turns graceful and I get into a rhythm that melds me, this machinery, the road, the jukebox, approving audiences, trucker lore, memories, and my ability to cheat death. On a desolate stretch of America, my hands on eighty thousand pounds moving sixty miles an hour, at one with my brothers in passing rigs, I think about all the sleeping people in those little towns and urban sprawls I pass by, straight, square people whose lives I sometimes envy for their routine, predictability, and connectedness with others. Now, locked in this rhythm and enveloped in night, I do not envy them at all. I laugh at them, at their world. I am not lonely. I feel free, masterful, totally alive, and absolutely content. I am high on the magic, and I am sorry for the squares who will never know it.

Many studies of work begin by assuming a labor contract that pits an employer who wants to get the most work for the least pay against workers primarily motivated by the desire to work the least for the greatest pay. Workers are said to assert their interests largely through withholding effort, restricting or degrading production, or resisting modernization. Employers seek advantage through coercion, charismatic leadership, or, in the typical large modern enterprise, sophisticated manipulations of the labor process. If, in these studies, workers are granted an active role beyond resistance to exploitation, it typically is limited to the pursuit of short-term economic advantages, a strategy that in turn is said to reproduce the conditions under which they are exploited.

Examinations of work that depict workers as primarily motivated by instrumental and fundamentally economic considerations often confuse employees' situations with qualities in the employee. For example, Blauner (1964) states:

> The average manual worker and many white collar employees may be satisfied with fairly steady jobs which are largely instrumental and non-involving, because they have not the need for responsibility and self-expression in work. . . . For those with little education, the need for sheer activity and for association are more important than control, challenge and creativity. (29)

Marxist and humanist theorists, while rejecting this view of workers, posit a worker whose natural creativity and need for self-expression is stunted or crushed by the structures of capitalism (Knights 1990).

In studies that look to the labor process to explain workplace behavior, workers are usually seen as enmeshed in a highly deterministic structure that is both the culmination of the history of capitalist production and the creation of local employers. In this view, workers typically are assumed to care mostly about making money to enhance nonwork life—whether through nature, socialization, or macro-economic forces—and manipulated by employers who, in modern work settings, nurture and take advantage of this orientation. While Burawoy's (1979) ethnography looked beyond a simple economic orientation and into social and psychological needs that motivated workers to produce at a high rate, he neither fully explored these needs nor convincingly moved beyond economic motivations (Finlay 1988, 28).

But the deep meanings work holds for nonunion drivers and the processes by which these meanings are constructed, maintained, and changed, show that explanations that rest on economic understandings of human action are not enough to account for their workplace behavior and choices. Certainly, the piecework systems at AgriHaul and SandHaul were compelling forces in shaping this behavior, but they do not explain the essentially similar behavior of PetroHaul's drivers, who were paid by the hour. The greatest difference between piecework and hourly pay was not in the amount of effort each elicited, but in the greater conflict piecework caused between drivers.

An alternative explanation is that drivers use work to construct a sense of self that satisfactorily locates them in the social world. They are motivated by far more than economic concerns, valuing intrinsic rewards such as autonomy, variety, and excellent equipment for their own pleasures, and because these rewards enhanced self-esteem and lent meaning to life.

Contrary to popular depictions of self-esteem as a psychological state produced for and within one's self, the concept is used here in its sociological sense. That is, self-esteem is produced in interactions with others and takes into account cultural prescriptions for human conduct. In the case of these truckers, self-esteem is the sum of a driver's understanding of feedback regarding his on-the-job performances from co-workers, owners, managers, and the different audiences that lie beyond the company gate. In interpreting and negotiating this feedback, traditional definitions of masculinity play a central role.

The obvious basis for occupational esteem is mastery of the

occupation's work skills and control over their application. Drivers, however, face a serious problem in grounding esteem in their work skills: most of these skills are not readily observable by fellow drivers. Consequently, drivers turn to production as a direct measure of skill. Drivers measure one another by their ability to sustain effort, especially in situations that call for heroic effort. Production through high effort proves a suitable basis for positive esteem for several reasons: it is observable, can be quantified, requires some skills, is consistent with the employer's definitions of skill, and incorporates traditional definitions of masculinity. Further, effort implies the worthiness of labor. If work worth doing is work worthy of high effort, then perhaps work done with high effort is work worth doing. Gender prescriptions for traditional manhood support the use of effort as a measure of worth by positively valuing the capacity for high, sustained, and effective physical effort. At the onset of this exploration, I asked, Why do drivers work as hard as they do, and how do they make sense out of their efforts? One question largely answers the other. Drivers work as hard as they do because effort is a way of making sense of their work (and of themselves). Effort was so compelling that there were virtually no norms among drivers restricting it.[5] And one of the most common frustrations among drivers, as for the wire assemblers and mechanics studied by Juravich (1985), was with management ineptitude that caused drivers to work inefficiently.

However, the expenditure of effort is problematic for employees. High effort extracted by the tip of a whip spoils the equations between effort and work's worthiness and between effort and masculinity. To be forced into high effort, especially at one's own expense and another's profit, is ignoble, dishonorable, and unmanly. Workers in general appear most reluctant to expend effort after it has been made dishonorable.

Owners of competitive sector trucking companies have a difficult time resorting to the whip as a means of extracting effort, although they have the power to make rules, set quotas, and fire and suspend violators. The owners at PetroHaul, SandHaul, and AgriHaul, however, understood there were better ways to insure high effort: recognizing the desire of drivers to work as if they were the owners of the trucks they drove—that is, recognizing the desire to control the application of their skills as if they were self-employed; assisting drivers in ways that allowed them successfully to act out prescriptions for manhood and trucker myths; and honoring drivers' interpretations of skill. Through these, agreements, the dishonor inherent in employment was mitigated, and high effort became possible.[6]

As a point of comparison, it seems to me that the machinists described by Burawoy (1979) worked hard not only for extra income or to relieve boredom but because "making out" made effort honorable. The term "making out" implies honor in the context of employment: the machinists took advantage of the company rather than the reverse. In turn, effort cleansed of its dishonor makes work seem worthy. And engagement in worthy work enhances life. At the least, these machinists had the satisfaction of knowing that they were (traditional and probably effective working-class) men.

Finlay (1988, 94–106) reported a similar situation. In order to extract a high level of effort from West Coast longshoremen, employers made deals in which effort was rewarded by shorter working hours. For example, if a crew of ten was sent to unload cargo, five might work while the other five relaxed for two to four hours. After the agreed-upon time had elapsed, the two groups of five would switch places. To make this deal work, the crew of five had to be able to do the work of ten, and thus the five worked very hard indeed.

The most obvious element of this deal is that workers exchanged effort for "free" time. That is, the deal makes sense because it allows longshoremen to get out of work. But there is another way to see this deal: it is also a way to get *into* work. By making employers give up something—money for time spent loafing—longshoremen were able honorably to expend the sort of effort that enhanced the worthiness of their work, attested to their masculinity, and thus added to their own valuation of themselves.

The cases of the machinists and longshoremen suggest that a key to making effort honorable is the opportunity for workers to see high effort as a way of taking advantage of their employers. This seemed to be the case at SandHaul and AgriHaul, where working fast had the effect of raising drivers' hourly pay *rates.* High effort at SandHaul and AgriHaul could be seen as honorable because owners were given less time for the same amount of pay. But seizing advantage is not a necessary condition for mitigating employment's dishonor. At PetroHaul, high effort meant doing more work for the same amount of pay, or doing the same amount of work for less pay, yet drivers worked diligently. The behavior of PetroHaul drivers, given the absence of notable coercion, attests to the high value drivers placed on occupational esteem, traditional masculinity, and the opportunity to be a somebody; to the ability of the informal, competitive sector contract to counter employment's ignobility, thereby allowing drivers to use high effort as an indicator of skill and masculinity; and to the joys of trucking when performed with excellent equipment, some variety, and reasonable autonomy.

Also making employment less dishonorable was the owners' and drivers' habit of blaming the market for much of the exploitation that could not be masked.[7] It was easier for drivers to acquiesce to owners' requests or demands if they could see them not as personal impositions but as necessary responses to market conditions.

Company owners offered the informal contract I have specified not simply because they were insightful and manipulative but also because drivers actively sought the rewards found in the contract. Most drivers accept work as a given. Why not seek work that is enjoyable, that they have control over, that attests to their masculinity and worth, and lets them see themselves as folk heroes? When the union organizer comes around trying to sign up these drivers, he is correct in assuming that their fears must be addressed: fear of the unknown, of losing their jobs, of being discriminated against by the owner should he find out they signed a petition. The organizer is also correct in touting the worth of workers' rights; fewer work hours; and more money, insurance, and vacations. But the union organizer's pitch is likely to fail if it remains at this level and ignores other fears, the ones drivers are unlikely to talk about—of no longer being able to control their work, operate excellent equipment that they can personalize, work as if effort was sensible and honorable rather than something employers extract from unwilling employees as spelled out in a formal contract, work as if the individual driver is more than just another face, negotiate man-to-man with an owner who respects effort, access the materials and conditions necessary to construct themselves as the men they want to be, and know the magic in trucking.[8] Though work in these small nonunion companies is very demanding, the super trucker and trucker have much to think about before answering the question Would I be better off with a union job?

I graduated from high school and went to work as a telephone installer. Supervisors rarely observed us while we worked and only occasionally reviewed our installations; mainly they watched to see if we completed our assignments. This situation seemed ripe for exploitation, and, from my schoolboy point of view, exploiting it seemed the honorable thing to do. I wanted to do my work well—it was work done with my hands and requiring some skill, thus it was honorable—but why overdo it? I soon learned that as long as I thought and acted this way, my workmates and foreman saw me as a boy.

Later, after a stint in the army, I went to work at a warehouse that paid me at the end of each day. Most of my workmates were recently released convicts living in a nearby halfway house. Our supervisor was a teenager and a tyrant. We did our best to loaf, drag our feet, interfere with production, break rules for the sake of it, and insult the kid. As in high school, we congratulated and respected one another for this behavior.

I began trucking. As at the telephone company, there was little supervision. Again, I wanted to master the work. Again, why not stop at a coffee shop whenever I felt like it, take a noon nap, or run a few errands? True, I was not paid an hourly wage and lost money by loafing, but I was making more than enough and often did not care about getting every available load. Again, I was considered a boy.

Both the telephone and trucking companies presented me with an opportunity not available in school (or at the warehouse): to be a man. But it was not enough simply to show up each day. The deal was this: if I worked hard and effectively in these workplaces, which did not dishonor effort by acting as if it were in need of forceful extraction, I would be seen as possessing traditionally masculine qualities associated with both physical exertion, such as strength and stamina, and the mastery of my environment (if only to the extent of conquering whatever would interfere with my attempts at high production). Virtually everyone—owners, managers, and fellow workers—had this understanding, but it was communicated most effectively by my workmates. I also believe that at a less conscious level there was a similar inducement, one based in social class but still intertwined with gender: we are a class of men that, unlike the desk jockeys in suits, get things done; don't disgrace us. This orientation seemed to be embraced not only by my workmates but also by most of the foremen and trucking company owners, though less straightforwardly, because they shared our social class origins and had once done our work.

The trucking company offered even more in terms of self-identity. Here was the chance to embody, or at least appear to embody, qualities associated with some of this country's most treasured male icons: cowboys, frontiersmen, explorers, adventurers. Truck driving at these companies, though often boring and routine, provided sufficient danger, variety, spontaneity, travel, autonomy, solitude, associations with deviance, opportunities for individualism, and need for self-reliance for a driver to deliver a convincing performance both to his audiences and, often, to himself. That we operated in a frontier of sorts—night—and, symbolically, on horseback only served to underscore these iconic associations. And the magical experiences we found on the road confirmed for us that we were engaged in something special.

Drivers always ask me if I miss trucking. We talk—sometimes at length, sometimes briefly—and almost unfailingly reach the same conclusion: the attraction to driving, whether it's something to be applauded or cursed, runs deep. "Yeah, brother, I guess it's in the blood."

NOTES

Chapter 1

1. I modified the original paradox as formulated by Sennett and Cobb to include the issue of effort marking one "as having surrendered to those in authority."

2. Most issues of trade magazines serving the trucking industry (e.g., *Heavy Duty Trucking; Go West*) have articles, or at least advertisements, suggesting how to increase profits by restraining drivers from using too much fuel or prematurely wearing out the trucks they drive.

3. When I formulated this research, I had enough involvement with blue-collar work to believe that treatments of the subject usually paid inadequate attention to the actual experience of work. As an alternative, I wished to explore in depth how workers felt about their work and themselves as workers, and how these feelings shaped their work world. Thus, in addition to addressing the social structural elements of work and the rational constructions that inform workers' behavior, I wanted to delve into the realms of human conduct ruled by feelings and emotion. To accomplish these goals, I returned to trucking and adopted a complete membership role as defined by Adler and Adler (1987): "Rather than mere participatory involvement, complete-member-researchers (CMRs) immerse themselves fully in the group as 'natives.' They and their subjects relate to each other as status equals, dedicated to sharing in a common set of experiences, feelings, and goals. As a result, CMRs come the closest of all researchers to approximating the emotional stance of the people they study" (67). I use pseudonyms to identify the companies and people that appear in this book.

4. The exception was my brother, a driver at SandHaul. In 1977 I taught my brother to drive a heavy-duty diesel truck and later helped him get his first job. Eventually he joined SandHaul, where he worked until the mid-1980s. Between 1986 and 1988, he worked full- and part-

time for several trucking companies and a cement batching plant. In late 1988, he became a full-time firefighter but continues to drive trucks part-time. He also contemplates buying a truck and going into business for himself. While my brother served as my most trusted source of information at SandHaul and as a check on my perceptions and analytical notions, he was not my main source for understanding work at this company. We worked on different shifts, and I saw him only occasionally while on the job. Most of what I know of SandHaul came from my own experiences and my observations of and interactions with the drivers with whom I shared the night shift. For objections to covert research see Erikson (1967) and Gold (1958).

5. Kotarba (1977, 260) lists four advantages in using one's own experience in conducting research: experience is a first source of data; it provides a basis for comparison with the experiences of others; it generates points of inquiry; and it helps the researcher attain a more complex theoretical understanding of real events rather than settle for simplistic explanations of other people's behavior.

6. My reference at PetroHaul was a respected mechanic who worked at a nearby company and operated several of his own trucks. My Sand-Haul reference was my brother. Neither had the sort of relationship with company owners that would have helped me get hired while in an overt research role.

7. In the entire time I drove trucks, I worked with only two women who were employed as full-time drivers. One worked the day shift at SandHaul (I worked the night shift) and was fired after having an accident shortly after I was hired. The other worked for a competitor of one of my employers not featured in this study. I was able to talk with her only on the occasions we shared loading sites or destinations.

Chapter 2

1. Describing the industry is complicated, because deregulation, which was initiated shortly before I began working at PetroHaul and SandHaul, dramatically transformed large areas of trucking. Since I accrued most of my experience before deregulation, I describe the industry as it existed under those conditions and cite some differences brought about by the new rules. That the impact of deregulation was greatest after I ceased driving does not make this investigation irrelevant. In many cases, intrastate trucking has not been deregulated to the same extent as has interstate trucking; it is therefore still much like what I experienced and describe. Moreover, deregulation encouraged the founding and growth of companies more like the three in this study than the large unionized companies they replaced.

2. Beyond these major divisions are many subdivisions (most are organized around hauling specialties) that have their own rules and concerns. However, these subdivisions are not relevant here and will be ignored.

3. I believe drivers do not see differences in CDL qualifications as meaningful skill gradations, because the differences do not reflect significant variations in real-world occupational skills. Further, in order to attain additional CDL qualifications, veteran drivers need only pass written tests that are no more difficult than the basic CDL exams.

4. It is possible to pay truckers in a manner akin to factory piece-rate workers. Drivers could be paid per mile hauled, with a bonus for miles beyond a prescribed minimum, and this could be underpinned by a guaranteed hourly or daily wage.

Chapter 3

1. The hourly equivalents of the piecerates varied considerably, depending on the method of calculation. Drivers computed hourly equivalents by dividing a shift's gross income by the number of hours between their departure and return to the yard. In doing so, they ignored time spent in the yard waiting for or working on trucks, and they did not assume the existence of an overtime differential. Using the drivers' method, hourly pay ranged from approximately $8.50 to $13.50, depending on the haul and the driver's seniority. Drivers with more than twelve months' tenure were paid the top rate of 31 percent, which they believed averaged about $10 an hour. If unpaid working time (waiting in the yard for a truck, swapping trailers, servicing and washing trucks) is added to the calculation, hourly wages are considerably lower. For example, if a driver finished a $100 haul in ten hours, by his calculation he earned $10 an hour. If, in the course of his shift, the driver waited thirty minutes before getting a truck and spent seventy-five minutes exchanging trailers and inspecting, servicing, and washing the truck (these are normal times and activities), the hourly rate falls to $8.51. If an overtime differential is assumed, the rate of pay is further diminished: in the first example, hourly pay falls from $10 to $9.09; in the second example, from $8.51 to $7.34.

The only exception to being paid according to output was standing time, that is, time spent loading or unloading in excess of one hour. Drivers were paid $5 an hour for standing time, which they thought equal to about half the normal pay rate. I never saw a driver try to accumulate standing time, and drivers complained incessantly about these delays.

2. Some loads netted drivers more money, while others took less

time than loads that paid the same. In the second case, the effective rate of pay, though not net pay, was higher and thus more desirable.

3. I doubt that the reason I witnessed few instances was because drivers were hiding these attempts or intentions from one another or from me in particular. While in my presence and the presence of one another, drivers were not at all shy about engaging in the offense most likely to bring dismissal, stealing gasoline.

Chapter 4

1. Drivers earned approximately 125–235 percent of the 1980 median income of $19,243 for full-time employed males fifteen and older.

2. The presence of a competitive environment would lead one to suppose that rate cutting within companies was common as they went about underbidding one another and the railroad. However, it was rare for a company to cut a rate and announce that it had done so in order to keep a haul. Instead, hauls were lost to other companies that were said to have undercut the current rate. The owners of AgriHaul and SandHaul explained the loss of hauls by noting that current rates were often close to the margins of profit and thus the company would not agree to a lower rate. Occasionally, the owners announced that the customer had dissatisfactions beyond the price for services, such as undependable delivery scheduling. Most often, hauls that were lost were said by owners and drivers to have been stolen by fools who were pricing themselves out of business and made it hard on everyone else. Hauls won away from competitors almost always were explained by my employer's ability to deliver better service; owners virtually never admitted to undercutting a current rate to obtain hauls. And, with the exception of exempt commodities, this competition was conducted above the safety net of price regulation that put a limit on how much prices could be slashed.

3. The refusal to exploit opportunities to load slowly did not appear to be a consequence of drivers prefering other work activities such as driving. By loading slowly drivers could, through a snowball effect, get time for reading, napping, eating, and other leisure activities while still being paid.

4. When pay is based on a percentage of the gross, owners claim that activities such as truck washing are computed into the percentage. Drivers are not so sure, aware, for instance, that drivers of chronically dirty trucks do not have any pay withheld as a consequence.

5. At times, day-shift drivers took their trucks as soon as the night-shift drivers returned them to the yards, but often they did not need to depart until several hours later.

6. Regarding "anarchy in the market," the markets serviced by SandHaul and AgriHaul were, for the most part, regulated, so state-imposed price minimums and restrictions on entry softened competition somewhat. This was not the case at PetroHaul.

7. Concerning job security, AgriHaul rarely fired drivers, and, when work was slow, assignments were distributed evenly so that no one was laid off. SandHaul was somewhat more inclined to fire drivers, but the three firings I observed occurred after several warnings and in the wake of offenses most drivers considered reasonable grounds for firing. One ex-union driver who worked at SandHaul said he felt more secure at SandHaul than in a union job. PetroHaul's owner was tolerant of errors and appeared slow to fire drivers. When business slowed, however, he laid off low-seniority drivers rather than distribute the available work between all drivers.

PetroHaul had some consciously bureaucratic features that protected drivers, including at least one formal rule that restricted the dispatcher from impinging on drivers' off-duty time.

Chapter 5

1. Travel may heighten the esteem bestowed on business persons, but it does so by being a measure of their organizational importance.

2. During the 1970s, the idea of convoys captured the public's imagination to the extent that both a movie and a popular song about truckers had "convoy" in their titles.

3. At SandHaul, twenty-two drivers (79 percent) were at the age of fifteen being reared by a primary wage earner who was a blue-collar worker or a foreman of blue-collar workers. Flittie and Nelson (1968) found in a survey of two hundred cross-country haulers that the fathers of 48 percent were in blue-collar occupations, while those of another 38 percent were "agriculturalists." An early attraction to trucking was common at all the companies I worked for, but only at SandHaul did I quiz drivers directly. Eighteen of twenty-two SandHaul drivers reported being attracted to trucking by at least some of its mythic images.

4. Those who cannot or do not engage in paid work are nonetheless measured by the relationship of their activities to paid work.

5. This is not to say our society is bereft of ideologies that encourage loyalty and effort in workers; the difference is a matter of degree.

6. For two examples of such situations see Burawoy's (1979) account of machinists at Allied Corporation and Juravich's (1985) examination of assemblers at National Wire and Cable. The machinists appeared to be almost uninterested in the quality of their work, while the

assemblers often had to fight management to insure even minimal levels of quality.

7. Baffles are wall-like constructions placed inside trailers to check the movement of liquid loads.

8. After drivers learn what they need to know for the most common breakdowns and safety hazards, the division of labor and the pay for extended breakdowns removes much of the incentive to learn more about their vehicle. Management rarely demands or encourages drivers to learn more than the basics, because either company mechanics or readily obtained outside mechanics can handle the problems. Older truckers brag about the days when there were few truck mechanics, especially on the road, and drivers were expected to make at least enough repairs to drive the truck back to the yard.

9. After we successfully negotiated the worst part of the mountain pass, two drivers passed me, apparently either feeling that I was going too slow or perhaps making a claim to greater skill than would have been implied by their following me all the way.

10. The issue of braking a heavily loaded truck while descending long, steep grades continues to be debated. For example, a recent study by the University of Michigan Transportation Research Institute (Spencer 1992, 32) contradicts the braking style described by the Sand-Haul driver, which is approximately that prescribed in manuals used to prepare drivers for the commercial drivers license exams. For an earlier example of this argument see *Go West* (June 1986, 10).

11. Since the late 1960s, private truck-driving schools have come into being. I did not examine this mode of training and entry, partly because, with one exception, no one at any of the companies I worked for went to such a school. Some of these schools do seem to be providing an entry into trucking, and certain large, nonunion companies were using them as sources of cheap labor. However, among the companies in this book, the impact of truck-driving schools was negligible except at SandHaul. After losing most of its core-group drivers and many recently hired drivers, SandHaul apparently out of desperation began hiring drivers from truck-driving schools. Recently departed core-group drivers and their friends who continued to work for SandHaul reported that this decision turned into a fiasco because of the ineptness of the new hires.

12. The recent adoption of a national commercial driver's license that requires new drivers to take detailed written exams and a driving test supervised by a state examiner has made it harder for a minimally skilled driver to get a license. In the remainder of the book, my statements about the consequences of having a license are based on my experiences with drivers in states that issue special licenses and re-

quire for their procurement written tests and either driving tests or certifications by employers.

13. The Motor Carrier Safety Act of 1986 caused all states to demand that commercial truck drivers pass nationally uniform written
tests. In addition, all new drivers and, under certain conditions, some
veteran drivers have to pass state-administered driving tests that conform to nationwide standards.

14. By 1993, the industry was so desperate for drivers that some
employers were calling for lowering the age limit for a commercial
driver's license from twenty-one to eighteen. Among the reasons for this
shortage are the increased difficulty in obtaining a license, and changes
brought by deregulation that have made driving much less desirable.
For example, the pay at some of the companies where I worked more
than ten years ago is barely higher now than it was then. Employers
now also have access to technologies that appear to give them greater
control over drivers.

15. There appears to be a contradiction between my contention that
drivers typically have limited direct exposure to one another's driving
skills, and my claim to have made numerous such observations. I believe I saw more truckers at work than did the average driver, because I
worked at eight companies where I made an effort to drive with new
workmates, particularly at SandHaul and PetroHaul, and I had two jobs
in which I drove long-distance with co-drivers.

Chapter 6

1. For example, PetroHaul and eventually AgriHaul would not hire
novices, but SandHaul during my tenure trained one driver and hired
two others with little experience, even though the labor market was favorable to employers. Later, when quitting soared at SandHaul, the
company resorted to hiring recent graduates of truck-driving schools.

2. For example, the Highway Patrol found that 11 percent of the 131
tank truck accidents in California during 1980 were directly the result
of mechanical problems (*Los Angeles Times*, March 5, 1982, sec. 5, p.
8). It is reasonable to assume that mechanical problems indirectly contributed to an even larger percentage of accidents.

3. In the following description, I am not asserting that these are
work characteristics that all, or even most, drivers attempt to acquire.
Family pressures, injuries, and interests outside trucking push drivers
into looking for jobs that, for example, involve shorter hauls and get
them home daily. What I am suggesting is that if drivers had only work
to consider, these are the characteristics they most value.

4. Because of the trailers they are hauled in ("portable parking

lots"), automobiles are thought by many to constitute an ugly load. Another example of an ugly load is wrecked cars that have been smashed flat and loaded onto a flatbed trailer.

5. A long wheelbase provides a better ride and generally is thought to be better looking. For the same reasons, most drivers prefer conventional cabs to the cab-over-engine ("cabover") design. Conventionals are also thought to be safer in front-end collisions.

6. I have heard of union companies that hired people wishing to be drivers and put them to work in a company warehouse before training them as drivers. However, these were not the larger companies, and I did not personally know anyone that entered trucking in this manner.

7. Deregulation led to the demise of most of the largest trucking companies regulated by the ICC. For example, of the 30 largest companies in 1979, only 10 were operating in 1992. Of the 20 no longer in existence, 17 failed and three merged with another company (Barlett and Steele 1992, 112). My observations of these large carriers were made, for the most part, prior to deregulation. Today, the largest unionized carriers might be somewhat more enlightened about providing drivers with a few amenities, but for the most part the descriptions here still apply.

Chapter 7

1. For example, the Environmental Protection Agency regulates hazardous wastes, the Air Control Board enforces certain regulations concerning the loading and unloading of gasoline, and agricultural officials inspect produce.

2. Large carriers can arrange to have state officials inspect their equipment while it sits at company terminals.

3. Out-of-state drivers in some states are jailed until they pay fines levied against them. Other truckers subject to jailing include those who carry guns, drugs, or multiple logbooks; those who drive in a reckless manner; and those who dump loads illegally.

4. There is a certain irony in listening to politically conservative drivers who have nothing but disdain for the police, a group typically championed by U.S. conservatives. I would guess that some of the political conservatism reputed to exist among truckers derives, not from their having been bought off by middle-class wages, but from their experiences with regulatory agencies and the appeal of conservatives' promises to free society from "overregulation."

5. Though many of these workers may have devalued statuses, drivers also see them as blue-collar workers. In addition, while many

jobs are filled by members of other groups, there is no shortage of blue-collar, white male workers, especially at large union plants.

Chapter 8

1. For example, adding extra lights may take twenty to sixty minutes a light, and at least one driver at SandHaul spent two hundred dollars on lights. Regarding sitting positions, "low riding," sitting very low in the seat of an automobile, is popular among working-class whites, blacks, and especially Mexican Americans, the style's apparent originators. Low-riding became popular among younger California truckers in the mid-1970s. In a truck, low riding was usually accomplished by letting all the air out of the seat's supporting air bag, a clear sacrifice of comfort in return for appearance.

2. In my experience, drivers who spend most of their time on city freeways are more likely to encounter female exhibitionism, while road drivers are more likely to encounter overtures by homosexuals. City freeway drivers are also more likely than road drivers to see on-the-road sexual behavior, if for no other reason than they pass many more motorists.

3. In trucking, and I suspect in many occupations, equipment is an important consideration for the worker. However, sociologists seem to have difficulty categorizing equipment as it relates to job satisfaction. For example, Mottaz (1985) suggests equipment is a relatively minor extrinsic reward, but he offers no rationale. I suggest that equipment be treated as an intrinsic reward; the very operation of a truck is one of trucking's joys, and the quality of the truck can add to or detract from that enjoyment. Further, equipment quality suggests to workers their employer's commitment to workmanship.

4. Some of the rankings in the table, especially regarding accessories, vary according to geographical region. For example, chrome rods with a light in the tip that are attached to each end of the front bumper are popular in many nonwestern states, but many California truckers think they indicate a "hick." The table most reflects California, the West Coast, and western states.

Chapter 9

1. The industry, at least before deregulation, had many companies and offered drivers widely varying combinations of extrinsic and intrinsic rewards. However, few companies were high on both types of rewards. For example, in 1981, union drivers who worked a typical sixty-

hour week (Wyckoff 1979, 36) could earn more than $45,000 a year (*Go West*, April 1981, 16), but they probably would operate inferior equipment over comparatively shorter routes and in highly routinized operations. In comparison, a year of sixty-hour weeks at PetroHaul paid $32,760, but drivers at such nonunion companies typically drove nice trucks that they could personalize, hauled many different loads over a variety of routes, and had near total autonomy in executing their work.

2. Among drivers, "super trucker" is usually a somewhat pejorative term connoting a driver who totally identifies himself with and is totally absorbed in truck driving, but whose skills fall short of his commitment, or who behaves in a stupid fashion to further his trucker image. For example, a driver fastidious to the point of washing his truck before driving it in rain or snow might be labeled "super trucker." However, some drivers reject the derogative elements of the definition and openly identify themselves as super truckers by, for example, displaying a badge that says "Super Trucker." My use of "super trucker" signifies only extremely high commitment; it implies nothing about a driver's skills; however, I acknowledge the negative elements of the term when it is used in that fashion by other drivers. "Trucker" does not have a special meaning among drivers, although it is sometimes used to distinguish drivers of large trucks from those operating small trucks. "Worker" also has no particular meaning in trucking. While I discuss each role as if it were discrete, in reality they shade into one another and are more accurately viewed as points on a continuum.

3. Among large unionized companies there are a few exceptions. In particular, some oil companies, after the huge influx of cash they experienced in the 1970s, purchased first-rate equipment with many custom accessories. The super trucker, though attracted to such equipment, might also assume that the decision to purchase it had more to do with the way the companies wanted to present themselves to the motoring public (beautiful, *clean* trucks) than with how they felt about their drivers. Such an assumption may well be correct; four drivers for the unionized company offering the best equipment told me that drivers were very dissatisfied with an oppressive management.

4. There are two exceptions worth noting. One is the SandHaul super trucker I describe in Chapter 6 who went to a small, unionized company that, in many ways, was comparable to SandHaul before its original owner's son redefined work relations in a way that devalued super truckers; that this company was unionized had nothing to do with his decision to seek work there. The second exception is an educated guess. I suppose that occasionally a PetroHaul super trucker quit in order to join the large unionized oil company to whom PetroHaul leased several trucks and drivers. In this case, the driver moved to a

company whose equipment was comparable to PetroHaul's and simply continued performing the same work for greater extrinsic rewards.

5. Norms specifying appropriate rates of production and sanctions prohibiting "rate-busting" are said to exist in most occupations and at many levels within occupations (Runcie 1971, 42). However, among truck drivers it typically takes a rather extreme situation before a driver is said to be doing too much work. For example, someone who works seven days a week, week after week, is likely to be identified as overdoing it. At SandHaul and AgriHaul, such drivers usually were owner-operators who leased to the company. I do not recall instances where drivers were seriously criticized for doing too much work in a given time period, such as a day or a week, though a driver who increased production by speeding excessively and driving recklessly probably would be considered stupid. The most common criticism regarding excessive effort had to do with working while off duty (usually to enhance a truck's appearance), which was seen by some drivers as overcommitment. Among SandHaul's night-shift drivers, arriving too early at the yard was seen both as overcommitment and as cheating other drivers out of their rightful dispatch positions (in deciding which motivation got the greatest emphasis, drivers considered the violator and the situation). In the uncommon cases where drivers were thought to be working too much, other drivers expressed no animosity and instead felt sorry for the driver, guessing that domestic or financial problems caused this situation.

6. SandHaul's problems in retaining veteran drivers arose when the owner, who was the original's owner's son and fairly new at running the company, became inconsistent in upholding the implied contract drivers had made with his father. It is interesting to note that the son was honored by at least one industry association for his modern methods of management.

7. The reader might suggest that PetroHaul's drivers worked hard because, among the three companies, they were in the most deregulated and therefore most competitive sector. In this case, drivers might be expected to labor intensely simply to keep the company afloat and preserve their jobs. While it is true that PetroHaul was in the least price-regulated sector, PetroHaul's owner and managers were the least likely to cite competitive pressures as a means of pacifying drivers, I believe because PetroHaul saw deregulation—at least in its early stages—as an opportunity more than a threat.

8. Most of these truckers' and super truckers' understanding of union jobs is based not on direct experience with union work but on what they see of it and, for some, on discussions with union drivers or other unionized workers. Direct experience may positively alter their

valuation of unionized trucking, as the super trucker explained who left SandHaul for a union job only because it provided equivalent intrinsic rewards: "The union? That really wasn't an issue then [when I applied for this job]. Later, after I had been there a while, I came to appreciate being union. In the union I have retirement, medical, overtime. Now, I like being in the union." In this case, the super trucker was able to find a union company that operates equipment and has a management style consistent with his orientation (Chapter 6), but where drivers also reap the benefits of being in a union. Though I did not survey the super truckers and truckers who knew of this driver's new job, I would guess that most would think it a good find but too uncommon to serve as a model of what is possible.

REFERENCES

Adler, Patricia A., and Peter Adler. 1987. *Membership Roles in Field Research.* Newbury Park, Calif.: Sage.

Argyle, M. 1972. *The Social Psychology of Work.* London: Penguin.

Barlett, Donald L., and James B. Steele. 1992. *America: What Went Wrong?* Kansas City: Andrews and McMeel.

Becker, Howard S. 1963. *Outsiders.* New York: Free Press.

Blauner, Robert. 1964. *Alienation and Freedom.* Chicago: University of Chicago Press.

Braverman, Harry. 1974. *Labor and Monopoly Capital.* New York: Monthly Review Press.

Burawoy, Michael. 1979. *Manufacturing Consent.* Chicago: University of Chicago Press.

Chinoy, Ely. 1955. *Automobile Workers and the American Dream.* Boston: Beacon.

Daily Northwestern. 1985. Evanston, Ill.: Northwestern University.

Douglas, Jack D. 1976. *Investigative Social Research: Individual and Team Field Research.* Beverly Hills, Calif.: Sage.

Douglas, Jack D., and John M. Johnson, eds. 1977. *Existential Sociology.* Cambridge: Cambridge University Press.

Dubin, Robert. 1976. *Handbook of Work, Organization, and Society.* Chicago: Rand McNally.

Edwards, Paul, and Hugh Scullion. 1982. *Social Origin of Industrial Conflict: Control and Resistance in the Workplace.* Oxford: Blackwell.

Edwards, Richard. 1979. *Contested Terrain.* New York: Basic Books.

Erikson, Kai T. 1967. "A Comment on Disguised Observation in Sociology." *Social Problems* 12:366–373.

Etulain, Richard W. 1982. "Westerns." In *Concise Histories of American Popular Culture,* edited by M. Thomas Inge. Westport, Conn.: Greenwood.

References

Film Center Gazette. 1983. Film Center of the School of the Art Institute, Chicago. June.

Finlay, William. 1988. *Work on the Waterfront: Worker Power and Technological Change in a West Coast Port.* Philadelphia: Temple University Press.

Flittie, Edwin G., and Zane P. Nelson. 1968. "The Truck Driver: A Sociological Analysis of an Occupational Role." *Sociology and Social Research* 52:205–210.

Friedman, Samuel R. 1982. *Teamster Rank and File.* New York: Columbia University Press.

Gold, Raymond. 1958. "Roles in Sociological Field Observations." *Social Forces* 36:217–223.

Goldthorpe, John, David Lockwood, Frank Bechhofer, and Jennifer Platt. 1968. *The Affluent Worker: Industrial Attitudes and Behavior.* New York: Cambridge University Press.

Haraszti, Miklós. 1978. *A Worker in a Worker's State.* New York: Universe.

Harper, Douglas. 1987. *Working Knowledge: Skill and Community in a Small Shop.* Chicago: University of Chicago Press.

Hayano, David M. 1979. "Auto-Ethnography: Paradigms, Problems, and Prospects." *Human Organization* 38:99–104.

Hirszowicz, Maria. 1981. *Industrial Sociology.* Oxford: Martin Robertson.

Hodson, Randy. 1991. "The Active Worker: Compliance and Autonomy at the Workplace." *Journal of Contemporary Ethnography* 20:47–78.

Howe, Louise Kapp. 1977. *Pink Collar Workers.* New York: Avon.

Hughes, Everett C. 1958. *Men and Their Work.* Glencoe, Ill.: Free Press.
———. (1970) 1984. *The Sociological Eye.* New Brunswick, N.J.: Transaction.

Juravich, Tom. 1985. *Chaos on the Shopfloor.* Philadelphia: Temple University Press.

Kaprow, Miriam Lee. 1991. "Magical Work: Firefighters in New York." *Human Organization* 50:97–103.

Kehr, Dave. 1984. "Mythic West." *Chicago Reader,* September 14, 14.

Kerr, Clark, John T. Dunlop, Frederick H. Harbison, and Charles A. Myers. 1960. *Industrialism and Industrial Man.* Cambridge, Mass.: Harvard University Press.

Knights, David. 1990. "Subjectivity, Power, and the Labour Process." In *Labour Process Theory,* edited by David Knights and Hugh Wilmott, 297–335. Basingstoke, England: Macmillan.

Komarovsky, Mirra. 1962. *Blue Collar Marriage.* New York: Random House.

Kotarba, Joseph A. 1977. "The Chronic Pain Experience." In *Existential*

Sociology, edited by Jack D. Douglas and John M. Johnson, 257–272. Cambridge: Cambridge University Press.

Lamphere, Louise. 1979. "Fighting the Piece-Rate System: New Dimensions of an Old Struggle in the Apparel Industry." In *Case Studies on the Labor Process*, edited by Andrew Zimbalist, 257–276. New York: Monthly Review Press.

LeMasters, E. E. 1975. *Blue-Collar Aristocrats*. Madison: University of Wisconsin Press.

Liebow, Elliot. 1966. *Talley's Corner*. Boston: Little, Brown.

Linhart, Robert. 1981. *The Assembly Line*. Amherst: University of Massachusetts Press.

MacAvoy, Paul W., and John W. Snow. 1977. *Regulation of Entry and Pricing in Truck Transportation*. Washington, D.C.: American Enterprise Institute.

Manwaring, Tony, and Stephen Wood. 1984. "The Ghost in the Machine: Tacit Skills in the Labor Process." *Socialist Review* 74:55–94.

Marx, Karl. 1977. *Capital*. Vol. 1, 8th ed. New York: International Publishers.

Mayo, Elton. 1933. *The Human Problems of an Industrial Civilization*. New York: Macmillan.

———. 1945. *The Social Problems of Industrial Civilization*. Cambridge, Mass.: Harvard University Press.

Mehan, Hugh, and Houston Wood. 1975. *The Reality of Ethnomethodology*. New York: Wiley.

Melbin, Murry. 1978. "Night as Frontier." *American Sociological Review* 43:1–22.

Merton, Robert K. 1938. "Social Structure and Anomie." *American Sociological Review* 3:672–682.

Mottaz, Clifford J. 1985. "The Relative Importance of Intrinsic and Extrinsic Rewards as Determinants of Work Satisfaction." *Sociological Quarterly* 26:365–386.

Ouellet, Lawrence J. 1981. "Job Satisfaction and Occupational Prestige: The English Lorry Driver, 1967–1980." Master's thesis, Northwestern University.

Pfeffer, Richard M. 1979. *Working for Capitalism*. New York: Columbia University Press.

Pleck, Elizabeth, and Joseph Pleck. 1980. *The American Man*. Englewood Cliffs, N.J.: Prentice-Hall.

Pleck, Joseph. (1981) 1983. *The Myth of Masculinity*. Cambridge, Mass.: MIT Press.

Poulantzas, Nicos. 1975. *Classes in Contemporary Capitalism*. London: New Left.

Reiss, Albert J. 1961. *Occupations and Social Status.* New York: Free Press.

Riemer, Jeffrey W. 1979. *Hard Hats.* Beverly Hills, Calif.: Sage.

Rose, Michael. 1985. *Re-working the Work Ethic.* New York: Schocken.

Roy, Donald. 1952. "Quota Restriction and Goldbricking in a Machine Shop." *American Journal of Sociology* 57:427–442.

Rubin, Lillian Breslow. 1976. *Worlds of Pain.* New York: Basic Books.

Runcie, John F. 1971. "Social Group Formation in an Occupation: A Case Study of the Truck Driver." Ph.D. diss., University of Michigan.

Sennett, Richard, and Jonathan Cobb. 1972. *The Hidden Injuries of Class.* New York: Vintage.

Shapiro-Perl, Nina. 1979. "The Piece Rate: Class Struggle on the Shop Floor. Evidence from the Costume Jewelry Industry in Providence, Rhode Island." In *Case Studies on the Labor Process,* edited by Andrew Zimbalist, 277–298. New York: Monthly Review Press.

Smith, H. W. 1978. "The CB Handle: An Announcement of Adult Identity." *Symbolic Interactionism* 3:95–107.

Smith, Henry Nash. 1980. "The Mountain Man as Western Hero." In *The American Man,* edited by Elizabeth Pleck and Joseph Pleck, 159–172. Englewood Cliffs, N.J.: Prentice-Hall.

Special Task Force. 1973. *Work in America.* Cambridge, Mass.: MIT Press.

Spenser, Todd. "Downhill Braking." *Landline* 17(5): 31.

Stinchcombe, Arthur L. 1983. *Economic Sociology.* New York: Academic Press.

Taylor, Fredrick Winslow. 1947. *The Principles of Scientific Management.* New York: Harper.

Taylor, Laurie, and Paul Walton. 1971. "Industrial Sabotage: Motives and Meanings." In *Images of Deviance,* edited by Stanley Cohen, 219–245. Hammondsworth, England: Penguin.

Thomas, James H. 1979. "Truckstops, Truckers, and Trucks: 1976." *Journal of Popular Culture* 13:221–228.

Tolson, Andrew. 1978. *The Limits of Masculinity.* New York: Harper and Row.

Turkel, Studs. (1972) 1974. *Working.* New York: Avon.

Van Maanen, John. 1988. *Tales of the Field: On Writing Ethnography.* Chicago: University of Chicago Press.

Veblen, Thorstein. (1899) 1905. *The Theory of the Leisure Class.* New York: Macmillan.

Watson, Tony J. 1980. *Sociology, Work, and Industry.* London: Routledge and Kegan Paul.

Willis, Paul. 1977. *Learning to Labor.* New York: Columbia University Press.

Wyckoff, D. Daryl. 1979. *Truck Drivers in America.* Lexington, Mass.: Lexington Books.

Wyckoff, D. Daryl, and David Maister. 1977. *The Motor-Carrier Industry.* Lexington, Mass.: Lexington Books.

INDEX

Accidents, 31, 32, 107, 121, 130, 138–139, 154–155, 157–158, 161–163, 216
Adler, Patricia A., 225
Adler, Peter, 225
AgriHaul, organization of work at, 27–31, 56–60
Al, 78, 79, 108–109, 136, 152, 196
Alan, 51
Andy, 54
Arnie, 147
"Asphalt Cowboy," 105
Audience: company support personnel as, 154, 163–166; management as, 129; motorists as, 170–182, 215–216; motorists compared to jazz fans as, 181; other truck drivers as, 125, 128, 182–196, 214–215; police/government officials as, 122, 137, 154–163; as source of truckers' self-esteem, 20, 100, 108–110, 112–113, 117, 128, 153; workers who load/unload trucks as, 154, 166–168

Barney, 47, 49, 56
Becker, Howard S., 181, 198
Bentley, Clark, 105
Big George, 195
Blauner, Robert, 218
Bobby, 85

Brown and Williamson Tobacco Corporation, 106
Burawoy, Michael, 8, 9, 10, 11, 71, 97, 99, 134, 221, 229

Charisma (as form of control), 8, 97–98
Claude, 135
Cobb, Jonathan, 5
Commitment to occupation: in conflict with commitment to family, 204–206, 210; debased at Sand-Haul, 150; as enabling, 150, 220–221; high level of, 199; indicated by equipment, 193; loss of, 203, 209; as overcommitment, 235; as problematic, 112, 150, 183–188; union job as implying less, 210
Conflict between drivers, 40, 44, 45, 46–56, 57, 62–64, 68, 78–79, 87, 235; norms mitigating, 45–46, 48, 62–64
Conflict between drivers and management, 11, 42, 58, 64–66, 68–70, 98–99, 235; absenteeism as cause of, 87–88, 96; by driver type, 200–201, 202, 204, 206–207; and quitting, 88–95, 98, 149, 152; and sabotage, 85–87, 96; and strikes, 95. *See also* Effort, role of, in bargains with management; Effort, withdrawal of (foot-dragging)